Climate

Change

in the

Adirondacks

Cedar River Flow, August, 2009

South Inlet of Raquette Lake, March, 2009

CLIMATE CHANGE IN THE ADIRONDACKS

THE PATH TO SUSTAINABILITY

JERRY JENKINS

FOREWORD BY BILL McKIBBEN

COMSTOCK PUBLISHING ASSOCIATES, A DIVISION OF CORNELL UNIVERSITY PRESS
ITHACA AND LONDON

A PROJECT OF THE WILDLIFE CONSERVATION SOCIETY ADIRONDACK PROGRAM

Copyright © 2010 by Wildlife Conservation Society

First published 2010 by Cornell University Press
First printing, Cornell Paperbacks, 2010

This book is made possible through the financial support of The Wild Center, the Adirondack Nature Conservancy, the Adirondack Council, the Open Space Institute, several private donors, and, through a parallel project, the Institute for Ecosystem Studies. The Wildlife Conservation Society and the White Creek Field School have underwritten additional research and writing.

Printed in China

Library of Congress Cataloging-in-Publication Data

Jenkins, Jerry (Jerry C.)
    Climate change in the Adirondacks : the path to sustainability / Jerry Jenkins ; foreword by Bill McKibben.
        p. cm.
    "Published in association with the Wildlife Conservation Society, Bronx, New York."
    Includes bibliographical references and index.
    ISBN 978-0-8014-7651-8 (pbk. : alk. paper)
    1. Climatic changes--New York (State)--Adirondack Mountains Region. 2. Energy consumption--Environmental aspects--New York (State)--Adirondack Mountains Region. 3. Energy policy--Environmental aspects--New York (State)--Adirondack Mountains Region. 4. Sustainable development--Environmental aspects--New York (State)--Adirondack Mountains Region. 5. Environmental policy--New York (State)--Adirondack Mountains Region. 6. Adirondack Mountains Region (N.Y.)--Environmental conditions. I. Wildlife Conservation Society (New York, N.Y.) II. Title.

QC984.N7J46 2010
363.738'746097475--dc22

                    2009053992

Cornell University Press strives to use environmentally responsible suppliers and materials to the fullest extent possible in the publishing of its books. Such materials include vegetable-based, low-VOC inks and acid-free papers that are recycled, totally chlorine-free, or partly composed of nonwood fibers. For further information, visit our website at www.cornellpress.cornell.edu.

Paperback printing   10 9 8 7 6 5 4 3 2 1

CONTENTS

Sugar maple on Ampersand Mountain, October, 2009

FOREWORD

More than two decades ago, sitting in my house deep in the Johnsburg woods, I wrote the first account of climate change for a general audience, a book called *The End of Nature*. At the time, we knew enough about global warming to worry deeply about the future—but not enough to worry in specifics. I realized that in some sense wildness was coming to an end, and that even the Blue Line couldn't hold at bay the outsized impact of the rest of the planet. But no one knew what it would look like in any detail, or what exactly we could do about it.

Now, thanks to Jerry Jenkins, I think the future has been plotted more firmly for the Adirondacks than perhaps any other region on the planet. With his trademark ability to work across disciplines, he has taken from every branch of the sciences, including the social sciences, to paint a devastating picture of where we are headed. These are the biggest changes the park has faced since the last Ice Age, and if we allow them to play out in full, many of the glories of the Adirondacks will simply be gone.

We don't control our own destiny, of course. Since the Adirondacks represent a vanishingly small percentage of the world's CO_2 emissions, we can't head off change by ourselves. That's why I've spent much of my time building big, global grassroots campaigns to try and do that work on the only scale possible: one planet at a time. But, of course, those changes must be reflected close to home, and this book's careful considerations of our indigenous options for energy are both apt and welcome. I can remember the hey-day of giant satellite dishes across the north country; it will be nice when there are as many solar panels.

And as becomes very clear in these pages, even if we do everything right, there are some changes we won't head off. The world will become a tougher place, with wilder and more erratic swings of weather. To deal with that, we'll need stronger, more intact communities, able to support each other through thin times. The process of building and strengthening those communities begins with information. Jerry Jenkins has emerged as the information source for our mountains, a kind of one-man Adirondack Google who has done the work to understand what makes this place tick. This book is a great resource, and a great gift; we are all in his debt.

Bill McKibben

Climate change is a world problem that is usually discussed on a world scale. When we do—speaking of billions of tons of carbon in the atmosphere, ice-shelves disintegrating in the Antarctic, the sea flooding Pacific islands—so we capture its size and severity. But in doing so, we can also give the impression that climate change only concerns far-away places and that it is too big for us to do anything about.

Both impressions are wrong. Climate change will affect northern New York too. We are not likely to have big floods and storms or devastating heat waves. But we could easily see large changes in how we live our lives and what kind of places we live them in. And we could, also easily, lose much that we love and many of the things, both human and natural, that give our lives meaning.

Furthermore, climate change, though a big problem, is a solvable problem. We have created it through a century of using fossil fuels. We can solve it by spending the coming century learning not to use them.

I believe that we have strong reasons to do this. As Americans, we have historical responsibilities: 36% of the carbon now in the atmosphere was emitted by us. As Adirondackers, we have a motive: our home and our culture are at risk. And we have an opportunity: if we act, and act soon, we may be able to do something about it.

Before we can act, we have to understand our situation and our options. This book is a start in that direction. It is of course limited—there is only so much that one person can think about, and only so far into the future that he can see. But it is a start and will, I hope, allow others to think better and see farther.

The book has two parts. Part I, The Climate Problem, asks how climate change will affect the Adirondacks. Part II, An Adirondack Strategy, asks how we might reduce our carbon emissions in response.

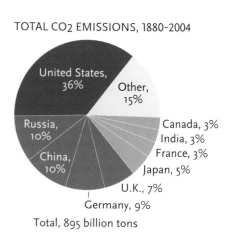

TOTAL CO2 EMISSIONS, 1880-2004

Total, 895 billion tons

The word *strategy* comes with a disclaimer. The climate problem is global and can't be solved by individual communities. But nonetheless, because the global problem is the sum of thousands of local ones, local action still matters. Fossil fuels are woven into local economies all over the world, and the world problem won't be solved until they are unwoven.

This is the reason I have written an Adirondack book about a global problem. We need to do something about carbon emissions and to do it now. We can do little about world emissions. We can do a lot about the emissions of the Adirondacks. That seems, for the time being, worth focussing on.

This book has been two years in the making. It began as a report commissioned by The Wild Center in Tupper Lake, New York, in 2008. In 2009, I rewrote and enlarged it, focussing on how we use energy and what we could do to use less. While researching energy use, I realized that the technology already exists to allow us to eliminate fossil fuels and to become carbon-negative in 20 years. This is the book's main conclusion, and I hope that you find it as exciting as I do.

Like my other Adirondack books, this book is a primer. The text is intended to give you the facts and concepts you need to think about a complicated issue.

The illustrations are there to make the story real and convey some of its detail and complexity.

Short books on large subjects need clear boundaries. My boundaries are these: My subjects are climate and energy in the Adirondacks. My goal is to figure out what is physically possible for us to do, how we might start doing it, and what it might cost. But it is not to offer a detailed plan, or to tell you how to make it happen.

As a result, many important things—politics, leadership, institutions, policy, planning—have been left out. All of these are important and could easily fill another book. Perhaps one of you will write it. My subject here is narrower, and I have stuck to it as well as I could.

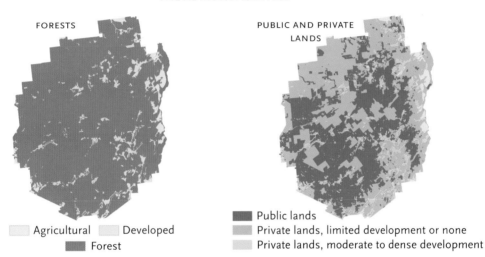

THE ADIRONDACK PARK

FORESTS

PUBLIC AND PRIVATE LANDS

◻ Agricultural ◻ Developed
■ Forest

■ Public lands
■ Private lands, limited development or none
◻ Private lands, moderate to dense development

About the Adirondacks

The Adirondacks are a temperate forest landscape with unusually high amounts of protected land and unusually low amounts of development. As such, they have a special importance in the climate story.

For readers unfamiliar with them, I give a brief account here. For more detail, see Phillip Terrie's *Contested Terrain*, Barbara McMartin's *The Great Forest of the Adirondacks*, Porter, Erickson, and Whaley's *The Great Experiment in Conservation*, and my first Adirondack book, *The Adirondack Atlas*.

Formally, the Adirondacks are a 6-million acre state park, created 118 years ago. About 5-million acres are forested; the rest are open, developed, or water. The openings are scattered and the forests are, to an extent that is rare in the United States, continuous and connected.

The lands in this park divide, roughly equally, between the public lands held by the State of New York and the private lands held by timber companies, nonprofit organizations, and individuals. The public lands are protected by a 1894 amendment to the state constitution which says that they shall be "forever kept as wild forest lands"; that they may not be leased, sold, or exchanged; and that the timber on them may not be sold, removed, or destroyed.

This amendment—Article XIV— is the strongest forest-protection law ever passed in the United States. It currently protects about 2.5 million acres of forested land, including at least 400,000 acres that were never logged for hardwoods and contain old forests with large old trees.

By protecting trees, Article XIV also protects climate. The state forests have been adding to their carbon stores for over 100 years. The stored carbon is now a major climate asset, and, because few if any large forests in the United States have been allowed a comparable period of undisturbed growth, also a unique one.

The private lands, which lack constitutional protection and can be harvested, are younger and faster growing than the state lands. They hold less carbon than the state forests, but have a higher rate of carbon storage and can supply forest products, which the state forests can not.

Both the forest products and the high storage rate are climate assets too. To develop a low-carbon economy we will need green materials, green jobs, and ways of offsetting carbon emissions that we can't avoid. The private lands, through their products and storage, can supply us with all three.

OLD FORESTS

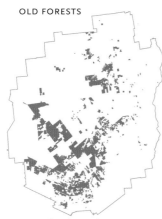

State lands, no harvests or limited harvests before 1900.

PERMANENT PROTECTION

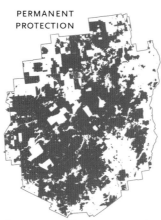

State ownership or conservation easement, no development (60%)

LIMITED DEVELOPMENT

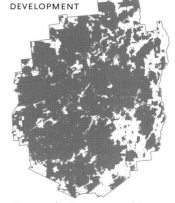

State and private ownership, 15 houses per square mile or less (85%)

Like the public forests, private Adirondack forests have significant protection. Development is regulated through a state land-use plan. Most large private timberlands may have at most 15 houses per square mile. Additional protection is provided by conservation easements that prevent development altogether. Easements of this sort now cover around 700,000 acres and constitute the most rapidly growing category of protected lands in the park.

The combination of the various sorts of protection guarantees that 60% of Adirondack lands will never be developed at all and another 25% will have at most low-density development. As with the supply of forest products, these restrictions will be important in developing a low-carbon economy. Development releases carbon (p. 144) and any truly low-carbon society will have to limit it. Societies that, like the Adirondacks, have already limited it, have taken a big step toward carbon neutrality. Those that haven't, have much farther to go.

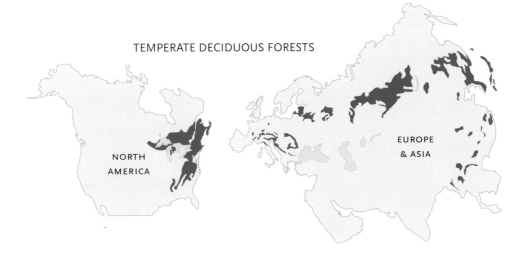

TEMPERATE DECIDUOUS FORESTS

NORTH AMERICA

EUROPE & ASIA

And Why They Matter

It is my belief that the Adirondacks have an importance in the climate story that extends beyond their boundaries. I can't prove this, but I can offer two arguments in its support.

The first is that temperate forests in general, and the Adirondacks in particular, are powerful symbols of the danger the natural world faces from climate change.

Temperate forests are among the world's oldest and most distinctive living communities. They evolved over 30 million years ago and have been the northern home of our species for 50,000 years. They are home to tens of thousands of animal and plant species and to hundreds of human languages and cultures. They have, for millennia, removed carbon from the air, and supplied fuel, materials, and clean water for the use of these cultures.

Over time, however, they have been much diminished by agriculture and settlement, and their capacity to store carbon and supply forest products correspondingly reduced. North America has some of the largest surviving examples; among these the Adirondacks, by virtue of their size and degree of protection, have a special place.

All temperate forests, large and small, are threatened by climate change. Because they are intrinsically northern in their composition and biology, climate change will come fast to them and have large effects. If we limit carbon emissions soon, they can survive. If we don't limit emissions, many may not.

Both the richness of temperate forests and their vulnerability make them symbols of the danger the living world is in. If we want a compelling example of how our carbon emissions are putting nature and humanity at risk, we have only to look about us.

The second argument for the Adirondacks' importance is that they, or someplace like them, could be the first place in America to demonstrate that a modern society can live without fossil fuels.

This kind of demonstration is urgently needed. The United States has pledged to reduce its greenhouse emissions by 80% from 2005 levels by 2050. Since cutting emissions from agriculture and long distance transport will be difficult, this will mean that ordinary communities, which is to say places like the Adirondacks, will have to eliminate all but the most necessary uses of fossil fuels.

We know that, in principle, this can be done. What we need is proof-of-concept: an example of some place, in America, that has actually done this.

After a year of looking at numbers and strategies, I think it possible that the Adirondacks, or some forested region like them, could be the first place to do this. Forested regions tend to have thrifty communities with modest energy needs. They have the resources—the land, water, and wood—needed to build green economies and the traditions of competence and independence needed to put the resources to use. They are, in other words, culturally and naturally rich, and rich in precisely those ways that energy independence will require.

If energy independence can be achieved, in America and by average Americans with average carbon needs, it will be a powerful example and a hope for the world.

My belief is that it can be done, and done here, and done more quickly than we think. This is of course romantic, but I will argue that it is quantifiably romantic. If the Adirondacks can produce 1 gigawatt of carbon-free power, they can eliminate petroleum and become energy independent. If they can cut their power use in half first, they can do it with just 500 megawatts. And 500 megawatts, as I will try to show you, is a large number but an achievable one.

Numbers and Units

My telling of the climate-change story has, deliberately, a lot of numbers. I don't think you can do it otherwise. The numbers matter because they establish scale and separate the possible from the impossible. *How much might we warm?* Less than 5 degrees if we are lucky, over 10 if we are not. *How big are the energy savings from passive solar houses?* Very big: a passive solar house may use less than one-fifth of the energy of a conventional house of the same size. *Can we make enough ethanol in the park to power our current fleet of cars and trucks?* No: our cars and trucks need 400 megawatts of power. The most we could make, using all the private lands, is around 200 megawatts.

Because numbers matter, I have used them freely, especially in the diagrams. You can skip them if you are not interested, but I hope you will be.

The energy literature is a hodgepodge of units from different systems (watts, joules, BTUs, horsepower, barrels, mets, calories,…), plus uninformative *ad hoc* concoctions ("enough fuel for all the trucks in Westchester"). A significant part of the work in preparing this book was converting energy data to a uniform system of units and trying to avoid the mistakes that plague such conversions. I do my own work in SI (*Système Internationale*) units because they are the world standard, but use English units in the book because they are the ones commonly used in the Adirondacks.

In particular, note that temperatures are always in Fahrenheit degrees (which matters) and weights in U.S. tons (which doesn't).

Carbon flows are measured in two ways, as pounds of carbon and pounds of carbon dioxide (CO_2). One pound of carbon equals 3.7 pounds of CO_2. When dealing with flows of carbon in and out of forests, pounds of carbon are the appropriate units: there is, after all, no carbon dioxide in a log or a roll of paper. When talking about carbon emissions, pounds of CO_2 are the appropriate units, because that is what is being emitted.

Emissions of other greenhouse gases like methane are conventionally measured in carbon dioxide equivalents, $CO_2(e)$, which is the amount of CO_2 that has the same warming effect.

Energy, which, even more than climate, is the central topic of this book, is measured in kilowatt-hours (kWh). The kilowatt-hour is used in both metric and English systems and is familiar from electric bills. A moderately efficient refrigerator, for example, might use a kilowatt-hour per day. A thrifty household of four persons might use 5,000 kilowatt-hours of electricity in a year.

The great utility of having a single unit of energy is that it can express the equivalence of different energy sources. A gallon of gasoline can be burnt to produce 37 kilowatt-hours of heat. So can 0.9 gallon of diesel fuel, 1.4 gallons of propane, and roughly 22 pounds of dry hardwood.

ENERGY CONTENT OF FUELS

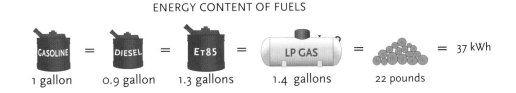

| 1 gallon | 0.9 gallon | 1.3 gallons | 1.4 gallons | 22 pounds | = 37 kWh |

Readers who balk at measuring wood or gasoline in kilowatt-hours may want to reflect that energy is not a substance but, like price or weight, a functional or transactional value that is specifically designed for comparing unlike things.

In much of this book we are concerned with power, the rate at which energy is used, rather than with energy itself. The kilowatt-hour is a unit of energy. The watt (W), 8.77 kilowatt-hours per year, is a unit of power. Human societies use a lot of power, and so we make frequent use of kilowatts (kW), thousands of watts, and megawatts (MW), millions of watts.

HOUSEHOLD POWER USE

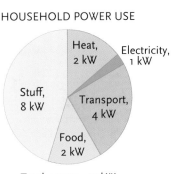

Total power = 17 kW

As with energy, having a single unit for power makes it possible to compare unlike things. The diagram at right shows the energy flows for a hypothetical Adirondack family. It makes the point that the energy used in the production of our nonfood purchases ("stuff") is a major part of many families' energy use. If treating the purchase of clothing or computers as an energy flow seems odd, please realize that we live in an odd world where buying shoes in Saranac Lake makes power plants in China burn more coal.

Averages, Ratings, and Calculations

A lot of the things we measure in this book are variable or intermittent: temperatures go up and down, furnaces and cars are sometimes running and sometimes stopped. In many cases the variation is not interesting, and we need some sort of average or summary. The numbers in the pie graph above, for example, are averages. The furnace in the house uses 20 kilowatts when it is running and nothing when it is not; the 2 kilowatts for heat is an average of the furnace's ons and offs over a whole year.

Graphs showing climate trends, like the temperature graph on the top of the next page, use a form of double averaging called a sliding average. First, the summer temperatures for each year are averaged, producing the pale red dots. Then the averages for the years in the green window are averaged again, producing a dark red dot. The

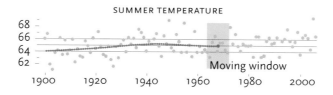

SUMMER TEMPERATURE

window is slid to the right one year at a time and the process is repeated, producing a string of dark red dots that trace out a smoothed curve of average temperature.

Another kind of summary, especially useful for motors, heaters, and generators, is a rating that expresses how good the unit is, compared to how good it might be. For heaters and engines we speak of efficiency, which is the ratio of the heat energy we put in to the useful energy that comes out. In the diagram below, the efficiency is 25%, typical of many internal combustion engines. For generators, we speak of the capacity factor, which is the ratio of the average power the generator produces to its peak power when running full out. For the Bergey wind turbine in the diagram below, the capacity factor is 15%, typical of small wind turbines and about half that of commercial ones.

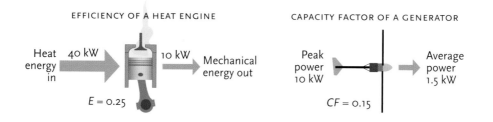

The diagrams also show, and alert readers may have already noticed, that the word *power*, by itself, is dangerously ambiguous. Engines have an input power and an output power; generators have a peak, or *nameplate* power and an average power. I have tried to be as clear about this in the text as I can, but readers should be aware that all authors occasionally forget to specify what kind of power they mean, and this can make it hard to compare numbers from different sources.

One further word about numbers. Many of the numbers in this book are based on fairly complicated calculations. The statement on p. 76 that producing $1,000 of sneakers results in the emission of 0.7 tons of carbon dioxide comes from an input-output model for carbon emissions of the entire U.S. economy developed by researchers at Carnegie-Mellon University. The statement on p. 125 that shallow geothermal heat can yield about 5 watts per square meter of surface comes from my application of a solution of the 1-dimensional heat-flow equation given by the English physicist David MacKay to our climate and soils.

Like the results of almost any real-world calculations, these numbers are necessarily based on many simplifications and assumptions. The estimate of the emissions associated with shoes averages over all the different types of shoes and different shoe makers. The estimate of available geothermal heat assumes a particular type of soil and a particular value for temperature difference between the warmest and the coldest months. The soil and temperatures I used are common in our area, but not necessarily the ones you will find in your yard.

The point here is that we are doing a kind of rough-and-ready estimation—MacKay calls it "guerilla physics"—and not precise engineering. The results are, I hope, approximately true for the particular examples I examine. But they are certainly not generally true, and they may be *very* wrong in situations where the assumptions are not met.

Thanks and Acknowledgments

This book is a project of the Wildlife Conservation Society Adirondack Program. Zoë Smith directed the project and Leslie Karasin managed it. Jerry Jenkins did the analyses and wrote, illustrated, and designed the book. Elizabeth McKenna and Carrianne Pershyn helped with research, and Michale Glennon and Heidi Kretser supplied ideas and comments. Jodi Hilty, director of the Wildlife Conservation Society North America Program, supported and encouraged us throughout.

We thank The Wild Center, the Adirondack Nature Conservancy, the Adirondack Council, the Open Space institute, several private donors and, through a parallel project, the Institute of Ecosystem Studies for financial support and the Wildlife Conservation Society and the White Creek Field School for underwriting additional research and writing.

We thank Stephanie Ratcliffe of the Wild Center for initiating the project, and Paul Alioto, Colin Beier, Debbie Benjamin, Bill Brown, Charlie Canham, Mike Conway, John Davis, Mike DeWein, Levi Durham, Howard Fish, Kate Fish, Mark Hall, Ann Ingerson, Larry Master, Kara Page, Vic Putnam, Don Reid, Curt Stager, Steve Trombulak, Amy Vedder, Bill Weber, Chris Westbrook, Ross Whaley, and Dave Ziemba, for discussions, advice, and information.

We thank Art DeGaetano and Cameron Wake for permission to reprint two graphs in Chapter 2, Tim Howard for the data on alpine plants on p. 35, the Saranac Lake Free Library and the New York State Archives for permission to use historical photos, Jason Smith for the photo on p. 32, and Nancie Battaglia for the photos on p. 47.

And we thank our friends at Cornell University Press—Heidi Lovette, chief science editor, Candace Akins, senior manuscript editor, Scott Levine, senior designer, and their colleagues—for their support of this book, and for the hard work they have done to make it better and bring it to press.

And an Exhortation

The climate change story is challenging to think about because the problem is large and the future uncertain. My response to this is pragmatic. Yes, we have a large problem, and yes, we have no idea whether we can solve it. But we know a lot of things that can be done, and so let's get started and do them. Being hopeful will help a lot. A whole generation of Americans—my parents, many of your grandparents—had a large problem in 1939 and faced a future that was much darker and more frightening than ours. They stayed calm and went to work. We can too.

Osgood River, March, 2008

1 INTRODUCTION: WE HAVE A CLIMATE PROBLEM

The Adirondacks, like much of the rest of the world, has a climate problem. The problem is that average temperatures are gradually rising. So far the rise is small and has caused only small changes. But, extended over a century, it will be larger and cause correspondingly larger changes.

Part I of this book, The Climate Problem, which includes this chapter and the next five, summarizes what we know about the changes that have already happened and what we may expect in the next century and beyond.

AVERAGE ANNUAL TEMPERATURE, 19 NORTHERN NEW YORK HCN STATIONS

Degrees °F

46
44
42
40

1900   1920   1940   1960   1980   2000

• Average for a single year
— Running average

The yearly temperatures (brown circles, above) for northern New York are estimated by averaging data from the 19 stations of the Historical Climatology Network (p. 4). They show no clear pattern. But when we average them again, using a sliding window that looks at them in groups, a clear pattern emerges (dark line). The smoothed temperatures rose slowly in the first part of the century, leveled off in the middle, and rose again, more rapidly, after 1970. The total rise is about 2 degrees.

The Adirondack temperature increases are part of a world-wide temperature increase, and have the same cause: increased amounts of carbon in the atmosphere, coming from fossil fuels and land-use changes.

YEARLY FLOWS OF CARBON INTO AND OUT OF THE ATMOSPHERE IN 1990S

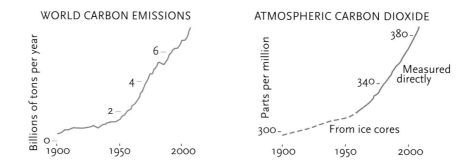

In the 1990s, humans released about 6.4 billion tons (GT, for gigatons) of carbon a year into the air by burning fossil fuels and another 1.6 billion tons by converting natural vegetation to farms and settlements. About half of the carbon was removed by forests and oceans. The rest stayed in the atmosphere.

The carbon in the atmosphere is in the form of carbon dioxide. Carbon dioxide acts as a blanket, trapping heat that would otherwise leave the earth. The more of it there is in the atmosphere, the hotter the earth becomes.

World carbon emissions rose rapidly after 1950 as the human population grew and the world industrialized. Atmospheric carbon dioxide concentrations, which are the result of carbon emissions, rose with emissions. Adirondack and world temperatures, delayed because the climate system takes time to respond, lagged about 30 years behind carbon dioxide concentrations and now are rising rapidly.

Just how much they rise will depend on how much fossil fuel we burn. Computer models adapted by the Northeast Climate Impacts Assessment predict, as shown on p. 3, that if we lower world carbon emissions immediately, northern New York will warm about 5 degrees from 1960 levels in the coming century. If, on the other hand, we continue to use large amounts of fossil fuels for 50 years or more, northern New York will warm about 11 degrees from 1960 levels.

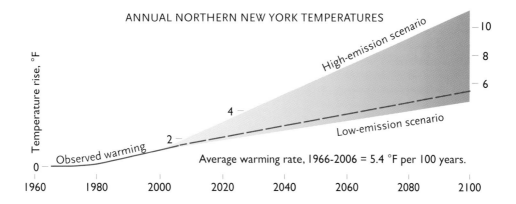

ANNUAL NORTHERN NEW YORK TEMPERATURES

Average warming rate, 1966-2006 = 5.4 °F per 100 years.

Currently northern New York temperatures are rising at a rate of 5 degrees per century. Since emissions remain high, and since the rate of warming will increase as carbon dioxide concentrations rise, it seems likely that we may end up in the top half of the colored figure rather than near the bottom.

The longer we delay in reducing emissions, the worse the prospects get (p. 27). If fossil fuel consumption rises for 30 years more before leveling off, we could see a temperature rise of 10 degrees in the 21st century. If it rises for 60 years more, we could add another 10 degrees more in the 22nd century.

Because the Adirondacks are a northern landscape with a northern culture, temperature rises of this magnitude will change them greatly (Chapter 6). With 5 to 10 degrees of temperature rise, they will lose much of their ice and snow. With the ice and snow will go the cultures, human and wild, that need cold winters. Winter sports, and the winter economy based on them, will decline. Boreal landscapes, like the open meadows along the Osgood River shown on p. 1, will turn to woods or thickets. Boreal animals like the marten and loon and boreal plants like the bog aster and purple saxifrage will decline or vanish.

With 10 to 20 degrees of temperature rise, the Adirondacks will become un-recognizable. Ice and snow will be gone. Our winters will be warm, our summers subtropical. Over half of our birds and trees will be beyond their current climatic limits. Our forests will likely decline and may be adding carbon to the atmosphere rather than removing it.

An Adirondack temperature rise of 10 degrees will be part of a world temperature rise of 6 degrees. If we reach this point, the world will be greatly changed. Seas will be rising, storms and droughts intensifying, and many human and natural ecosystems stressed or collapsing. The pace of change will be accelerating, and feedbacks in the climate system may make further change inescapable.

These predictions are from the 2007 consensus report of the Intergovernmental Panel on Climate Change, the largest international scientific body ever assembled on our planet. If they are even approximately correct, they suggest a simple conclusion: *only a low-emission scenario, keeping the rise in world temperatures to 4 degrees or less and the rise in Adirondack temperatures to 6 degrees or less, offers us a reasonable chance of escaping dangerous climate change.*

This conclusion is now widely accepted by climate scientists. The purpose of this book is to translate it into Adirondack terms. It asks two questions: "What might dangerous climate change mean for us?," and "What can we do to help put the world on a low-emission path?"

Hudson River Ice Meadows, Warrensburg, March, 2008

2 THE WEATHER IS CHANGING

How much has Adirondack weather changed over the last century and in what direction do the changes point?

To answer this we need long-term weather records that have been reviewed for consistency and adjusted for bias. In northern New York, our best long-term records come from the 19 northern New York stations of the U.S. Historical Climatology Network (HCN) shown in the map below. Six of these stations are within the Adirondack Park, and the remaining 13 outside. Because the Adirondack stations are too tightly clustered to give an accurate picture of the entire park, in most of what follows I use the full set of 19 stations, and give the average results for all of northern New York.

The annual temperature trend for northern New York is shown on p. 1, and the seasonal trends on p. 5. The annual, spring, summer, and winter averages show statistically significant increases. The increase in annual and winter temperatures over the whole period of record have been 2.7 degrees per 100 years. The increases in spring and summer temperatures have been 1.5 degrees per 100 years.

The annual, summer, and winter records show a slight mid-century cooling followed by a rise from the 1970s on. This pattern is seen in many temperature records, and is thought to represent a transient cooling caused by natural cycles and sulfur aerosols from fossil fuels, followed by an accelerating warming caused by increases in greenhouse gases.

THE HISTORICAL CLIMATOLOGY NETWORK
FOR NORTHERN NEW YORK

• Data from 1910 or before   • Data from 1931 or before

MEAN SEASONAL TEMPERATURES, NORTHERN NEW YORK

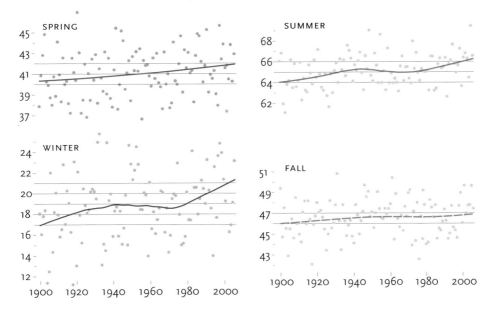

The temperature trends at the five central Adirondack stations, shown below, have been quite similar to those for northern New York as a whole. Since fewer stations are used, the individual data points scatter more than those for all northern New York. But the trend lines are similar, and, once again, the annual, summer, and winter trends are statistically significant. The increase in annual temperature has been 2.3 degrees per 100 years. Summer increases have been 2.1 degrees per 100 years and winter 3.0 degrees per 100 years.

The rise in Adirondack temperatures is part of a regional pattern of recent temperature increases. The map shows temperature changes at 137 stations for which

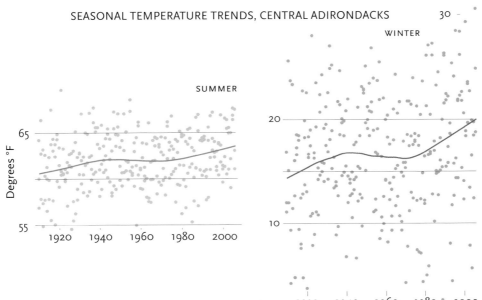

SEASONAL TEMPERATURE TRENDS, CENTRAL ADIRONDACKS

there are good records. At 75 of them the average temperature has risen by 3 degrees or more in the last 40 years. At 20 of them it has risen by 4 degrees or more.

The increases are fairly uniform across New England and New York with perhaps a slight tendency, confirmed in other studies, for greater rises in inland areas than in coastal ones.

As the winters warm, the last frosts are coming about a week earlier in spring and the first frosts about a week later in the fall than they did 50 years ago. As a result, the average growing season has lengthened by two weeks. Currently the last frost in spring, averaged over the region, is around May 2. The first frost in fall is around September 15, and the average growing season about 136 days.

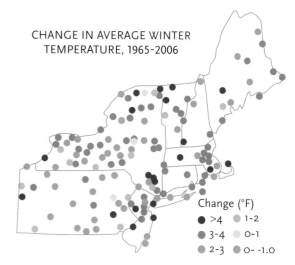

CHANGE IN AVERAGE WINTER TEMPERATURE, 1965-2006

Change (°F)
- ● >4   ● 1-2
- ● 3-4   ○ 0-1
- ● 2-3   ● 0- -1.0

Graph by Elizabeth Burakowski and Cameron Wake, University of New Hampshire

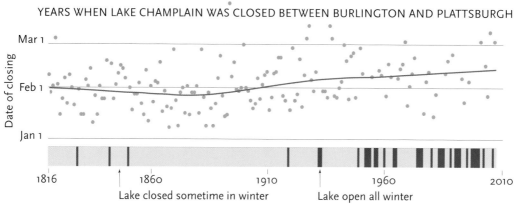

YEARS WHEN LAKE CHAMPLAIN WAS CLOSED BETWEEN BURLINGTON AND PLATTSBURGH

Date of closing
Mar 1
Feb 1
Jan 1

1816   1860   1910   1960   2010

Lake closed sometime in winter   Lake open all winter

Lake Ice

The warming temperatures have changed the freezing and thawing dates of lakes. Lake Champlain, which is large and doesn't freeze till midwinter, has responded strongly to the warmer winters. In 1900 it usually froze around January 30, and it had been 50 years since its widest point, between Burlington and Plattsburgh, had been open all winter. In 2008 it tended to freeze around February 13, and its widest portion had been open 15 out of the last 30 winters.

As a result of the late freezes and warm years, the fraction of the winter when the lake is completely frozen has decreased from over 60% to under 20%. This has obvious consequences for the recreational use of the lake and perhaps biological consequences as well.

The other Adirondack lakes for which we have records are smaller and still freeze most winters. Their freezing and thawing times depend on their size and depth, and differ from lake to lake. Some show clear trends. Schroon Lake and Mirror Lake now have three weeks less ice cover than they used to. Others, like Lake George and Lake

ICE-IN AND ICE-OUT DATES

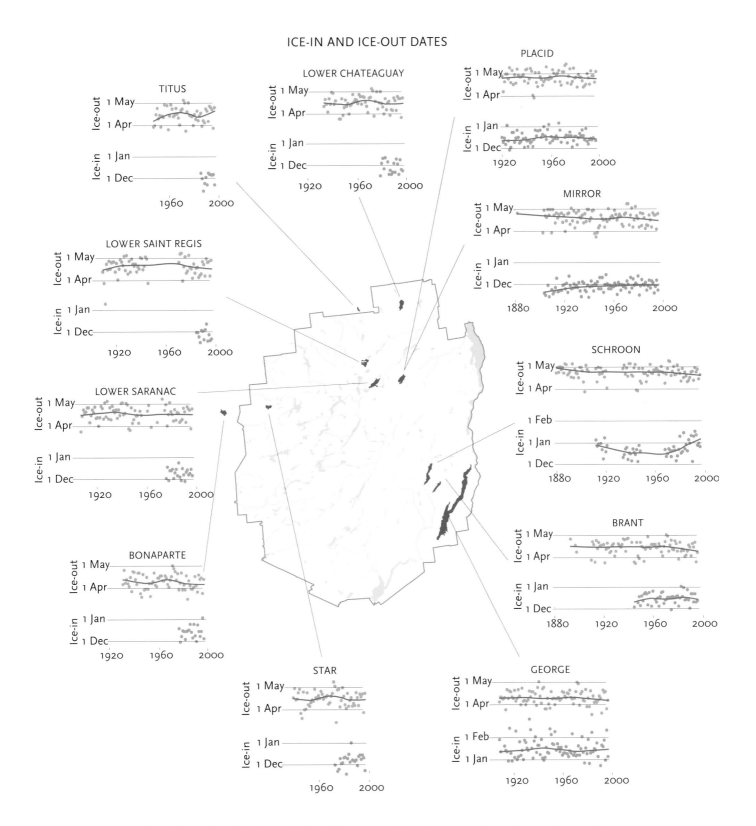

Placid, have hardly changed. And for many others the records are incomplete, and we have no way of knowing whether there is any pattern at all.

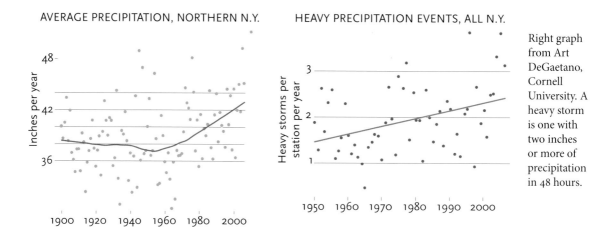

AVERAGE PRECIPITATION, NORTHERN N.Y.

HEAVY PRECIPITATION EVENTS, ALL N.Y.

Right graph from Art DeGaetano, Cornell University. A heavy storm is one with two inches or more of precipitation in 48 hours.

Rain, Snow, and Snowmelt

Changes in precipitation have been smaller than changes in temperature and less in accord with what regional climate models are predicting.

Overall, total precipitation has increased and is about 13% greater than it was in 1960. With this increase has come an increase in the frequency of heavy storms. In 1950 each New York weather station experienced, on average, 1.5 heavy storms per year. By 2006, each station was experiencing 2.5 heavy storms per year.

Since it is heavy storms that cause floods, wash out crops, and kill aquatic animals and plants, this increase is significant. Highly damaging storms, with four inches of rain or more, are still rare. But the probability of one occurring is nearly twice as high as it was 60 years ago and apparently getting higher.

The increases in storms and general wetness were expected. What was not is the seasonal pattern. Climate models suggest that we will have wetter winters and dryer summers. Instead, over the last 50 years, our summers and falls have gotten wetter and our winters have hardly changed.

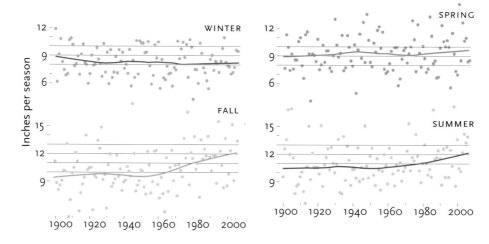

AVERAGE SEASONAL PRECIPITATION, NORTHERN NEW YORK

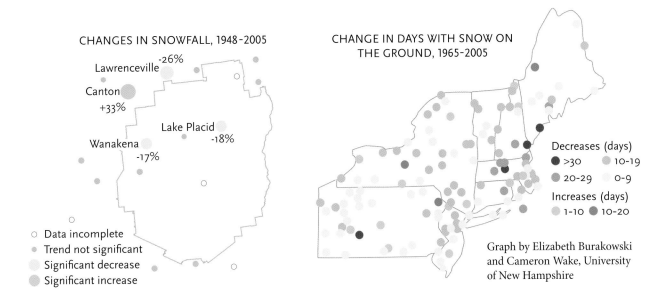

CHANGES IN SNOWFALL, 1948-2005

-26%
Lawrenceville
Canton
+33%
Lake Placid
-18%
Wanakena
-17%

○ Data incomplete
• Trend not significant
  Significant decrease
  Significant increase

CHANGE IN DAYS WITH SNOW ON
THE GROUND, 1965-2005

Decreases (days)
● >30   10-19
  20-29 0-9
Increases (days)
  1-10 ● 10-20

Graph by Elizabeth Burakowski
and Cameron Wake, University
of New Hampshire

The patterns in snowfall are less clear, partly because the data are much less complete, and partly because snowfall is increasing in some places and decreasing in others. In the Adirondacks (left graph), three stations have shown significant decreases, one a significant increase, and nine no change.

If we look, instead, at the number of days in which there is an inch of snow or more on the ground, there is a clear regional pattern (right graph). Most of New York and New England have lost, on average, 2 to 4 weeks of snow cover in 40 years. Depending on the station, this is a decrease of 15% to 30% in the number of days with snow.

Some of the decrease in snow cover has been caused by winter thaws, and some by precipitation falling as rain rather than snow. Either way, more water is running off in the winter and less accumulating in the snow pack. This is shown by the shift in the center-of-volume (cv) dates, the dates when rivers have carried half the water they are going to carry that year. The cv dates for large New England rivers without dams, after being constant for much of the 20th century, have become 10 to 12 days earlier in the last 30 years.

Earlier cv dates mean more water—sometimes a lot more—in the winter and early spring and less in the summer. Both have important consequences. More water in the winter means more winter flood events and more transport of the nitrogen acids that accumulate in forests impacted by acid rain when the vegetation is dormant. Less

CENTER-OF-VOLUME DATES FOR 10 NORTHERN NEW ENGLAND RIVERS

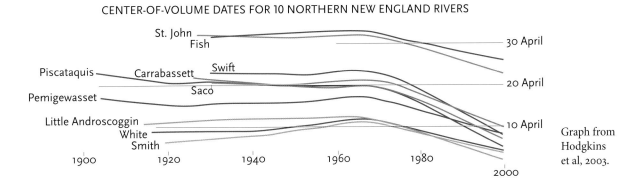

St. John
Fish
Piscataquis
Carrabassett
Swift
Pemigewasset
Saco
Little Androscoggin
White
Smith

30 April
20 April
10 April

1900   1920   1940   1960   1980   2000

Graph from
Hodgkins
et al, 2003.

water in the summer means dryer watersheds, lower flows, higher temperatures, less water for wetlands, more problems from pollution, and less habitat for animals dependent on cold water and steady flows.

Summary

Currently the Adirondacks are experiencing the beginnings of climate change: warmer summers and winters, earlier springs, longer growing seasons, and more rainfall. Falls last longer and springs come earlier. Lakes freeze later and sometimes not at all. Snow doesn't last as long and runs off faster. Summers are wetter and intense rain events more common, but average summer river flows are lower.

The warming has accelerated since 1970. The summer warming rate, from 1966 to 2006, was 3.5 degrees per century. The spring warming rate for this period was 4.4 degrees per century, and the winter warming rate a noteworthy 8.8 degrees per century.

Taken together, the climate records show that the kind of warming we experienced in the last century—about 2 degrees total—has been largely benign. It has caused noticeable changes but does not represent a major shift in climate.

We should not take much comfort from this. Climate warming has arrived faster in northern New York than anyone expected. The current warming rate is twice as fast as that of the last century, and is in fact already equal to what climate models predict for the next century under a low-emission scenario.

Because of lags in the climate system, the current warming rate reflects the atmospheric carbon levels of several decades ago. Since atmospheric carbon has risen since then and will likely continue to rise for several decades more, the warming we have already seen may only be a taste of the warming that is coming.

Lake Champlain at ice-out, March, 2008

3 THE CLIMATE PROBLEM IS AN ENERGY PROBLEM

The climate problem is caused by the carbon we are releasing into the atmosphere. Most of the carbon comes from the burning of fossil fuels. We burn these fuels to get energy, and the climate problem will only be solved if we can use less energy or produce energy without using fossil fuels.

This chapter is about fossil fuels and the alternatives that may replace them. How much do we use, and what do we use them for? What did we do before we had them? Can we replace them with other fuels?

World Energy Use

For context, we start with the whole world. In 2006, humans used 15 trillion watts of power. Four-fifths of this came from fossil fuels. Oil contributed a third of the power and coal and natural gas about a quarter each.

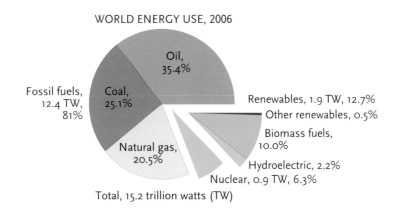

WORLD ENERGY USE, 2006

Oil, 35.4%

Fossil fuels, 12.4 TW, 81%

Coal, 25.1%

Renewables, 1.9 TW, 12.7%
Other renewables, 0.5%
Biomass fuels, 10.0%

Natural gas, 20.5%

Hydroelectric, 2.2%
Nuclear, 0.9 TW, 6.3%

Total, 15.2 trillion watts (TW)

The amount of fossil fuel required to produce 12 trillion watts is very large. The world produces about 40 million tons of fossil fuels each day. This is about 7 times greater than world grain production (5.5 million tons per day) and represents 15 times as much energy.

The emergence of the fossil fuel economy took about 200 years. In 1800 the human energy supply was 90% biomass, augmented with small amounts of coal. By 1900 we derived about half our energy from biomass and half from fossil fuels. Now 81% of world energy comes from fossil fuels, 10% from biomass, and 9% from nuclear and renewables.

On the world scale, nuclear energy supplies only 6% of total energy use. But this understates its importance. Nuclear power is used exclusively to generate electricity, and electricity is the cleanest and most flexible kind of energy we have. World-wide, 16% of electricity comes from nuclear power. France generates 79% of its electricity from nuclear power, Belgium 56%, and Sweden 46%. The United States generates 19% of its electricity from nuclear power, and New York State a nontrivial 29%.

The renewables supply about 13% of total world energy. Most of this comes from biomass and hydropower—the old renewables that civilization has used for millennia.

Wind, solar, and geothermal, the new renewables on which much hope is pinned, currently supply only 0.5% of world energy.

On close inspection, some the old renewables turn out to be more polluting and less renewable than we hoped. Far from being clean and permanent, many have significant greenhouse emissions and useful lives of less than a century. Forests that are harvested unsustainably generate carbon emissions. New hydroelectric reservoirs emit greenhouse gases; old ones fill with sediment and generate less power. They are still better than fossil fuels, but are neither permanent nor carbon-free.

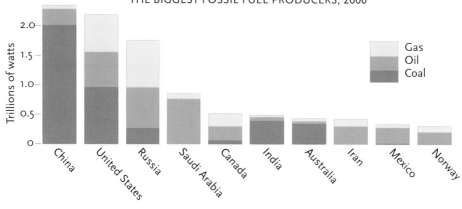

THE BIGGEST FOSSIL FUEL PRODUCERS, 2006

Energy Equity: Is there enough energy to go around?

Fossil fuel resources are unevenly distributed. The top ten producers, shown above, supply over three-quarters of the world's fossil fuels. The top three produce half. The list of large producers is thus a quick guide to 21st-century economic power. It says, explicitly, that China, the United States, Russia, and Saudi Arabia are fuel rich and likely to remain powerful, and, given the special importance of oil, that Iran, Mexico, and Norway are more important than their size might lead us to think. And it says, by omission, that Europe, South America, and Africa are at a geopolitical disadvantage, and may suffer because of it.

The list can also be read in a darker way. If reducing fossil fuel use becomes a 21st-century priority, the list tells us who stands to lose the most from reductions and hence who will be most likely to oppose them. The United States, the world's second largest fossil fuel producer, is high on that short list.

Distributed evenly, the average human would use 2.3 kilowatts of power or 20,000 kilowatt-hours per year. This is about one-fifth of what an average American uses, and is, by our standards, not very much power. It is enough to put several thousand calories of vegetarian food on the table, heat a small house in a mild climate, and perhaps drive a small car a few thousand miles a year. But it is not enough to support a meat and dairy diet, or heat a medium-sized house in our climate, or drive a large car or travel by air.

Actual use, of course, is uneven, and so some of us have meat diets and large cars and some don't. Wealthy countries, and especially those that have cold climates or are major energy producers themselves, tend to use over 7 kilowatts per person.

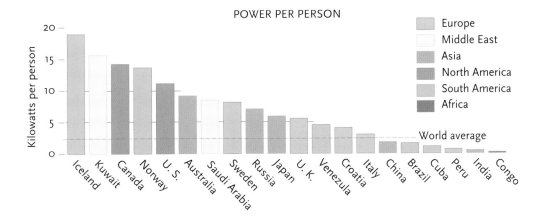

POWER PER PERSON

Kilowatts per person

- Europe
- Middle East
- Asia
- North America
- South America
- Africa

World average

Iceland, Kuwait, Canada, Norway, U.S., Australia, Saudi Arabia, Sweden, Russia, Japan, U.K., Venezuela, Croatia, Italy, China, Brazil, Cuba, Peru, India, Congo

Poorer and warmer countries use half this or less. China, for example, uses about 2 kilowatts per person, just below the world average.

The poorest countries use too little to show on the graph. Ethiopia has 47 watts per capita, enough to light a small incandescent bulb. Chad, the poorest country in the International Energy Agency database, has only 10 watts per capita, barely enough to make a few pieces of toast a day.

How much power do humans really need? The graph suggests that, at least in Japan and the U.K., it is possible to have a comfortable life in a modern economy on 5 to 7 kilowatts of power. But it does not appear possible to have a comfortable life and a western life-style on 2 to 3 kilowatts of power.

Since many of the people in the world aspire to a western life-style, this is a sobering conclusion. *At present, there is not enough energy to go around.* If current world energy supplies were shared equitably, we would not starve, but neither we nor anyone else would have the kind of lives most people want.

What this means is that there are two world energy problems, not one. To prevent dangerous climate change we need to use less fossil fuel. To give people comfortable lives we need to increase the world energy supply.

The only way to solve both energy problems will be with new, carbon-free energy sources. Cutting energy consumption will be necessary, but will not be enough. For a stable climate, the rich countries will need to cut their fossil fuel use by 90% or more. Doing this without new sources will be impossible. No matter how much we conserve, the United States will never cut its energy use to the level of Cuba or Peru; thus to reduce fossil fuel use we need to find fossil fuel replacements.

The problem for the developing countries is to find more power for their people without emitting more carbon. Energy equity—the principle that every country should have an equal per capita energy supply—says that they have a right to do this. The question is how they will do it. Currently China's and India's economies depend on coal. They will never leave this coal in the ground unless they have something equally cheap and useful to replace it with.

A useful way of visualizing world energy needs is to plot per capita power against population, creating rectangles whose area is proportional to the total power used (p. 14). Such a plot divides the world into tall skinny regions (North America, Eurasia) of high per capita use and low population, and broad low ones like Asia, where per capita use is low and population is high.

The red line separates the energy rich from the energy poor. The regions left of the line contain about a quarter of the world's population, have over 4 kilowatts of

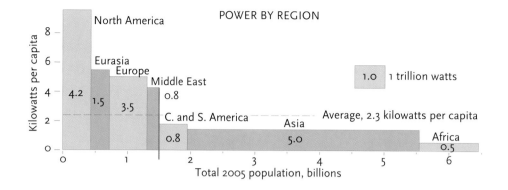

power per capita, and consume about two-thirds of the world's energy. Those to the right contain three-quarter's of the world's population, have less than 2 kilowatts per capita, and consume only about a third of the world's energy.

This graph quantifies what the previous one suggested: if 5 kilowatts per capita is the minimum power needed for a comfortable life, two-thirds of the people in the world do not have enough to live comfortably. Further, if energy were equally distributed, everyone would be energy poor. There would simply not be enough to provide the kind of amenities—central heating, private cars, electric appliances, air travel—that the countries on the left of the graph take for granted.

Thus population and inequality complicate the climate problem, as they do many other problems.

What Energy Equity Would Require

A world with energy equity would have to support the present population, 6.5 billion, and give them enough energy for healthy and fulfilling lives. This might not need an American or Swedish level of consumption, but it would probably need more than a Brazilian or Chinese level. Let us assume that, with improvements in efficiency, it could be achieved with 4 kilowatts per person. Achieving this would require us to modify the population and energy diagram above until it looked like this:

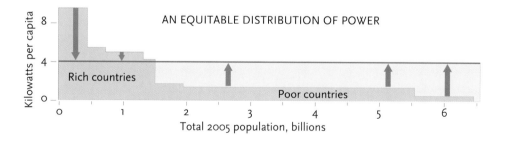

Use by the rich countries would contract and use by the poor ones grow, and both would end up with 4 kilowatts per capita. Overall, the world energy supply would have to increase from 15 trillion watts to 26 trillion watts. To do this while stabilizing climate might require cutting fossil fuel use to, say, 2 trillion watts. This would require creating 21 trillion watts of new, nonfossil power, as in the diagram to the right.

The central question that everyone who thinks about the climate problem wrestles with is whether we can come up with this much new carbon-free power before our fossil fuel use commits us to dangerous levels of climate change.

This question is too large for an Adirondack book. But it poses a related question. If the developed world is to cut its carbon emissions, we must cut ours. The logical place to start is by cutting our energy use. To do this, we need to know how much we use. Are we really using 10 kilowatts of power per person? What do we use it for? How could we use less?

New nonfossil, 21 TW

Fossil, 2 TW

Existing nonfossil, 3 TW

Total, 26 trillion watts (TW) for 6.5 billion people

HORSEPOWER AND PERSON POWER

3,000 watts input, 600 watts output

400 watts input 80 watts output

Energy Before Fossil Fuels

One way of understanding why we use as much energy as we do is to look back to when we didn't.

Consider a small Adirondack town, perhaps North Elba, in 1840. It had a few-dozen households, most of which farmed. Heat was from wood, motive power from muscles, and lighting, such as it was, from candles or whale oil lamps. Grain was ground locally, and the iron for horseshoes and farm tools was produced by small forges in the nearby towns. Sugar was produced from sap. Cobblers still went from town to town, and some spinning and weaving was still done locally. Manure and compost were the only fertilizers, and seeds were saved from previous crops.

Some manufactured goods and commodities—textiles, cookware, glass, crockery, salt—were brought in by wagon. But the cost of overland transport was high, and the total amounts were small.

There were probably no fossil fuels in the town. Coal was too heavy to transport through the mountains; kerosene was unknown in the United States. It would be another 18 years before the first North American oil wells were drilled in Ontario and, a year later, in Pennsylvania.

There were, however, water-powered machines and wood-fired heaters. Most towns had water-powered gristmills or sawmills. The iron-making towns had water-powered trip hammers and bellows. Iron box and parlor stoves were in wide use by the 1830s and would have been found in stores and inns and at least some of the houses.

How much energy was there in such a town? What was the average energy use, and what kind of peak power might a settlement muster?

For a farm family, the largest energy input would be firewood. A family of five might use 15 cords of wood a year for heat and cooking. This would be a total power of 10,000 watts, or 2,000 watts per person. Much of this was wasted: fireplaces and early stoves typically sent 90% of the energy of the fuel up the chimney.

The next, and only other, large input would be food for themselves and their animals. Their basic metabolic needs, averaged over resting and working, might be 100 watts per person and 500 watts per horse.

In addition, there would be some embedded energy in the things they bought. Textiles might have been made by water-powered machinery, horseshoes made in a forge heated by charcoal. But in those days farm families bought little, and the embedded energy flow of the household was small.

Putting this all together, the direct household energy use would be 12.5 kilowatts, or 2.5 kilowatts per person. The indirect use, through embedded energy, would have been much smaller, perhaps a few thousand watts or 0.5 kilowatt per person.

Very little of this energy became useful work. Viewed as heat engines, animals are only about 20% efficient. Put 500 watts of food into a farmer or a horse and you get about 100 watts of work out. A person working moderately hard does a little over half of a kilowatt-hour of mechanical work in a day. This is less than the mechanical energy we can get from 10 cents' worth of electricity or a pint of gasoline.

WATER POWER AND WOOD HEAT, CA. 1840

Waterwheel, 10 kilowatts input, 6 kilowatts output

Bloomery forge and trip hammer, 250 kilowatts heat input, 100 tons iron per year

Parlor stove, 5 kilowatts heat input, 2 kilowatts heat output

What about machines and massed power? The small waterwheels used in country mills produced 5 to 10 kilowatts of mechanical power. The charcoal fires in blacksmith shops and small forges produced ten times or more this amount of heat, but no mechanical power. The combined muscle power of the town, say 50 men and 10 horses working together at a barn raising, might have been 20 kilowatts.

What these numbers tell us is that an early Adirondack town, while rich in land and fuel wood, was poor in mechanical energy. A man and a team, working steadily, could do less work than a medium-sized riding lawn mower. A week of eight-hour days netted them less useful work than we get from 5 gallons of gasoline. The town gristmill, or the massed person-power and horsepower of the town, had less mechanical power than a small motorcycle.

Mechanical power is what enables us to move freely and do hard work easily. Without it, early Adirondackers worked hard and moved with difficulty. It took them perhaps 50 hours to raise and harvest an acre of wheat. It takes us one. They could travel 25 miles in a day. We can go halfway around the world.

These numbers are important because they show us how far we have come and caution us about where we do not want to go. The early Adirondacks, after all, were a solar society. All their energy came from the sun, collected by green plants and water, and converted to mechanical energy by muscles and waterwheels. As a result, they were energy poor and their lives were hard.

One widely advocated way of solving our energy problem is to build a new solar society. What the past tells us is that if we want to do this without sacrificing our material welfare, we are going to have to find better collectors and converters. Otherwise we could be back at 3 kilowatts of power per person, a level that, given our climate and our needs, none of us would willingly choose.

What Fossil Fuels Have Done

Fossil fuels changed the Adirondacks, as they did the world.

The obvious ways were heat engines and electricity. Small steam engines, with outputs of 10 kilowatts or so, had arrived in the Adirondacks in the early 1800s. By 1900 steam engines were the dominant form of mechanical transport, and their size and power had increased by over 100 times. Their use was largely commercial. Only the rich—the Durants and Vanderbilts and their peers—had private steam engines.

By 2000 steam engines had been replaced by internal combustion engines and gas turbines. The largest ones—big aircraft engines, the giant diesels used in container ships—were again 100 times more powerful than the engines of a century before. And, perhaps even more important, the smallest ones were light and cheap, and made personal transport and personal power sources a way of life. Today a homeowner with a chain saw has more power at her or his disposal than a farmer had with a heavy team. A kid on an ATV has more power than William Durant did at the wheel of his steam yacht.

If fossil fuels and internal combustion made it possible for everyone to have heat engines, electricity made it unnecessary to have them. Electricity was the first kind of power that could be generated in one place and used in another. And it was, and still is, the only kind of power that can be changed easily into every other sort of power. With electricity you can make heat or light, run machines, or store and transmit information. You can produce steel or silicon, mix bread, show a movie, or power

ADIRONDACK HEAT ENGINES, CA. 1900

Steam yacht, 60,000 watts heat
input, 15,000 watts output

Shea logging locomotive, 150,000 watts
heat input, 37,000 watts output

Steam donkey engine, 30,000 watts
heat input, 7,500 watts output

Early trolley, 100,000 watts electric
input, 80,000 watts output

a trolley or a submarine. You can even make a river run uphill, storing power until you want it again. Our civilization is defined by its abundance of electricity and will only persist in present form as long as electricity remains plentiful.

Commercial electrical generation began in the 1880s and spread rapidly. As with combustion engines, electrical generators rapidly became bigger and more efficient. Thomas Edison's first U.S. powerhouse, in New York City, had six 100-kilowatt generators and an efficiency of 4%. A hundred years later the largest individual generators produce 1.5 billion watts each, equivalent to 15,000 of Edison's first machines, and are 40% efficient. The largest power stations today produce over 10 billion watts, again about 15,000 times larger than Edison's first station.

ADIRONDACK HEAT ENGINES, 2000

400 kilowatts input,
100 kilowatts output

200 kilowatts input,
50 kilowatts output

100 kilowatts input,
25 kilowatts output

50,000 kilowatts input,
15,000 kilowatts output

0.5 kilowatt input,
0.1 kilowatt output

50 kilowatts input,
15 kilowatts output

Energy in Food and Goods

Heat engines and electricity are obvious signs of a fossil fuel culture. Large flows of food and goods are equally important but less obvious ones. The food and goods require energy to produce and transport. We call this energy *embedded energy*. Strictly speaking, the energy should be called something like production energy, but *embedded* is widely used and I use it here.

The food and goods used in our 1840 Adirondack town had little embedded energy. Most of what the town used was made or grown locally. Farmers could not invest more energy in a crop than the crop returned to them without starving. Manufacturing did use energy, but the amounts of energy involved—a few kilowatt-hours per pound for pottery or textiles or iron—were modest by modern standards.

Today, farming and manufacturing are energy intensive. In modern farming, fertilizer is usually the largest energy input. Farmers, charged with feeding 6.5 billion people, are producing four to five times as much food per acre as they did in 1900. To do this they use artificial fertilizers made from methane and nitrogen gas via the Haber-Bosch process. These fertilizers contain 10 kilowatt-hours of embedded energy per pound, six times more than steel. They were uncommon 60 years ago, and are now ubiquitous: world-wide about 30% to 40% of the nitrogen in proteins and 50% of the nitrogen in crops comes from synthetic fertilizer.

Besides fertilizers, producing foods requires seeds, chemicals, irrigation, machinery, and transportation, and all of these require energy. As a result, conventionally produced food contains large amounts of embedded energy. Meat, sugar, and whiskey all require more energy per pound to produce than steel.

Like modern food, modern materials like aluminum, plastics, and silicon are energy intense and the things manufactured from them even more so. Plastics use 5 times as much energy per pound as steel. The silicon in chips and solar panels requires 100 times as much energy as steel. As a result, the computer on which I work has about 1,500 kilowatt-hours of embedded energy, equal to 5 years of hard manual work. My small station wagon has perhaps 30,000 kilowatt-hours of embedded energy, equal to several lifetimes of manual work. This is why computers and cars are not made in barns with hand tools.

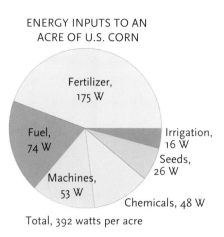

ENERGY INPUTS TO AN ACRE OF U.S. CORN

Fertilizer, 175 W

Irrigation, 16 W

Seeds, 26 W

Chemicals, 48 W

Machines, 53 W

Fuel, 74 W

Total, 392 watts per acre

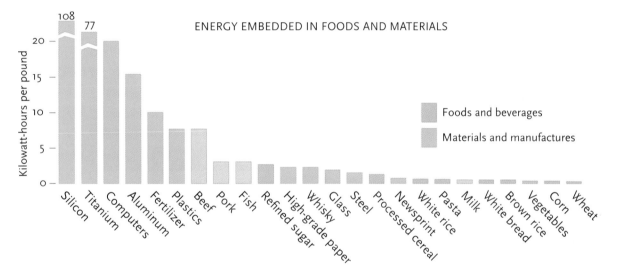

ENERGY EMBEDDED IN FOODS AND MATERIALS

Foods and beverages

Materials and manufactures

Embedded Energy Adds Up

If we look at an Adirondack town and try to visualize the energy flowing into it, the direct energy flows—the power lines, the filling stations, the hydroelectric plant, the fuel oil and propane trucks—are most obvious. But depending on the size of the town, the embedded flows may be as large or larger. Every truck that comes into town represents a flow of embedded energy. Every warehouse, loading dock, and store is part of a hidden grid that enables us to use embedded energy. Until we understand this, we will not understand how deeply fossil fuel energy is woven into our communities or how hard it will be to remove it.

Consider, for example, a medium-sized department store that sells a ton of manufactured goods a day. If the average energy in the goods is 10 kilowatt-hours per pound, the average flow of energy in these goods is then 600 kilowatts, the size of a small hydroelectric station. Or imagine a town of 10,000 people, eating an average American diet. The town will have a flow of 6 or 7 million watts of embedded energy for its food. Now add the flows in clothing, furniture, cars, building materials, electronics, and all the other things we buy. The total could easily go to 20 or 30 million watts. This is a big hydro station, running 24/7.

Embedded energy, in other words, adds up. If we care about energy issues, we ignore it at our peril.

THE DIRECT ENERGY USE OF AN ADIRONDACK FOSSIL FUEL HOUSEHOLD

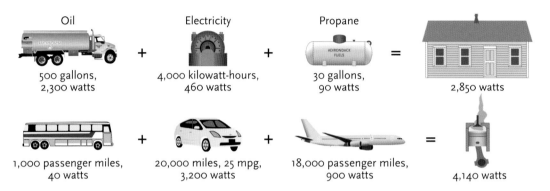

Oil		Electricity		Propane		
500 gallons, 2,300 watts	+	4,000 kilowatt-hours, 460 watts	+	30 gallons, 90 watts	=	2,850 watts
1,000 passenger miles, 40 watts	+	20,000 miles, 25 mpg, 3,200 watts	+	18,000 passenger miles, 900 watts	=	4,140 watts

Measuring Household Energy Consumption

To reduce energy consumption, we must measure it. Our starting point is the household—a group of people sharing food, heat, and transport. How much energy might an Adirondack household use?

The answer depends on how many people are in the household and what they do. The diagram above, based on a small survey we took in 2008, shows the direct energy consumption of an idealized Adirondack family. The family has three people, lives in a well-insulated house of about 1,500 square feet, commutes to work by car, and makes one cross-country plane trip a year. They eat an average American diet, mostly from the supermarket, and spend about $10,000 per year on goods and services besides food and energy. With these assumptions, their direct energy consumption for heat, electricity, and transport is about 7,000 watts.*

Compared to the farm household of two centuries ago, this household is thrifty in its use of heat, and lavish in its use of mechanical energy. Because of an efficient house, it uses less than a quarter of the energy the 1840 family did for heating and cooking. Because of fossil fuels and electricity, it has over ten times as much mechanical energy available as they did. The mechanical energy cuts wood, tills the garden, pumps water, does laundry and dishes, circulates heat and air, and provides 29,000 miles a year of travel, something that would have been inconceivable in 1840. Probably no generation prior to our own traveled as far in their lives as we do, or emitted as much carbon doing it.

The budget shown above is for direct energy use, and does not include the energy embedded in food and stuff. My best estimate of food, explained in the chapter notes, is that an average American diet represents an energy flow of about 750 watts per person. I have no good way of estimating the energy in the goods that the family buys. David MacKay, in a careful estimate for Britain, suggests that miscellaneous purchases and their packaging and transport represent an energy flow of 2,000 watts

*To calculate the energy budget for your own household, see pp. 69-77 and 169-170.

per Briton. I have used his estimate, but increased it to 2,500 watts per American out of national pride.

ENERGY BUDGET OF AN ADIRONDACK HOUSEHOLD

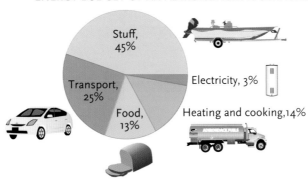

With these assumptions, the total household energy use, direct and embedded, is 17 kilowatts. Household energy—heat, light, and food—are only about a quarter. Transport is another quarter. Purchased goods—stuff—are the remaining half.

The energy per person is about 5,600 watts. This is half the U.S. per capita average of 11,500 watts, but we deliberately picked a thrifty country household and have not included the energy embedded in vehicles or buildings, or the household's share of the energy used by governments and schools. So the result seems reasonable for a quick estimate.

Thrifty or not, if the 111 million households in the United States used 17,000 watts each, they would use 1.9 trillion watts of power, or 55% of U.S. consumption. This suggests that despite the size and complexity of the U.S. economy, it is in some sense a large village of energy-using households, whose consumption drives national consumption. If this is true it means that our houses and food and furnaces matter, and that to reduce national consumption we must reduce personal consumption.

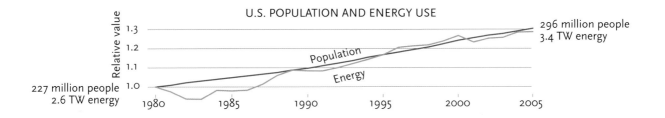

National Consumption and Personal Consumption

This is an important enough conclusion to be worth a careful look. Currently the United States uses about 3.4 trillion watts of power, or about 11 kilowatts per person. For the last 25 years U.S. energy use has been growing about 1% a year. This is not a big growth rate, but since we started off as the largest energy users in the world, it has required that we add nearly a trillion watts of power in that time.

Over that period, the U.S. population growth has also been 1% per year. Energy growth has been somewhat variable, population growth more steady. But even so, the ratio between the two has not varied by more than about 5% in 25 years, suggesting that the two are closely related.

UNITED STATES ENERGY USE BY ECONOMIC SECTOR, 2005

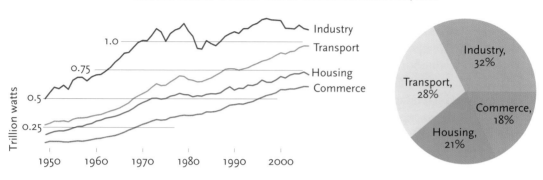

This makes sense if we think about how the economy is structured. About a third of U.S. energy (all household, half of transportation) is used directly by individuals. The rest is used by businesses and government. But, since businesses exist to serve customers, much of the remaining energy is related to personal consumption as well. Industry makes the things that people use and supplies the materials and tools to make them. Commerce finances and sells the stuff that industry makes, and transportation delivers it. The parallel curves of the housing, commercial, and transportation, all rising at about 1%, suggest that the growth rates of sectors are related to one another and to population growth.

There are, of course, energy uses that do not reflect personal consumption. The United States government, the largest buyer of fossil fuel in the world, uses about 36 billion watts of power, or 120 watts for each of us. This is impressive, but it is still only 1% of U.S. consumption. Add fuel for the industries that supply things to the government and you might double or triple that. Add the state and local governments, and all their suppliers, and you might double it again. But even so, total government-related energy use is going to be a small part of total national use.

And so it seems, the conclusion stands: *national energy consumption is driven by personal consumption, and to reduce national consumption we must reduce personal consumption.*

Replacing energy or reducing consumption?

There are two routes to lowering carbon emissions: reducing our energy use and replacing fossil fuels with renewables. Reducing our energy use is hard, because it means changing behavior, being more efficient, being content with less. And so it is tempting to think that we might avoid the hard work by greening our energy supply—simply replace fossil fuels with renewables and nuclear, and continue to use all the energy we want.

Imagine that we try this for the United States. The United States uses 2.8 trillion watts of fossil fuel. We decide to replace it with a mixture of solar, wind, nuclear, biomass, and biofuels. We decide to give them equal pieces of the pie, and so each must produce 560 billion watts. The graphs below show the facilities we will need and how much land it will take. The results are somewhat surprising.

RESOURCES REQUIRED TO REPLACE 2.8 TRILLION WATTS OF FOSSIL FUELS

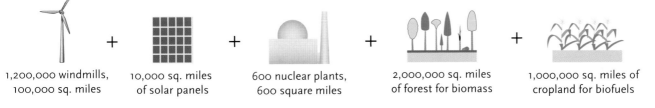

| 1,200,000 windmills, 100,000 sq. miles | 10,000 sq. miles of solar panels | 600 nuclear plants, 600 square miles | 2,000,000 sq. miles of forest for biomass | 1,000,000 sq. miles of cropland for biofuels |

Note the large areas: The solar panels need an area the size of Vermont, the windmills need an area the size of Oregon, and the biomass and biofuels an area comparable to the contiguous United States.

The reason for these large areas is that the power densities of renewables (the amount of power that can be recovered from a given area) are low. Solar panels in the United States produce, on average, about 20 watts per square meter (metric units are standard here) or 52 million watts per square mile. Windmills, which have to be spaced far enough apart so as not to interfere with one another, produce a tenth of this, 2 watts per square meter or 5.2 million watts per square mile. Croplands produce a quarter of this, 0.5 watt per square meter. We lose a lot of this energy when we produce biofuels, and so our net energy production is likely to be about 0.2 watt per square meter, or 520,000 watts per square mile. And finally, since forests are less productive than croplands, their energy production will likely average 0.1 watt per square meter at most, or 260,000 watts per square mile.

Taken together, the total area required to replace fossil fuels is just slightly smaller than the lower forty-eight states. We could reduce it by changing the mix and emphasizing wind and solar, or by using nuclear in place of renewables. But this would still not change a basic physical fact: *Renewable energy is dilute, and so renewable resources have large footprints.* To collect enough renewable energy for a high-energy country can take much of the area of the country.

LAND NEEDED TO REPLACE 2.8 TRILLION WATTS OF FOSSIL FUELS

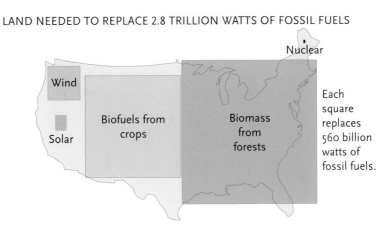

This has two important consequences. The first is that we are never likely to replace all of our current fossil fuel energy with renewables. Instead we are going to have to reduce our energy use, probably by a lot, to get it down to a level where renewables can take over.

The second is that if we are thinking about what a low-emission future might look like, we have to take the issue of footprint seriously. Many of us object to the footprints of oil and coal—the big mines, the roads and pipelines, the wells. But coal mines and oil fields produce energy at densities of 2,000 watts per square meter, and their footprints are thus a hundred times smaller than that of solar power and a thousand times smaller than that of wind power. If we object to the footprints of big coal and big oil, how will we feel about big sun and big wind?

Summary

The climate problem arises because energy consumption, at the personal, national, and world levels, is dominated by fossil fuels. Fossil fuel energy makes it possible to feed and shelter the world population. It also confers comfort, mobility, and wealth on societies like ours that have it in abundance.

Solving the climate problem will require reducing, and eventually eliminating, fossil fuel use. The international agreements that this will require will have to be based on some concept of energy equity, with the rich countries cutting their per capita energy use, and the poor ones being allowed to increase theirs.

Achieving this will require significant reductions in total energy use by the rich countries and widespread replacement of fossil fuels by renewables in both rich and poor countries. Since there does not seem to be enough energy to go around now, this may require, counterintuitively, an increase in total world energy use.

Because renewables are currently only a small part of total energy production, and because their power density is usually low, using them on the scale necessary to replace fossil fuels will be a very large undertaking. If we accomplish it, our lives and landscapes will be greatly changed, and not necessarily in ways that those of us who are advocating this course find it comfortable to think about.

Ice Flows on Hudson, April, 2009

Ross Mountain, Johnsburg

4 HOW MUCH COULD THE ADIRONDACKS CHANGE?

The Adirondacks are already warming, and will certainly warm more over the next century. How long will this warming continue, how warm will it be when it stops, and what will this do to the Adirondacks?

Since the warming is caused by the carbon dioxide in the atmosphere, the first question has a simple answer. The warming will continue as long as carbon dioxide concentrations continue to rise. It will stop when the world temperature stabilizes, perhaps 50 or 100 years after carbon dioxide stops rising.

Carbon dioxide, in turn, will only stop rising when we stop burning fossil fuels. Because there are still a lot of fossil fuels in the ground, this could take a long time.

ESTIMATED RESERVES OF FOSSIL FUELS

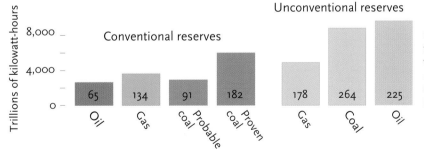

Unconventional reserves

Conventional reserves

Trillions of kilowatt-hours

8,000
4,000
0

Oil 65 | Gas 134 | Probable coal 91 | Proven coal 182 | Gas 178 | Coal 264 | Oil 225

Conventional reserves are those that can be mined economically with standard techniques. *Unconventional* reserves, like oil shales, need special and hence more costly extraction methods.

The graph shows estimated fossil fuel reserves. The numbers in the bars are the years of fuel remaining at the present rate of consumption. Thus we have enough easily accessible oil for 65 years, enough gas for over 100 years, and enough coal for 200 years or more. If we mine the more-difficult-to-extract unconventional resources, all three fuels could last for 300 years.

Thus, if temperatures stabilize in the next 200 years, it will be because the human race has chosen to get its energy from renewables and nuclear, and not because the supply of fossil fuels has run short.

THE CHEMICAL REMOVAL OF CARBON DIOXIDE FROM THE ATMOSPHERE

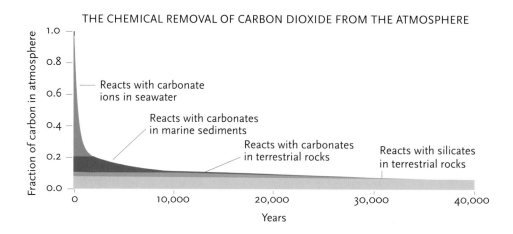

How long will the earth stay warm?

The earth will stay warm until the excess carbon dioxide is removed from the atmosphere. This will not be fast. The graph, based on calculations by David Archer, shows what happens when a large pulse of carbon dioxide, comparable to a century or two of burning fossil fuels, is added to the atmosphere. It doesn't include the storage of carbon in terrestrial vegetation, which happens quickly but has a limited capacity.

The long-term removal of the carbon involves three processes. About 80% is removed by reacting with carbonate ions in seawater. This starts quickly but, because of the slow circulation of the sea, takes nearly 1,000 years to complete. Another 12% is removed by reactions with carbonate rocks, both on land and in shallow seas. This is slower and takes perhaps 40,000 years. Finally, the remaining 8% is removed by reactions with silicate rocks. This is slower still, and takes several million years.

The conclusion is clear. The large-scale effects of global warming will last for several centuries after we stop adding carbon to the atmosphere. The smaller effects will last for thousands of years.

How high could carbon dioxide rise?

It depends on how much fossil fuel we burn. Currently carbon dioxide concentrations are about 387 parts per million (ppm). If we burn all the conventional reserves of fossil fuels, we will get over 700 ppm of carbon dioxide. If we burn all the unconventional reserves, we will get over 1,100 ppm.

These are large numbers. As we will see in a moment, if we wish to avoid ecologically dangerous climate change, we will probably need to keep carbon dioxide concentrations below 500 ppm.

To stabilize the carbon dioxide concentration, we have to reduce our carbon dioxide emissions to near zero. How fast we do this will determine how soon the concentration stabilizes and what level it stabilizes at.

RESULTS OF USING
UP FOSSIL FUELS

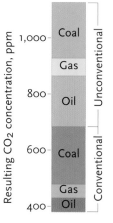

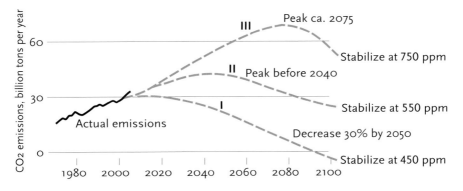

THREE SCENARIOS FOR STABILIZING CO₂

The graph shows three reduction scenarios out of many possible ones. They span the range from **I**, which is the best that we might hope for, to **III**, which was the worst that the scientists of the Intergovernmental Panel on Climate Change were willing to think about in 2002. Scenario **I**, with emissions decreasing almost immediately, gives us a final carbon dioxide concentration of 450 ppm. Scenario **III**, with emissions rising until 2080 and then decreasing sharply, gives us a final carbon dioxide concentration of 750 ppm.

World carbon dioxide emissions, shown by the black line, have been increasing rapidly for the last 5 years. In 2006 they were 32 billion tons of carbon dioxide, two tons higher than any of the scenarios. Scenario **III** may have been the worst-case scenario in 2002, but it is not the worst case now.

How are temperature and carbon dioxide related?

The temperatures that are the most concern to us are the final temperatures that will be reached after carbon emissions stop and CO_2 and temperatures stabilize.

For a given CO_2 level, the models predict a range of possible final temperatures. If, for example, we stopped emitting CO_2 today, the current CO_2 level of 387 ppm will result in an eventual Adirondack warming of 4 to 11 degrees over pre-fossil fuel levels. If instead we stabilize CO_2 at 600 ppm, the range of possible final warmings is 9 to 20 degrees.

The graph on p. 28, adapted from a similar graph for world temperature prepared by the IPCC, shows these relations. The x-axis is the final CO_2 level, the orange figure the range of final warmings. The notes to the left of the figure, which are my own, connect the temperatures to regional climate and biology.

Note that because the climate system responds slowly, it may take a century for temperature to catch up with CO_2. Thus actual warming at a given time is less than the eventual warming that CO_2 emissions have committed us to.

For example: currently we have warmed about 2 degrees from pre-fossil fuel levels. This is old news; it represents the warming that resulted from the CO_2 emissions of 30 or more years ago. The eventual warmings resulting from our present CO_2 level, shown by the red dashed line at 387 ppm, are predicted to be between 4 and 11 degrees.

Said another way, the climate system has momentum, and continues to move for some time after we have stopped pushing it.

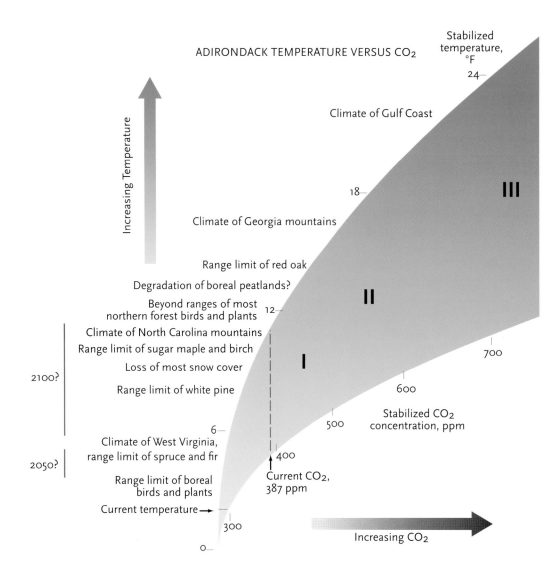

ADIRONDACK TEMPERATURE VERSUS CO₂

The bold numerals on the graph are the three scenarios illustrated on p. 27. They say that:

If we	The stabilized CO₂ will be	And final temperature rise will be
Do all we can fast	450 ppm	6°–14°
Reduce emissions by 2040	550 ppm	8°–18°
Reduce emissions by 2075	750 ppm	12°–25°

Note once more that these are the final temperature rises that will occur *after* emissions have stopped and the climate has stabilized. For Scenarios **II** and **III**, this may be 200 years from now. If we are concerned only with how climate change will affect us, they are not something we need to worry about. But if we are concerned, as citizens of the planet, with how our actions will affect the future of the earth, they have an important message for us: *The next 30 years are critical in the history of the world.* What we do, or do not do, in them may affect the climate and life of the planet for centuries to come.

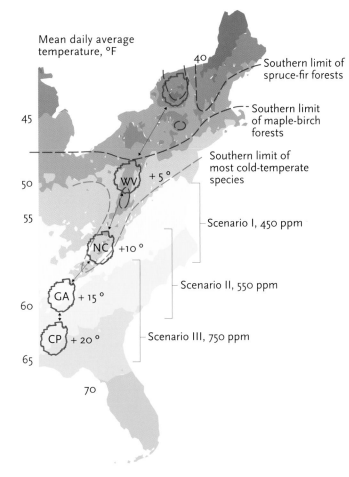

What might a warmer Adirondacks be like?

As temperatures rise our climate will become more southern, and our northern animals and landscapes will become more out of place in them. We can represent this by imagining the Adirondacks moving down the Appalachian mountain chain.

A warming of 5 degrees gives us a climate like that of West Virginia. A warming of 10 degrees or more gives us a climate like that of highland North Carolina. A warming of 15 or 20 degrees gives us a climate like that of highland Georgia or the Gulf coastal plain.

The analogy is only approximate. A temperature warming of 5 degrees will give us temperatures something like those of West Virginia, but will not give us Virginian day-length, sun-angles, or rainfall. A warming of 10 degrees will take us to the climatic limits of sugar maple and yellow birch, but it doesn't mean that all the maples and birch will die when we reach that temperature. Some will persist after we reach it. Others may die before we reach it.

The importance of this map is what it says about the biological and cultural effects of temperature change. The Adirondacks are a region of boreal and cool-temperate forests. They have big bogs, spruce-covered mountains, and snow and ice for much of the winter. They are a place where northern trees like yellow birch, sugar maple, and tamarack thrive, and northern animals like martens, loons, and snowshoe hares live among them. They are a place where people ski, snowmobile, climb, snowshoe, and ice fish, and where the winter economy is built around outdoor recreation.

Neither Adirondack biology nor Adirondack culture will survive the kind of climate changes the map on p. 29 suggests. In climates 5 degrees warmer than ours there are no big bogs, or spruce-fir forests, or mountains with continuous snow cover. Loons and tamaracks and martens are gone. Sugar maple and snowshoe hare are at the edge of their range, and only found in the mountains. Snowmobiling and skiing are limited, and snowshoeing and winter climbing almost nonexistent.

Climates 10 degrees warmer than ours are even more different. Southern Appalachian forests are oak and hickory dominated, and have little in common with Adirondack forests. Few of our common forest animals and plants live in them at all. The graph below shows that of 246 common Adirondack forest species, only 84 (34%) are found at temperatures 10 degrees or more warmer than ours.

NUMBER OF ADIRONDACK FOREST SPECIES FOUND IN CLIMATES 10 °F WARMER THAN OURS

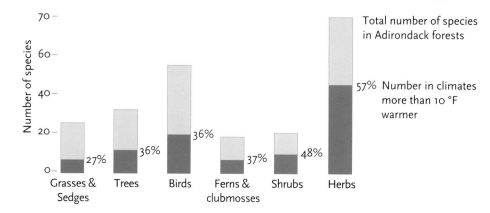

A warmer Adirondacks will have less snow and ice, and this will affect both the winter ecology and the winter economy. The maps at the top of p. 31, based on maps from the New England Climate Impact Assessment, show how snow cover might change with 5 to 10 degrees of warming. Historically most of upland New York had 6 weeks or more with snow cover in December, January, and February. The interior Adirondacks had 10 weeks or more, giving them more-or-less continuous snow cover. The low-emission scenario, with a 5-degree temperature rise, shrinks the 6-week area to the Adirondack highlands and the 10-week area to the highest mountains. The high-emission scenario, with a 10-degree temperature rise, shrinks the 6-week area further and eliminates the 10-week area.

Both winter sports economies and boreal animals seem to need continuous snow cover. The economies need it to attract their customers and pay their overhead. The animals seem to need it to eliminate their less boreal competitors. Either way both are mostly found in areas where there are 10 weeks or more of snow cover. Under the low-emission scenario, their New York habitat contracts by over 90%. Under the high-emission scenario, it disappears entirely.

PREDICTED CHANGES IN WINTER SNOW COVER

1960-1990

2070-2100,
SCENARIO I
LOW EMISSIONS

2070-2100,
SCENARIO III,
HIGH EMISSIONS

Winter days (DJF)
with snow cover
81—90 72—81 63—72 54—63 45—54 <45

Species loss or species replacement?

Over the next century we will likely lose northern species. How fast this will happen and what species will be most affected are unknown. The best we can do is to make simple models of their current distributions and assume, against the odds, that their relations to future climates will resemble their present ones.

The graph shows the results of one such model for forest trees in New York. It estimates how the habitat suitability of twelve common trees will change with a warming of 6 degrees. For all of our species except red oak, the model predicts a decrease of 50% or more in the suitability of the habitat over the next century.

CHANGES IN SUITABILITY OF HABITAT FOR NEW YORK TREES FOR A 6-DEGREE WARMING

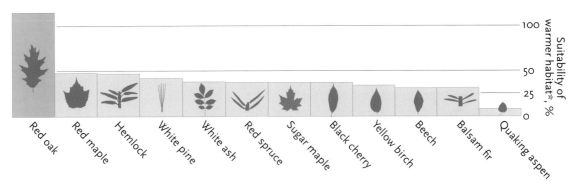

Suitability of warmer habitat*, %

100

50

25

0

Red oak Red maple Hemlock White pine White ash Red spruce Sugar maple Black cherry Yellow birch Beech Balsam fir Quaking aspen

Trees can endure unsuitable conditions for a long time and will likely decline slowly. Other species may go quicker. Biological history suggests that birds and animals can vanish quickly when their habitat ceases to support them. In the last 20 years the whippoorwill, nighthawk, meadowlark, and olive-sided flycatcher, all formerly common species, have vanished from significant parts of their New York range. It seems likely that others may follow them soon.

What is much less certain is how fast, if at all, southern species will replace them. If southern species were able to move north quickly, changing cold-temperate forests gradually into warm-temperate ones, climate change might not be so menacing. But this is unlikely to happen. Most of the plants and animals of the southern Appalachian

*The habitat suitability is defined as the ability of habitat to support populations similar to those that currently exist.

forests are hundreds of miles south of us. A few, mostly birds and butterflies, can migrate quickly. Most of the others migrate slowly, only 10 or 20 miles per century, and it may be hundreds of years before they get to us.

If the climate warms and stays warm, we will eventually have southern forests with southern animals to replace our old northern ones. But my guess is that it will not happen quickly, and in between there may be a prolonged period of loss and decline.

Summary

The fossil fuels we have already burned have committed us to a warming of 5 degrees or more in the coming century. This will be enough to warm our winters, decrease our snowfall, and make the Adirondacks less suitable for some of our animals and plants.

How much additional warming we get will depend on how much fossil fuel we burn. There is more than enough fossil fuel available to commit us to a total warming of 10 to 20 degrees and give us a climate comparable to that of the southern Appalachians. With such a climate there will be little or no ice or snow. Neither our winter recreation industry nor our boreal animals and plants will survive.

The exact amount of warming we will get and the rate at which it will happen are unknown. But the connection between fossil fuel and future warming is no longer in doubt. *If we burn as little as a third of the remaining fossil fuels, we will get carbon dioxide concentrations of over 600 ppm. If this happens, the Adirondacks that we know today will probably not survive.*

Griffin Smith, by Jason Smith

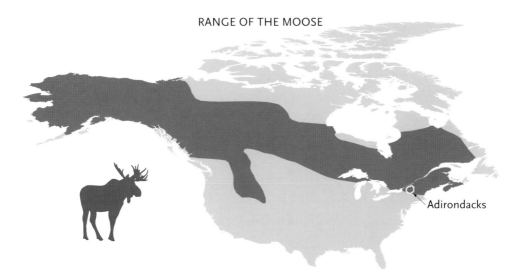

Adirondacks

5 WHAT WE MIGHT LOSE

Just how vulnerable are the Adirondacks to climate change? What parts of our landscape and culture will change the fastest? What parts may be the most resistant?

Our best answers to this come from climate models and geography.

The models suggest that the main changes here will be warmer temperatures, less ice and snow, and heavier rainstorms. We will not have to contend with rising sea levels or thawing permafrost. Our water supplies are probably secure, and our farms are capable of feeding us if farms elsewhere fail. We will probably not suffer violent storms, extended droughts, or gigantic fires.

What we will see is a gradual loss of the northern elements in our landscape. We will lose river ice, then lake ice, and then the ice and snow in the mountains. We will lose the deep cold, the boreal forests and wetlands that depend on it, and the boreal animals and plants that depend on them. We will lose the opportunities for winter recreation, the people—both visitors and residents—who come here for them, and the businesses and facilities that the recreationists support.

Our geography suggests that, because we are a northern landscape, these losses will be extensive. The Adirondacks have species, like moose and marten, that are most successful where there is continuous snow cover. They have winter activities like climbing, ice-fishing, and snowmobiling, that depend on ice and snow. They have landscapes like the open mountain summits and the great bogs that only develop in cold climates. And they have cultural traditions that value northern landscapes and northern activities and will be impoverished when these are gone.

Our geography also suggests that we may be vulnerable because many northern elements are at their climatic limits here. The Adirondacks are the southernmost place in North America where there are large bogs, or open river shores maintained by ice, or mountains with alpine tundra. They are the southernmost place in eastern North America where martens and mink frogs occur. And they are, along with southern Vermont, the southernmost place where there are towns whose winter economies are built around winter sports.

The Adirondacks, then, are a kind of climate frontier, beyond which northern species and northern cultures do not occur. This chapter is a tour of that frontier, looking at what it contains and trying to assess its vulnerability. It starts with natural communities and then looks at human ones.

Boreal Communities

Boreas was the north wind, and the boreal zone is where the north wind governs. The true boreal zone extends across Canada, north of the deciduous forest, where continuous conifer forests occur, and average summer temperatures are less than 64 degrees. Adirondack summer temperatures average around 67 degrees and so we are in the cold temperate zone rather than the boreal zone. But we have many places in the mountains and cold valleys that do in fact have boreal temperatures. These places are relatively small and do not form an extended boreal landscape. But they look and feel like the Canadian boreal when you are in them, and so may be thought of as boreal islands.

The boreal islands contain six kinds of natural communities. In the high mountains there is *krummholz*, the stunted forest of upper elevation, and open *alpine tundra*, the summit meadows and shrublands. In the valleys there are wooded *conifer swamps*, and open *bogs* and *fens*. And finally, along the northern rivers there are *open alluvial corridors*, containing a mixture of meadows, thickets, and wetlands.

All these communities are northern in their biology and geography. Large open bogs, open river corridors, and alpine tundra do not occur south of the Adirondacks. Small bogs do, but the difference in scale is great. A large bog in the Adirondacks may be 500 acres and have a dozen species of boreal birds. A large bog south of them might be 5 acres, and have one or two boreal species. Likewise, conifer swamps, krummholz, and open fens occur south of the Adirondacks, but again the difference in size, and with it the difference in the populations of boreal species they can support, is great.

Boreal Mountain Communities

The Adirondack mountains contain two boreal communities, krummholz and tundra. Krummholz, literally a crooked forest, is the stunted spruce-fir community that develops between about 3,500 feet in elevation and the timberline. It is a relatively common community, both in the Adirondacks and in the Northeast as a whole. It does not have unusual plants, but is important because it is the main New York habitat of the blackpoll warbler, an uncommon bird, and the only New York habitat of Bicknell's thrush, a rare one. The blackpoll warbler also lives around high-elevation ponds. Bicknell's thrush is a mountain specialist, and doesn't seem to breed below 3,500 feet.

ALPINE VEGETATION IN THE HIGH PEAKS

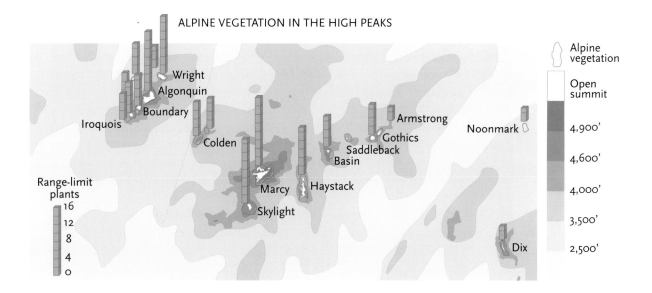

The *alpine tundra* is the low community that develops above timberline. It is a mixture of dwarf shrubs, grasses, sedges, herbs, mosses, and lichens. In northeastern North America, where mountains with timberline are rare, it is one of our rarest communities and contains some of our rarest plants. The Adirondack examples contain around 25 vascular plants and an equal number of mosses and lichens that do not occur outside the alpine zone. At least 20 of the vascular plants and 8 mosses are at their North American range limits here and do not occur south of the High Peaks.

For alpine tundra to develop, two conditions must be met. The climate must be harsh enough—cold, icy, and windy—to prevent trees from growing, and yet moist enough for low herbs to develop in shallow soils.

In the Adirondacks, these conditions are best met at high elevations. As the map shows, the largest examples with the most range-limit species are on the highest mountains. Tundra occurs at 3,500 feet, but is well developed only above 4,000 feet and reaches its richest development above 4,600 feet. On the lower mountains there is either too much competition from trees and shrubs or, because the mountain is below the average cloud height, not enough water. Thus most Adirondack mountains, even if they have an open rocky summit, do not have a tundra community and have few if any alpine plants.

PLANTS OF ALPINE TUNDRA

Lapland rosebay

Bigelow's sedge

Bilberry

Anastrophyllum minutum
(an alpine liverwort)

35

As a result, alpine tundra is one of our smallest and most isolated plant communities. Tim Howard of the New York Natural Heritage Program estimates that about 170 acres of alpine tundra occur on 21 Adirondack summits. Vermont has less than this, New Hampshire over four times as much, and Maine over ten times as much. No eastern mountain south of the Adirondacks has any at all.

How vulnerable will the alpine zones be to climate change? Probably very vulnerable, for several reasons. First, the area is small, and the populations of alpine plants are likewise small and to some extent isolated from one another. Second, the alpine plants are at their ecological limits here and a small change in conditions could make the habitat unsuitable for them. Third, the suitability of their habitat is tied to conditions—winter temperatures and snowpack, summer clouds and fog —that we know to be changing. And fourth, there are competitors from other communities ready to move into the alpine zone as the climate changes.

Much evidence from elsewhere in the world suggests that alpine zones are changing rapidly as climate changes. In both Europe and the Rocky Mountains, forest and krummholz plants are moving uphill and invading alpine zones, and shrubs and stunted trees within the alpine zones are growing taller. The alpine plants, which are low and slow-growing, are getting shaded out, and diversity is decreasing. When, as on the high mountains of Europe, there is open habitat further up the mountain, the alpine plants can move upwards. When, as in the Adirondacks, they are already on the mountain tops, they may die out.

The alpine area of Dix Mountain

Lowland Boreal Communities

The lowland boreal communities include bogs, fens, wooded wetlands, and open river corridors. Like the alpine communities, they are climate dependent and require low temperatures and year-round moisture. And again like the alpine zones, they contain boreal species at their southern range limits.

Where they differ is in their size. The wetlands maps prepared by the Adirondack Park Agency and the State University at Plattsburgh show over a quarter million acres of boreal wetlands in the Adirondacks. Conifer swamps are the commonest, with perhaps 200,000 acres; open bogs and fens and their associated thickets are second, with 50,000 acres; and open river corridors are a distant third, with under 10,000 acres.

The lowland boreal communities are of great biological and cultural significance. They are iconic landscapes with iconic species. They are where the moose, the loon, the beaver, the eagle, and the tamarack live, and where the lynx may once have lived. They were guideboat country once and are the wildest canoe country left to us today. They were also the headwaters of the log-drive rivers, and supplied much of the spruce and pine that built many Adirondack towns and fueled the Adirondack economy for a hundred years.

Today, though less harvested, the lowland boreal remains central to our sense of what the Adirondacks are. It is what the Adirondacks have that the lowlands around us do not have. And, as with the high mountains, it is one of the reasons that we perceive the Adirondacks as deeply and essentially northern.

The lowland boreal is large and complex, and I have written about it at length elsewhere. Here I treat it briefly, with a picture gallery, and a discussion of a few of its characteristic animals and plants and of what climate change may do to them.

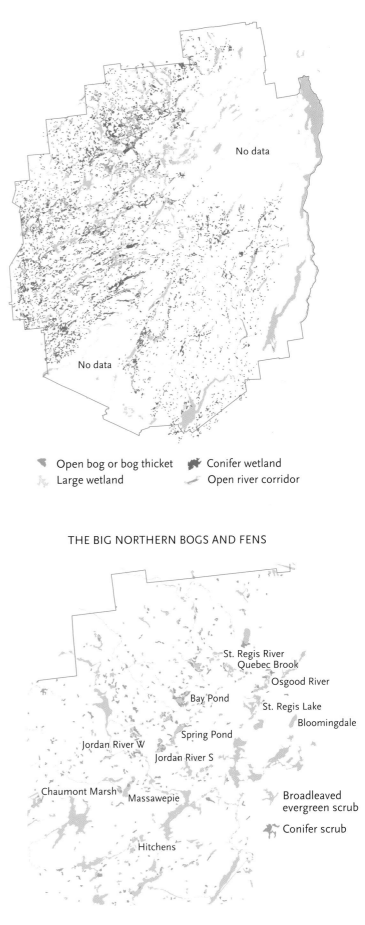

THE BIG NORTHERN BOGS AND FENS

Large open peatlands: Massawepie Bog

Open alluvial wetlands: confluence of Goodnough and Hudson

Black spruce-tamarack swamps and open shores: Osgood River

Open river shores: Oswegatchie River

Ice meadows: Hudson River in Warrensburg

Ice meadows: Hudson River in early spring

Bog rosemary, open bogs

Pod-grass, low wet bogs

White-fringed orchid, open bogs

Hare's-tail sedge, open bogs

Tamarack, bog thickets

Green alder, river shores and mountains

Canadian burnet, ice meadows

Kalm's lobelia, ice meadows

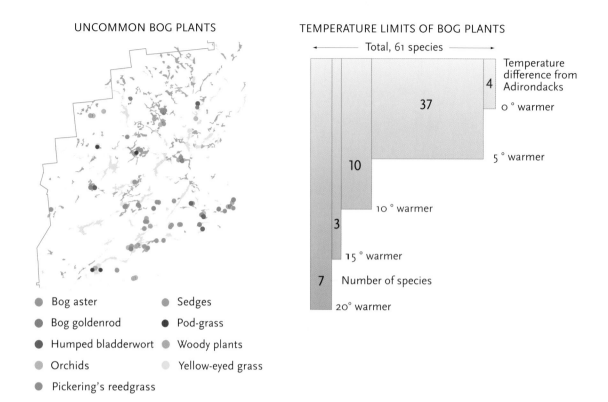

UNCOMMON BOG PLANTS

- Bog aster
- Bog goldenrod
- Humped bladderwort
- Orchids
- Pickering's reedgrass
- Sedges
- Pod-grass
- Woody plants
- Yellow-eyed grass

TEMPERATURE LIMITS OF BOG PLANTS

Total, 61 species

Temperature difference from Adirondacks

4   0 ° warmer
37   5 ° warmer
10   10 ° warmer
3   15 ° warmer
7   Number of species   20° warmer

Lowland Boreal Plants

Lowland boreal plants are, as a group, narrow-leaved, slow-growing, often evergreen, tolerant of wet peaty soils, and intolerant of heat. They dominate northern peatlands where nutrients are scarce but are replaced by taller and faster-growing species in warmer wetlands with more fertile soils.

Altogether the lowland boreal contains around 200 main species of vascular plants and about the same number of mosses and liverworts. This is low by temperate zone standards but typical of the boreal. Many of the plants are wide-ranging species like red spruce and blue-joint grass that occur in other communities. A smaller number, perhaps 100 species, are lowland boreal specialists and do not occur elsewhere.

For many of the boreal specialists, the Adirondacks are the southernmost place where they are truly common. Bog rosemary (top-left illustration, p. 39), which is found in hundreds of Adirondack wetlands and covers large areas, is rare outside of the Adirondacks. It occurs along mountains to West Virginia and the coast to New Jersey, but only in small populations in tiny bogs. Although its range extends further, the Adirondacks are its real ecological boundary.

This is part of a general pattern of thermal intolerance, shown in the graph above. Of 61 species of Adirondack bog plants, 41 do not occur in temperatures more than 5 degrees warmer than here, which is to say any warmer than West Virginia or New Jersey. Most of these, like bog rosemary, are rare south of the Adirondacks. Another 10 species extend to the North Carolina mountains, 10 degrees warmer than we are, but again only in small quantities.

Michaux's sedge

This has a clear implication for climate change. Bog communities, which cover over 50,000 acres of the Adirondacks and are among our most characteristic communities, exist south of us only as small relicts. They will be stressed by a 5-degree temperature change and greatly changed by a 10-degree one.

Because boreal habitats are ecologically specialized, they contain many species that are regionally uncommon. The map on p. 40 shows the distribution of 24 uncommon species in the northwest Adirondacks. The map to the right shows the distribution of 14 rare species in a short segment of the Hudson River Ice Meadows.

The unusual concentration of rare species in the ice meadows is the result of an ecological coincidence. This section of the Hudson has flat sandy shores that are underlain by a soft marble bedrock and kept open by pack ice (photos, pp. 24, 38). The ice grinds the marble up and mixes it with the sand, creating a fertile, prairie-like soil. The ice-meadow community, which is the most diverse river shore community that I have seen anywhere in the Northeast, is completely dependent on the ice. It will last as long as we have pack ice and no longer.

How vulnerable are lowland boreal habitats to climate change?

The open wetlands and river corridors are probably very vulnerable. Wetlands can remain open only where nutrients are locked up in peat and trees grow poorly. Warming releases nitrogen from the peat. Acid deposition adds nitrogen from the air. Trees and shrubs—which are great ecological opportunists—use the nitrogen to grow taller, shading out low plants. The open wetland becomes a shrub thicket or wooded swamp and plant diversity decreases.

Recent studies have found this happening in many places in the north. Open tundra is growing up to shrubs and trees, bogs becoming taller and turning into swamps. We do not know if it is happening in the Adirondacks. But the Adirondacks have been receiving excess nitrogen for 100 years and have been warming for 30 years, and so there is every reason to believe they are vulnerable.

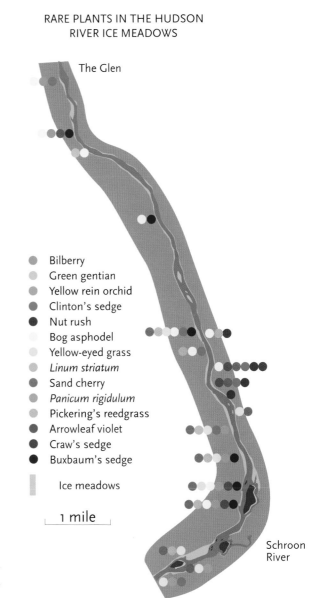

RARE PLANTS IN THE HUDSON RIVER ICE MEADOWS

The Glen

- Bilberry
- Green gentian
- Yellow rein orchid
- Clinton's sedge
- Nut rush
- Bog asphodel
- Yellow-eyed grass
- *Linum striatum*
- Sand cherry
- *Panicum rigidulum*
- Pickering's reedgrass
- Arrowleaf violet
- Craw's sedge
- Buxbaum's sedge

Ice meadows

1 mile

Schroon River

Buxbaum's sedge

Bog asphodel

Northern Mammals and Birds

Lincoln's sparrow

Gray jay

Bicknell's thrush

Spruce grouse

Common loon

Marten

Moose

The northern mammals tend to be ecological generalists. Two Adirondack species, the marten and the moose, occur throughout the boreal zone but are not restricted to it (maps, pp. 33, 43). Both formerly occurred south to Pennsylvania and are better considered wide-ranging sub-boreal species than strictly boreal ones.

The northern birds are more specialized. The Adirondacks have 23 boreal species, and 22 sub-boreal ones. The boreal species are restricted to boreal habitats. Twenty of them reach their southern range limit in or near the Adirondack park. The sub-boreal species are common in boreal habitats, but, like the moose and marten, also occur in cold-temperate ones.

With the exception of Bicknell's thrush and the blackpoll warbler (p. 34), which are high-elevation species, the boreal birds are largely species of the lowland boreal. The map, from records gathered by Michale Glennon of the Wildlife Conservation Society and her colleagues, shows the diversity at 7 northern Adirondack sampling sites. The highest diversities occurred in open bogs and on shores, in areas where there were many adjacent boreal wetlands.

As with the bog plants, the wetland birds as a whole have boreal distributions, and seem to need cold climates. Thirty-four of 53 species are restricted to climates that are 5 degrees or less warmer than the Adirondacks. Twenty of these, all true boreal specialists, barely occur outside of the Adirondacks at all.

How vulnerable are northern mammals and birds?

We don't know, and this is troubling. The marten and moose once occurred to the south of here. They were extirpated from much of the Northeast by hunting and trapping and have returned to part but not all of it. They may be

WCS BOREAL BIRD SURVEY RECORDS, 2003–2007

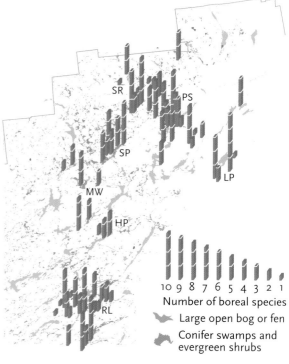

Number of boreal species

Large open bog or fen

Conifer swamps and evergreen shrubs

HP Hitchens Pond LP Lake Placid MW Massawepie
PS Paul Smiths   RL Raquette Lake SP Spring Pond
                  SR St. Regis River

TEMPERATURE LIMITS OF ADIRONDACK WETLAND BIRDS

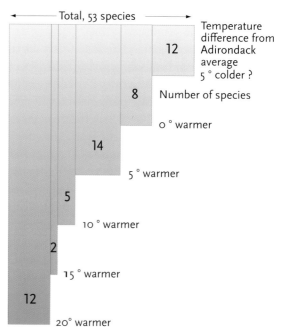

Total, 53 species

Temperature difference from Adirondack average

5 ° colder ?
Number of species
12
0 ° warmer
8
14
5 ° warmer
5
10 ° warmer
2
15 ° warmer
12
20° warmer

RANGE OF THE MARTEN

Adirondack
population

able to tolerate warmer temperatures, but are most abundant in places where there is continuous snow cover. Martens are believed to compete for habitat and prey with fishers, with the marten having the advantage where the snow is deep and the fisher where it is not. Our martens are an isolated population, separated by a hundred miles or more from populations in New England and Canada. If they decline here, they will not likely be replenished from elsewhere.

The boreal birds are closely tied to subalpine krummholz and open boreal wetlands. For now, the krummholz seems to be a stable habitat. The open wetlands may not be. As our wetlands warm, and as they absorb the nitrogen deposited from acid rain, they are likely to become more forested and less open (p. 41). Since many of the boreal birds seem to prefer open wetlands to forested ones, this could reduce the amount of habitat available for them. Several of the boreal bird species are already showing sharp declines (p. 62). We do not know what has caused them, or whether climate change and habitat loss are involved.

One advantage that both our birds and mammals enjoy, and that may make them less vulnerable to climate change, is the large amount of protected land in the Adirondack park. About 3.6 million acres—60% of the park—is either publicly owned or under easements that prevent development. This protection will ensure that much of the park will continue to have natural vegetation and be available for animals to use.

This freedom may be very important in the next century. As climate changes, habitats will change, and some animal populations will prosper and some will suffer. Animals that are free to move around may be able to find better habitats. Small populations may join with, or be replenished from, larger ones. Adirondack animals will have a large protected space—one of the largest in the United States—to move in, and with it, we hope, an exceptional chance to survive.

Unfortunately, their space may not be as large in 50 years as it is now. Another 26% of the park, which is largely undeveloped timberlands at present, is potentially developable and may have up to 15 houses per square mile. This density, research has shown, is enough to restrict the movements of animals, and with it the adaptability they may need to survive in a climate change century.

PERMANENTLY PROTECTED LANDS

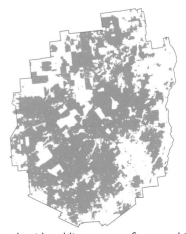

Lands with public or nonprofit ownership or conservation easements preventing development

Ice climbers on the Chapel Pond Slab

Winter Recreation

Winter recreation, including hiking, climbing, snowshoeing, bobsledding, tubing, alpine and nordic skiing, snowmobiling, and ice fishing, is relevant to the climate change story for three reasons.

First, it is embedded deeply in Adirondack history and culture. The Adirondacks were central in the development of winter sports in the United States. They had one of the first ski schools in the country, hosted the first and third of the country's four winter Olympics, and were among the first places to develop large, lift-serviced, downhill ski areas. They were one of the places where American winter mountaineering began a hundred years ago, and where, in the 1970s, the modern techniques for climbing vertical ice were developed and taken to world-class levels.

Second, winter recreation is the major winter industry of the Adirondacks. Winter recreation needs specialized skills and equipment and takes place in special venues. It also needs people to teach the skills, provide the equipment, and maintain the venues. The people and facilities represent a cumulative cultural investment, the human and physical capital that makes a winter economy possible. This investment is perishable: if the winters become too warm for winter sports, the skilled people will leave and the facilities will decay.

Third, all winter sports except ski jumping (which is now done year-round on wet plastic) need either cold weather or natural snow and ice. Downhill skiing and bobsledding, which use artificial snow and ice, are the least dependent on natural conditions. Snowmobiling, which requires both natural snow and sound ice for lake and river crossings, is perhaps the most so. But all require snow or cold to some extent, and so all will be vulnerable to warming climates.

In this section we try, through pictures and a chronology, to give some sense of what a hundred-year cultural investment in winter recreation means. We then look at the elements of the winter economy, and what climate change may mean for them.

The U.S. Olympic bobsled team, 1936; Donna Fox at right

Lake Champlain, 1920s

Historical photos courtesy of the New York State Archives, the Adirondack Collection at the Saranac Lake Free Library, and the 1932 & 1980 Lake Placid Winter Olympic Museum.

Lake Placid, 1932 Olympics

ADIRONDACK WINTER SPORTS, 1890–1980

1893 First known winter ascent of Mt. Marcy.

1897 The Pontiac Club inaugurates the Saranac Lake Winter Carnival.

1912 Fridtjof Nansen, the famed Norwegian arctic explorer, climbs Mt. Marcy on skis.

1914 First Mid-Winter Sports Festival in Lake Placid.

1917 Lake Placid Club builds a ski jump for its members.

1918 First eastern speed skating championships on Mirror Lake; ski jumping contests at Blood Hill at Saranac Lake.

ca. 1920 Herman "Jack Rabbit" Johanssen lays cross country ski trails around Saranac Lake and Lake Placid; the Lake Placid Club hires Henrik Jacobsen as the first paid ski instructor in the United States.

1921 First winter sport championships for women.

1922 The first meeting of Adirondack Mountain Club.

1924 The Sno Bird's Club ski tournament has 3,500 spectators.

1925 Earle Brinsmade skis 300 miles to Lake Placid to participate in the Sno Birds' club tournament; first Adirondack slalom competition; first Lake Placid-Saranac Lake race.

1926 First Adirondack downhill race.

1927 Lake Placid Club builds a 60-meter Olympic ski jump in North Elba.

1930 First race at the Mt. Van Hoevenberg bobsled run.

1931 Volunteers from the American Legion cut ski trails on Gore Mountain; Charles Martin and Otis King drive dogsleds to the top of Whiteface Mountain.

1932 Governor Franklin Roosevelt opens the third Olympic Winter Games at Lake Placid.

1934 Carl Schaefer installs a ski tow and starts a ski school ar Gore Mountain.

ca. 1935 "Powered sleds," the forerunners of the snowmobile, are first used in the Adirondacks.

1936 The Van Hoevenberg hiking trail is widened and becomes the Marcy Ski Trail; Jim Goodwin and Bob Notman make the first winter ascent of the Chapel Pond Slab.

1941 The New York State Constitution is amended to allow ski trails on Whiteface Mountain; in 1947 it is amended again to allow ski trails on Gore Mountain.

1947 Oak Mountain Ski Center in Pleasant Lake opens with two rope tows and a T-bar.

1949, 1969, 1973, 1978 World bobsled championships held at Mt. Van Hoevenberg.

1950 World ski jumping championship held at Lake Placid.

1952 David Bernays and his partner climb Rainbow Falls at Lower Ausable Lake.

1954 The first Appalachian Mountain Club winter mountaineering school.

1958 Whiteface Mountain Ski Center rebuilt.

1966 Gore Mountain Ski Center rebuilt.

1968 First Roger's Rangers Run cross-country ski race on Lake George.

1968 First Long Lake 100 Snowmobile Race.

1972 World University Winter Games at Lake Placid.

1975 John Bragg and John Bouchard climb *Positive Thinking* on Poke-o-Moonshine, the first Class 5 ice climb in the Adirondacks.

1977 First Alpo International Dogsled Races in Saranac Lake.

1978 Cross-country ski trails and biathlon range built at Mt. Van Hoevenberg.

1979 International luge competition at Mt. Van Hoevenberg.

1980 The thirteenth Winter Olympics are held at Lake Placid.

Mt. Marcy Bowl

Mt. Jo, North Elba

Joe McDonald and team, Mt. Van Hoevenberg

Pitchoff Mountain, Keene

Upper Saranac Lake

Lake Champlain

Titus Mountain, Malone

Santa Clara, Franklin County

Photos © Nancie Battaglia, Lake Placid, New York

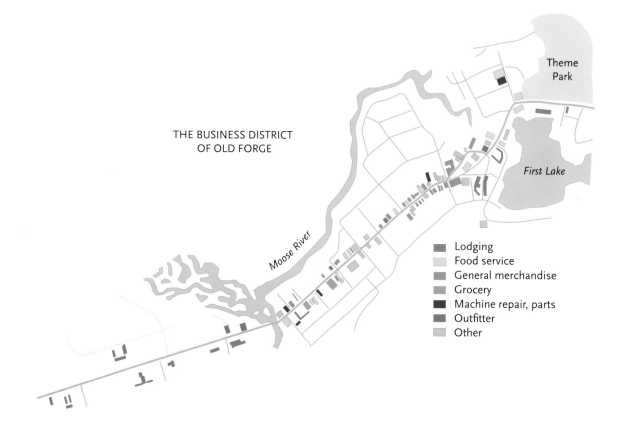

THE BUSINESS DISTRICT
OF OLD FORGE

Moose River

Theme
Park

First Lake

■ Lodging
□ Food service
■ General merchandise
■ Grocery
■ Machine repair, parts
■ Outfitter
□ Other

The Winter Economy

Winter recreation dominates the Adirondack winter economy. No town can really prosper without a year-round economy, and no Adirondack town can have a year-round economy without winter recreation.

The number and size of the venues involved is impressive. Area skiing takes place on over 300 miles of groomed trails at 29 different ski areas. Backwoods skiing uses several hundred miles more. Snowmobiling uses 800 miles of groomed trails on state land and several hundred miles of trails on private land. Ice climbing takes place on over 100 routes on 13 major cliffs. Ice fishing, not shown on the maps, is done locally on most lakes and is a major sport on the southern half of Lake Champlain.

To support this activity requires several hundred businesses to run the facilities and feed, house, and equip the participants.

We made an approximate estimate of the winter businesses near Old Forge, a snowmobiling and skiing center in the town of Webb. Webb operates its own snowmobile trail system and sells 10,000 trail passes a year. There are also three ski areas nearby. Seventy-eight of the 94 restaurants and inns in Old Forge and the adjoining towns are open in the winter; 6 businesses sell, repair, or rent snowmobiles; at least 20 businesses sell equipment, gifts, and general merchandise; and a dozen or more businesses offer professional services. Since retail, hospitality, and service businesses are labor intensive, this suggests that there may be over 500 to 1,000 people in the winter economy in the Old Forge area.

Besides the facilities and the service providers, the winter economy involves many user groups that build participation and sponsor events. Snowmobilers belong to clubs and are represented by snowmobile organizations. Nordic skiers are competition-oriented, and have teams and youth leagues and racing associations. Climbers

WINTER RECREATION

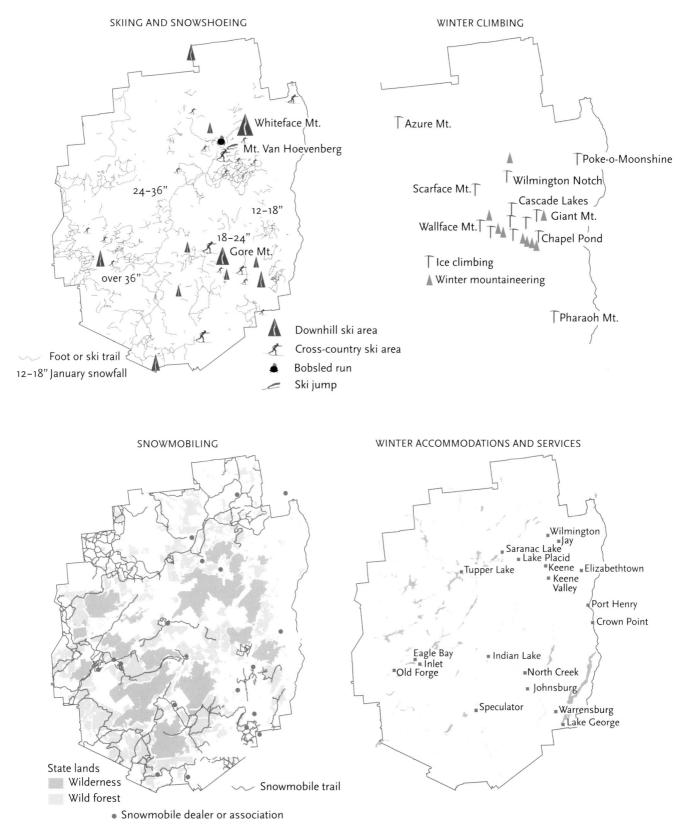

SKIING AND SNOWSHOEING

Whiteface Mt.
Mt. Van Hoevenberg
24–36"
12–18"
18–24"
Gore Mt.
over 36"

Foot or ski trail
12–18" January snowfall

Downhill ski area
Cross-country ski area
Bobsled run
Ski jump

WINTER CLIMBING

Azure Mt.
Poke-o-Moonshine
Wilmington Notch
Scarface Mt.
Cascade Lakes
Giant Mt.
Wallface Mt.
Chapel Pond

Ice climbing
Winter mountaineering

Pharaoh Mt.

SNOWMOBILING

State lands
Wilderness
Wild forest
Snowmobile trail
Snowmobile dealer or association

WINTER ACCOMMODATIONS AND SERVICES

Wilmington
Jay
Saranac Lake
Lake Placid
Keene
Elizabethtown
Tupper Lake
Keene Valley
Port Henry
Crown Point
Eagle Bay
Indian Lake
Inlet
Old Forge
North Creek
Johnsburg
Speculator
Warrensburg
Lake George

and snowshoers, traditionally the most solitary of the winter recreationists, still have clubs and schools.

Beyond the local level, there are the organizations that use the Olympic facilities in Lake Placid to train high-level competitors and hold national and international competitions. Their training programs and events are heavily staffed and are major economic drivers. A single major ski competition may cost its sponsors over a million dollars and bring thousands of spectators and participants.

All of these organizations represent significant investments of human and economic capital. This capital—the skills, facilities, experience, facts-on-the-ground—is the most concrete part of the Adirondack winter tradition. And it may be, as the climate warms, the most vulnerable part as well.

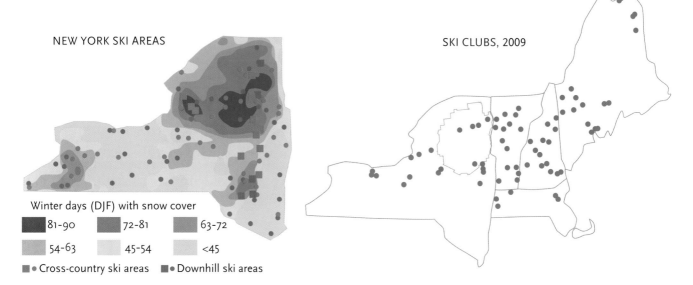

NEW YORK SKI AREAS

SKI CLUBS, 2009

Winter days (DJF) with snow cover

■ 81–90   ■ 72–81   ■ 63–72
■ 54–63   ■ 45–54   ■ <45

■● Cross-country ski areas   ■● Downhill ski areas

How vulnerable is the winter economy?

Because the winter economy is elaborate, it is interdependent. The users come not just because the cold and the snow are here, but because there are facilities for them, events for them to go to, and services in the towns where the events are.

This interdependence is both a strength and a vulnerability. Economies thrive on predictable resources. To disable a winter economy it is not necessary for the snow to vanish, but only for it to be less abundant or less reliable. If the winter season becomes short or unreliable, there will be fewer users and events. Without the users and events, the facilities will be abandoned, the service businesses will close, and the skilled people will move away. Without facilities and services there will be even fewer users. Winter sports may continue for some time, especially as snow vanishes outside the park. But they will not have the vitality they now have or support the communities they now do.

This has not happened in the Adirondacks yet, but it is happening not far to our south. Western Massachusetts, which formerly had reliable snow and a strong winter sports culture, now has increasingly brown winters and a noticeable decrease in winter sports and in the organizations and businesses that support them (p. 67).

The maps suggest that something similar may be happening in New York. Small ski areas occur all over New York, even in areas with less than six weeks of snow cover. Many of these operate intermittently; if western Massachusetts is any guide, many may not operate much longer. Large ski areas with continuous seasons are now restricted to the central Adirondacks and Catskills. Ski clubs, run by the dedicated skiers who train the kids who will be the next generation of dedicated skiers, are now all but gone from the southern half of New England and New York.

Summary

The winter communities in the Adirondacks, natural and human, are similar in several ways. They are old and have taken a long time to become what they are. They are, partly because they are old, complex and interdependent. And they all need, and in some sense welcome, deep cold, snow, and ice.

They also seem vulnerable in similar ways. Both are near their range limits: there are no big bogs, open rivers, bobsled runs, or big ice-climbing cliffs south of us. Both are losing their resource base as there is less snow and cold. And both are showing signs of decline elsewhere, and may soon decline here as well.

The long-term prognosis for our winter communities is almost certainly decline and loss. At first they will just lose elements—a species here, an outfitter or a trail or a ski area there. As the elements go, the communities that depend on them will become simpler and less vital, but will still function much the same.

At some point however, key elements will be lost, and when this happens the community may change rapidly. Trees may invade a bog, and the open-bog birds and sedges vanish. A winter may come when none of the river crossings freeze and none of the cliffs can be climbed. At this point the bog will be gone and climbing and riding will stop; effectively, the community will have collapsed.

Once they start, losses of this sort are hard to reverse. Natural communities may take hundreds or thousands of years to assemble their characteristic species and attain their mature form. Cultural communities develop faster, but still may take many decades to accumulate the economic strength and human resources that a complex community requires. Community-scale losses, either in towns or in the wild, will be long-lasting, and so particularly damaging.

Tullin Thams, gold medal winner in the 1924 Olympics, jumping at Lake Placid. Photo courtesy of the 1932 and 1980 Winter Olympic Museum.

The High Peaks from Bristol Mountain

6 BIOLOGY AND RECREATION ARE CHANGING

Compared to 30 years ago, the Adirondacks are warmer and wetter. Springs and falls are longer, winters shorter and warmer. The changes are not big, but they have come quickly.

When the climate changes, we expect culture and biology to respond. Northern institutions and species should decline, southern ones arrive or expand.

The changes will not be simple or predictable. A warmer climate may bring new birds and kill boreal trees, but the birds will take time to arrive and the trees even longer to die. Some institutions and species will prove unexpectedly resilient. Winter recreation will eventually suffer as cold and snow decrease, but in the short term it may prosper if we have snow and other places don't. Some northern animals and birds may do the same, temporarily increasing because they are doing better than their competitors and then declining as temperatures continue to increase.

Two conclusions follow from this, one encouraging and one cautionary. The encouraging one is that if culture and biology lag far enough behind climate, we may be able to stop climate change before its effects are irreversible. The cautionary one is that the short-term survival of a northern sport or species doesn't tell us anything about how it will do in the long term. And the climate problem, which has arrived quickly and will depart slowly (p. 26), is very much a long-term problem.

Either way, to prepare for the changes that are coming, we need to understand the changes that have already happened. This is not an easy job. For many changes that might interest us, like the number of school snow days or the former range of the marten, there are no historical data. For others, like fuel oil sales or visits to ski areas, the data exist but are inaccessible or have never been compiled.

Despite these difficulties, there is information that suggests that biological and cultural change is already occurring. We summarize it here, using Adirondack examples when they are available and examples from elsewhere when they are not.

CHANGES IN AVERAGE DATES WHEN FROGS BEGIN CALLING NEAR ITHACA, N.Y.

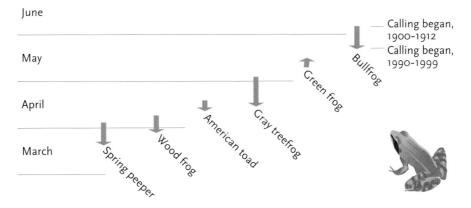

Seasonal Timing

Many biological events are tied to seasonal cycles, and there is now a considerable literature showing that many creatures are budding, flowering, migrating, singing, or breeding earlier in the spring. The changes in our area are typically 5 days or more in the last 30 years, and 10 days or more over the last century.

The graph above, from work by James Gibbs and Al Briesch in the Finger Lakes, shows a 100-year shift in the dates frogs began calling. The springs in Ithaca are about 3 degrees warmer than they were in 1900, and 5 out of 6 frog species are calling earlier than they used to. The average shift is about two weeks.

A similar example of changes in wild plants comes from Concord, Massachusetts, where Abraham Rushing-Miller and Richard Primack compared the flowering dates they observed between 2004 and 2006 with those observed by Henry Thoreau in the 1850s. The graph shows some of the species that had the most consistent changes. Other species changed less, or varied greatly from year to year.

CHANGES IN DATES OF SPRING WILDFLOWERS IN CONCORD, MASSACHUSETTS

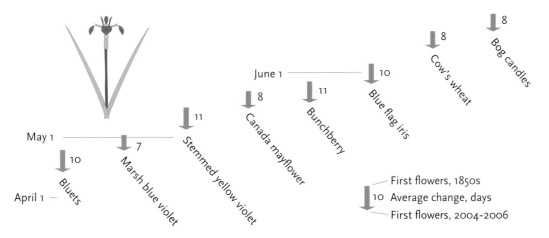

Bird migration dates are also changing, but here the story is more complex. In a study of 30 years of mist-net records from eastern Massachusetts, Miller-Rushing and his collaborators found that the *average* dates on which short-distance migrants passed through were getting earlier. This was as expected. But the numbers of migrants were also decreasing, and so the *first* dates on which species were seen were staying the same or getting later. And, adding further complexity, mid-distance migrants were responding more to general weather patterns than to temperature, and long-distance migrants were not changing their arrival dates at all.

It is reasonable to expect similar changes in the Adirondacks, but we have few long-term historical observations and so can't say much. Curt Stager of Paul Smith's College and his collaborators have reviewed several Adirondack data sets. They found a significant correlation between warmer springs and earlier flowering in white water lilies and apparent trends that were not significant in the arrival of blackbirds and the flowering of red trillium.

DAYS OF SNOW DURING DEER SEASON

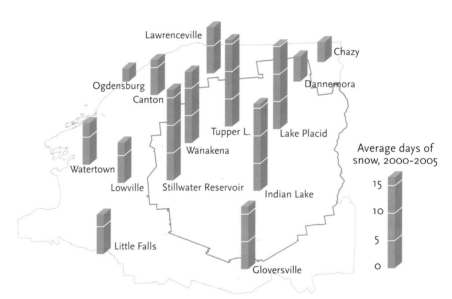

Recreation is also tied to seasonal cycles and seems to be changing as well. The evidence is anecdotal but interesting. Skiers, snowmobilers, ice climbers, and ice fishermen all report that they are starting later in the year, though (because snow and ice linger) apparently not ending earlier. Hunters report less snow in deer season. Gardeners, at least in the lowlands, are planting somewhat earlier and expecting frosts to come a week to two weeks later in the fall.

In the case of deer season, the climate records support the anecdotes. In the past, snow cover often arrived by late October or early November and stayed through winter. From 2000 to 2005, most of upstate New York had less than 10 days of snow cover in the 50-day deer season that starts in late October. Only the Adirondacks had 10 days of snow or more, and only the snowiest parts of them had 15 days or more.

Biological Significance of Seasonal Timing

The ecological success of many creatures depends on how well they can synchronize their biology to the timing of the seasons. Adult butterflies need to emerge when their nectar flowers are blooming. Flowers, in turn, need to bloom when pollinators are available. Insect-eating birds need to arrive on their breeding grounds as leaves are opening and insect populations are high, and vernal pool amphibians need to breed early so their tadpoles can mature before the ponds dry.

As climate warms, the seasons are changing. Some creatures, like the flowers and frogs shown on p. 53, are tracking these changes. But other creatures are not. An analysis of the Concord flowering dates (p. 53) by Charles Willis and his collaborators found that asters, anemones, and orchids, among others, did not shift their flowering dates as the temperature warms. A now classic study of the pied flycatcher by C. Both and M.E. Visser found that, like many long-distance migrants, its arrival dates in Europe depended on its departure dates from Africa, and these had not changed as Europe had warmed.

For the animals and plants that can track the changing seasons, climate change may not pose an immediate threat. But for those that can't, it may. Willis found that the greatest declines in Concord plants were in the species with the least ability to respond to climate change. Both and Visser found that breeding success of the inflexible pied flycatcher had declined greatly relative to more flexible species.

As yet we don't know if this is part of a general pattern, but these results are certainly suggestive. Compared to the natural rhythms of past climate change, the recent changes are coming very fast. It is not surprising that some species can respond to them and some can't. It is also not surprising that some of the ones who can't are suffering.

Edith's Checkerspot

Expansion of Southern Species

There is clear evidence, from all over the world, that animals are expanding their ranges northward as climate warms. But the expansions are selective. The largest changes are in big mobile animals, particularly birds and some marine fish. Smaller flying animals like butterflies and dragonflies are also expanding. Edith's checkerspot, a species of western North America, is a well-studied example.

Pedestrians and crawlers seem to be moving less than flyers, but this may be because they have been less studied. Red foxes have moved north in subarctic Canada, opossums in our area, and armadillos in the southwest United States. Small mammals have been reported to be moving upward on western mountains and northward into the boreal forest in the upper Midwest. A variety of small invertebrates (spiders, millipedes, beetles) seem to be moving north in Britain, perhaps the only place in the world that would notice. No reptiles or amphibians seem to be moving north, and in fact many of them are declining and contracting their ranges.

The evidence for northward expansions of plants is much more limited. Many plants are moving upwards in the mountains. Alpine tree lines are moving up and arctic tree lines moving north, and there is recent evidence that shows that many eastern trees are reproducing better at their northern range limits than their southern ones. But still, compared to birds, most plants have done little. In the last century the turkey vulture and the Carolina wren have expanded their range north by about 300 miles. The sweetgum and pawpaw, whose range limits in 1900 were similar to those of the vulture and the wren, do not seem to have moved at all.

EXPANSION OF SOUTHERN BIRDS INTO NORTHERN NEW YORK, 1900-2007

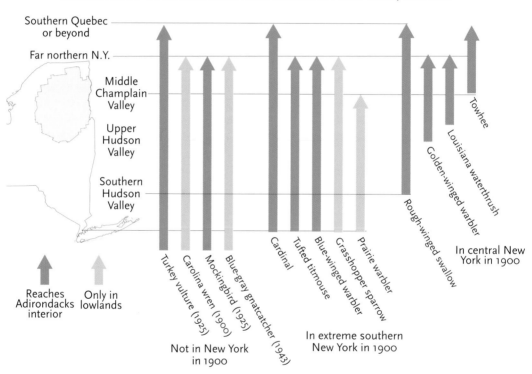

Movement of Birds in the Eastern United States

The northward movement of our birds has been particularly dramatic. About 25 new breeding birds have arrived in New York in the last century. Thirteen new breeding birds, shown in the graph above, have spread into northern New York. Nine of these, the left and middle groups in the graph, are southern species that have traveled the length of the state, 300 miles or more, in less than 100 years. Five of these are now in the Adirondack interior.

The northward movement of birds in New York is part of a larger pattern. Over the last century, most of the birds that have northern range limits in the eastern United States have extended their range northwards. The distances the birds have moved correspond to the amount that the temperature has changed, and suggest that birds are tracking climate change and moving with it.

The arrival of formerly southern birds like the turkey vulture and mockingbird in a northern landscape like the Adirondacks is noteworthy. The Adirondacks look the same as they did 100 years ago; our mockingbirds sit in spruces and maples, not in magnolias. But, without obvious change, the Adirondacks have become more hospitable to some southern species. An important question, which I will return to in a moment, is whether they may also have become, again without obvious change, inhospitable to some northern ones.

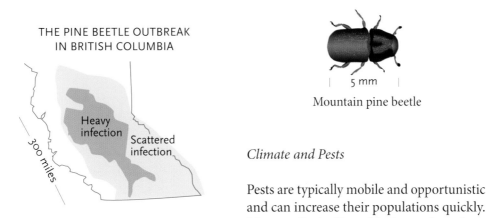

THE PINE BEETLE OUTBREAK
IN BRITISH COLUMBIA

Heavy infection

Scattered infection

300 miles

5 mm

Mountain pine beetle

Climate and Pests

Pests are typically mobile and opportunistic and can increase their populations quickly. Many are limited by cold winters. Some have already expanded their ranges and become more numerous as winters have become milder. Others may do so in the future.

One pest that has already expanded greatly is the mountain pine beetle, a native insect that kills pines by boring into them and transmitting a fungus. It occurs in the mountain forests of western North America, where it attacks ponderosa, lodgepole, and limber pines, which are dominant over large areas.

In the 1990s it was considered a locally important pest that had infected a few thousand square miles in scattered locations and was known to build up after mild winters. In the late 1990s, after a series of mild winters, it was able to shorten its life cycle from two years to one and start to spread. Its spread was facilitated by fire-suppression and harvesting patterns that created large continuous areas of the mature trees it prefers. By 2008 it had infected about 60,000 square miles of forests and had become the most damaging forest insect in North America.

It may also be the first forest pest to have direct effects on climate. The decay of the dead trees in forests affected by the beetle can release more carbon than the live trees can store. Researchers believe that, if the beetle continues to spread, 80% of the pines in British Columbia will die. As the dead trees rot, they will release something like 270 million tons of carbon over a 20-year period. This will be comparable to the amount of carbon released by all the forest fires in Canada, and equal to about 8% of Canada's fossil fuel emissions.

Closer to home, the hemlock woolly adelgid, an important forest pest, is known to be limited by winter temperatures and so is likely to expand its ranges as climate warms.

The adelgid is an Asian insect that was first recorded in the United States in Virginia in 1951. It spread northwards and now occupies about half the range of hemlock. In Pennsylvania, New Jersey, and Connecticut it moved rapidly, often killing the hemlocks in a stand within three years after it arrived. In New York and Massachusetts it encountered colder winters, which reduced its survival. As a result it is not spreading as fast and has been in some stands for five years or more without causing much mortality.

Currently, the winters in Massachusetts and central New York keep the adelgid population in check but do not eliminate it. Eliminating it requires extended periods with nighttime temperatures of -20 degrees or less. Since winter nights have warmed strongly, such temperatures now occur at only a few places within the range of hemlock. It thus seems likely that the adelgid will continue to spread north and that, as temperatures increase and its populations build up, it may eventually infest and kill hemlock throughout the range of the tree.

In the cases of the adelgid and the pine beetle, the relation between climate and the spread of the insect has been worked out. In many other cases, a climate relation is suspected, but has not been demonstrated.

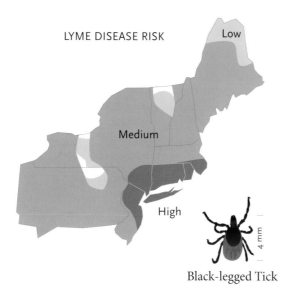

LYME DISEASE RISK

Low

Medium

High

Black-legged Tick

4 mm

An example of considerable importance to the Adirondacks is the black-legged tick (deer tick), which carries Lyme disease. The young ticks acquire Lyme disease from white-footed mice, the primary reservoir of the disease. They transmit it to humans and other mice. Adult ticks feed on large mammals, especially deer, and also humans.

Ticks, deer, and mice all seem to be increasing in abundance in the north part of their range. Climate change may well play a part in this, but just how much of a part, and for which species, no one knows for sure. The interactions between mice, ticks, and deer, which have been carefully studied by Rick Ostfeld and his colleagues at the Carey Institute, are complex. Climate enters, but so does habitat structure, food supply, and the presence or absence of hosts and predators.

Whatever the reasons, Lyme disease is spreading rapidly and is now a major public health concern. In the early 1990s it was mostly found south of our area. By the early 2000s it had reached northern New England and New York. It is now common in the St. Lawrence and Champlain valleys and starting to occur in the interior Adirondacks as well.

The hemlock adelgid and the black-legged tick are two pests that have recently arrived in our area from the south. Others, like the Asian long-horned beetle and emerald ash-borer, are near. We don't know how many of them will become significant problems within the Adirondacks. But apparently the northerness of the Adirondacks, which for many years we thought our strongest biotic defense, is weakening and increasingly breachable.

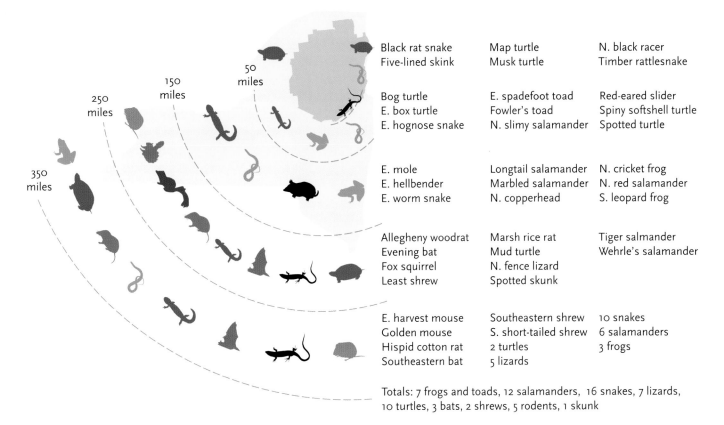

DISTANCES OF SOUTHERN ANIMALS FROM THE ADIRONDACKS

350 miles
250 miles
150 miles
50 miles

Black rat snake
Five-lined skink

Map turtle
Musk turtle

N. black racer
Timber rattlesnake

Bog turtle
E. box turtle
E. hognose snake

E. spadefoot toad
Fowler's toad
N. slimy salamander

Red-eared slider
Spiny softshell turtle
Spotted turtle

E. mole
E. hellbender
E. worm snake

Longtail salamander
Marbled salamander
N. copperhead

N. cricket frog
N. red salamander
S. leopard frog

Allegheny woodrat
Evening bat
Fox squirrel
Least shrew

Marsh rice rat
Mud turtle
N. fence lizard
Spotted skunk

Tiger salmander
Wehrle's salamander

E. harvest mouse
Golden mouse
Hispid cotton rat
Southeastern bat

Southeastern shrew
S. short-tailed shrew
2 turtles
5 lizards

10 snakes
6 salamanders
3 frogs

Totals: 7 frogs and toads, 12 salamanders, 16 snakes, 7 lizards,
10 turtles, 3 bats, 2 shrews, 5 rodents, 1 skunk

What southern species could come?

How many mobile species are there south of us and which ones might arrive in our area?

For birds, the answer is that there is a large pool of species and many species are already moving. The Carolina wren, blue-winged warbler, and red-bellied wood-pecker, for example, have been moving north rapidly. They are now fairly common at the Adirondack edge and starting to be found in the interior. The only questions about them are how much suitable habitat the Adirondacks contain and how soon the moderating climate will allow them to reach it.

The answer for mammals is more complicated. Most of the large mobile mammals in the eastern United States are already here. There are only two mammals—the fox squirrel and the eastern mole—in New York that aren't in the Adirondacks. Between New York and Virginia there are only 11 more: 5 mice, 3 shrews, 2 bats, and a skunk. All of them except the skunk are small animals, and many are uncommon. We have no idea which of them, if any, are currently expanding their ranges. We do know that there are many human and natural barriers between here and Virginia, and so it seems unlikely that they will reach us in the near future. But movements of small mammals are reported in other places, and they may surprise us.

There are far more southern reptiles and amphibians near the Adirondacks than there are mammals. The diagram shows 9 species at the edge of the Adirondacks and another 17 within 150 miles. But it is unclear whether we should expect to see any of them soon. Reptiles and amphibians, like most cold-blooded vertebrates, have little capacity for sustained motion. They do not migrate and typically travel only a few miles from the place where they were born. Many populations are small and isolated by habitat loss and fragmentation. The odds, at least in the short term, seem to be against their moving very far. The literature supports this, at least in a negative way: there seem to be no reports of reptiles or amphibians moving north as climate warms, and many reports of declining populations.

Taken together, these estimates of animal mobility say that, because there are a lot of southern bird species and because birds are highly mobile, we are likely to get many southern birds in the next century. Because there are fewer southern mammals and they seem less able to move, we will get fewer of them. And we may—though this is uncertain—get few if any new amphibians and reptiles because they have very limited mobility and are restricted to discontinuous habitats.

If this picture is correct, it poses a problem for conservation theory. Many conservation biologists recommend creating corridors to enable species to adapt to climate change. But corridors can only help species that have the capacity to move, and for whom suitable connecting habitats exist. They may not be necessary for able and adventurous species like birds and mice and squirrels. And they may not be helpful for dispersal-limited ones like salamanders and habitat specialists like turtles. The problem for conservation is whether there are species in the middle that are mobile enough to use corridors and choosey enough to need them.

So far as I can tell, no one has thought much about this problem. The most we can say is that if there are species that will need corridors to move north as the climate warms, we don't, as yet, know either who they are or what sort of corridors they will need.

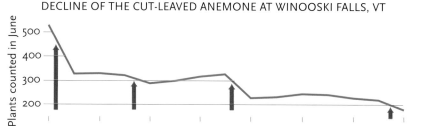

DECLINE OF THE CUT-LEAVED ANEMONE AT WINOOSKI FALLS, VT

↑ Year with an exceptionally hot or dry summer

Anemone multifida

Are cold-climate species dying off?

Some are, but others are not.

In the world as a whole there have been dramatic declines of Arctic bears and Antarctic penguins associated with losses of sea ice. There have been losses of mountain cloud forests in Africa and Central America, and with them some rare amphibians, including the golden toad, which is now thought to be extinct. There have been less dramatic but biologically important losses of low-altitude populations of mountain animals like pikas and ground-squirrels, and likewise of mountain butterflies and plants. And there is increasing evidence that as lowland species move higher up mountains, alpine species decline and diversity decreases.

Several examples suggest that similar declines may be happening in our area. For 15 years Debbie Benjamin and I monitored the cut-leaved anemone, a northern relative of our wood anemone, at Winooski Falls in Winooski, Vermont. The anemone is a subarctic plant. In Labrador and Alaska it lives in open tundra and on gravelly or ledge river shores. In Winooski it lives on rock cliffs and islands within a river gorge, where it is kept moist by spray from the falls. It may, like other glacial relics, have been here for thousands of years. The Winooski plants are the southernmost population in eastern North America, and are 400 to 500 miles from the nearest populations in Maine and Quebec.

As fits a boreal plant, the anemone tolerates cold and ice but is sensitive to heat and dryness. The Winooski plants survive severe winters and violent floods but can lose half of their population in a single dry summer. In wet summers they can recover, but wet summers are becoming less frequent and they barely start to recover before the next drought hits. The result is the staircase decline shown on p. 60. At the end of our study, in 2002, there were only a third as many plants as when we began in 1988.

A striking thing about the anemone, and one that may be characteristic of many species in decline, is how limited its reproduction is. It flowers and sets seed well, but few seedlings survive. Those that do are always near the parent plants: none of the hundreds of seedlings we counted was more than a foot or two from an adult plant. As a result, the population cannot spread. It occupies only a small fraction of the available habitat, and that fraction became smaller as our study progressed.

ADIRONDACK SPRUCE GROUSE IN DECLINE

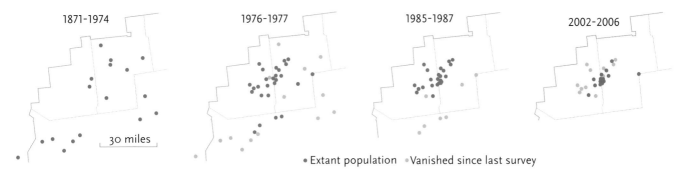

1871-1974   1976-1977   1985-1987   2002-2006

30 miles

• Extant population   • Vanished since last survey

The spruce grouse affords another example of the dramatic decline of a northern species. Like the anemone it is a subarctic species, occurring across the continent from north of the tree line to the southern edge of the boreal forest. Southwards it is found mostly in boggy black-spruce wetlands, leaving the upland forests to its southern relative, the ruffed grouse.

Our knowledge of its original distribution in the Adirondacks is incomplete. Early records are scattered over the northwestern quadrant of the park. We do not know how common it was, or how many other populations there were besides the ones on the map.

Since 1974 there have been three systematic spruce grouse surveys, by R.S. Fritz, R.P. Bouta, and A. Ross, all graduate students at the SUNY College of Environmental Sciences and Forestry in Syracuse. Their data show a steady decrease in the number of populations and number of individuals, with the outlying colonies going first, and the occupied area gradually shrinking.

The reasons for the decline are not known, but limited dispersal must certainly be a factor. Spruce grouse are mostly pedestrians; they fly short distances to escape predators, but walk the rest of the time. In her studies of radio-collared birds, Ross rarely found a bird more than half a mile from where it was first found, and never found one more than two miles from where it had been found. Since the dots on the maps are about two miles across, this means that any two populations that are not touching are effectively isolated from one another.

The spruce grouse and cut-leaved anemone are clearly northern species in decline. To what extent do they represent other boreal species, and to what extent are they exceptional?

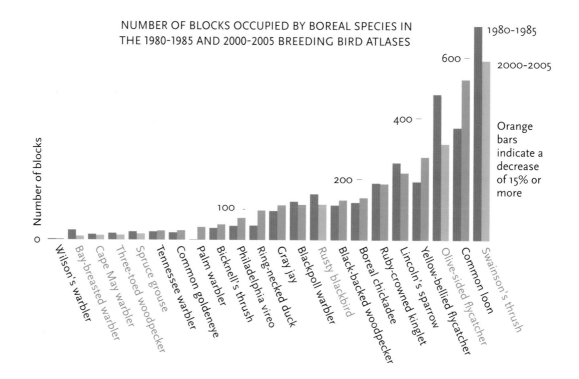

NUMBER OF BLOCKS OCCUPIED BY BOREAL SPECIES IN THE 1980-1985 AND 2000-2005 BREEDING BIRD ATLASES

Among boreal Adirondack birds, the spruce grouse is exceptional but not unique. The graph above shows the *occupancy*—the number of 5 × 5 kilometer survey blocks in which the species was seen—for 22 boreal species in 1985 and 2005. About two-thirds of the species maintained their occupancy or increased it. But roughly a third of the species had strong declines in occupancy, shown by the orange bars on the graph. These declines have been confirmed by recent field surveys by Michale Glennon and her co-workers, showing while many of the boreal species are easy to find in the right habitats, several of the ones in red have disappeared from habitats where they were formerly recorded.

Blue Ledge, Adirondacks

Mt. Horrid, Vermont

Mt. Hor, Vermont

Mt. Pisgah, Vermont

In the case of rare and hard-to-find species this might not mean much. Rare species often come and go. But in the case of easy-to-find birds like Swainson's thrush or the olive-sided flycatcher the decline can't be explained away. *At least three boreal birds that were formerly common and widespread in the Adirondacks have decreased sharply in the last 20 years, and now are increasingly rare and hard to find.* The reasons are unknown and no connection with climate has been shown. But they are boreal species near their southern range limits and, as such, potentially vulnerable to climate change. We are watching them to see what happens next.

Persistent Boreal Plants

Unlike boreal birds, most boreal plant species seem to be doing well. The decline of the cut-leaved anemone is unusual. The anemone may be particularly vulnerable because it lives at a low-elevation site that can get very dry in the summer. Most boreal plants live at moderate or high elevations, in sites where they are protected from drying by fog and clouds or seepage water.

The best foggy sites are in the alpine zone (p. 34). The best seepage sites are at the bases of cold limy cliffs where nutrient-rich water trickles over or through the rocks. Such cliffs usually accumulate ice in the winter and have ice avalanches and rockfall in the spring. They are active, violent places, with the kind of conditions that arctic species like and their competitors don't.

Mistassini primrose

Low braya

White mountain saxifrage

Roseroot

Brett Engstrom and *Eleocharis quinquefolia*

June Mendell and *Carex scirpoidea*

Less than a dozen cliffs in the Northeast are cold, wet, limy, and violent enough to have significant numbers of boreal species. The four shown on p. 63 are among the best. Each is big and limy and has active rockfall. Most stay wet year-round. Each has 10 or more rare arctic and subarctic plants, and the most diverse (Blue Ledge and Mt. Pisgah) have 20 species or more. They are thus, along with the alpine tundra and the big bogs (p. 37), our boreal plant diversity hotspots.

Because of this diversity, they are excellent places to learn whether climate is affecting boreal plants. Since we can't predict what species are going to be most sensitive to climate, we need a lot of species to look at. The cliffs and the alpine zones are our richest boreal communities, and so may be our best climate-change antennas.

If so, the signal they are thus far bringing in is hopeful. A 2007 survey of the Adirondack alpine zones by Tim Howard of the New York Natural Heritage Program relocated almost all the previously known species. A 2008 resurvey of plants on the Mt. Horrid cliffs by myself and June Mendell (shown at left counting plants on the main cliff) found that there had been very little change in the numbers of plants on the cliff since they had first counted them in 1991. Other revisits to boreal sites by the author, the Vermont Natural Heritage Program, and Vermont botanists (including Brett Engstrom, shown at left on Mt. Pisgah) have established that almost all of the boreal plants, except perhaps a few of the most rare, are persisting at their historical sites.

This reassurance comes with caveats. First, it is early in the climate change century, and things will get worse before they get better. And second, only the Mt. Horrid survey looked for changes in abundance as well as presence. A species usually declines for some time before it vanishes. We lack quantitative data for most boreal plants, and so have no way of knowing if, like the roseroot and saxifrage at Mt. Horrid, they are holding their own or if, like the anemones at Winooski, they are already in decline.

Changes in Boreal Communities

Elsewhere in the world, boreal communities are changing. The treeline is moving north and open tundra and open bogs are becoming more shrubby. Alpine and peatland communities are becoming less diverse.

Similar things could be happening here. We don't have a community-level monitoring program and so don't know if they are. But we do have two pieces of evidence that suggest that they may be. The clearest one comes from a study by Brian Beckage and his colleagues of the transition zone between hardwoods and conifers on three mountains in Vermont. By using historical air photos and duplicating previous studies, they have found that the high-elevation trees—spruce, fir, and white birch—have become less abundant at their lower elevation limits, and the hardwood-conifer transition has shifted upwards about 200 feet in 50 years.

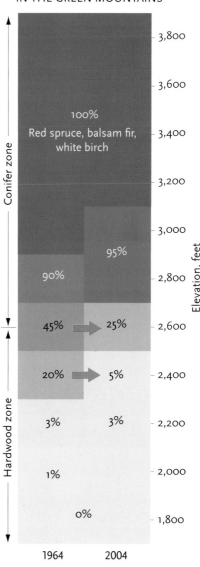

RETREAT OF BOREAL TREES
IN THE GREEN MOUNTAINS

Conifer zone

Hardwood zone

Elevation, feet

3,800
3,600
3,400
3,200
3,000
2,800
2,600
2,400
2,200
2,000
1,800

100%
Red spruce, balsam fir, white birch

95%

90%

45% ➔ 25%

20% ➔ 5%

3%   3%

1%

0%

1964   2004

Regenerating black spruce at Spring Pond Bog

A more ambiguous piece of evidence, suggesting changes in peatlands, comes from a study by the author on black spruce and tamarack on the mat of Spring Pond Bog, the Adirondacks' largest bog. We found many young black spruces, mostly arising as sprouts from older trees, and hypothesize that a pulse of vegetative reproduction started about 30 years ago. But since we have not measured the rate at which young trees are appearing or looked for dead trees buried in the peat, we do not know for sure that the rate of tree growth on the bog has changed.

Changes in Winter Recreation

Winter recreation has always been dependent on the weather, especially in early winter. Natural snow comes and goes, lakes freeze later or earlier, the ice on climbing routes forms or doesn't form, migratory fish populations do or do not show up.

Against this background variability, individual warm years and the cancellations of events that result from them do not count for much. In 2002–2003, the warmest Adirondack winter on record, snowfall was low, and many events were cancelled. On January 10, 2007, it was 60 degrees in the Adirondacks and there was no snow or ice anywhere. In 2006 and 2007 the Lake Champlain Ice Fishing Championship was cancelled for lack of ice. The pond hockey tournament in Lake Placid has been held on artificial ice in two of the last four Januaries because Mirror Lake was not frozen. All these are interesting, and may someday be seen as early warnings, but as yet they are not a trend.

SNOWMOBILE TRAIL PASSES SOLD BY THE TOWN OF WEBB

Likewise, anecdotal information from participants is valuable but hard to evaluate. We have been told, for example, that rivers are freezing less than they used to and that snowmobile crossings are correspondingly more dangerous; that rainbow smelt, a coldwater fish, are no longer making their winter migration to the shallow parts of Lake Champlain where they were traditionally fished; that no major ice-climbing routes in the Keene Valley area have passed out of use in the last decade; and that the total number of skier-days at Mt. Van Hoevenberg has not changed much in the last 15 years. All these are interesting, but none have been verified.

Thus far we have found only a little quantitative data on winter recreation. The town of Webb, a major snowmobiling destination, maintains its own trail system and sells passes to users (p. 48). The numbers of passes was high in the 1970s, declined in the 1980s, and recovered (after a data gap) after 1995. Why the decline occurred and what happened between 1985 and 1995 we don't know; in any event there is no long-term trend.

In western New England, one of the places where American downhill skiing developed, the story is different. In the 1940s and 1950s almost every town had a ski area. All of these were on natural snow, and all but a few were small rope-tow areas—often a steep pasture on a working farm, with a home-made tow powered by an old car.

The small areas came and went, and many were replaced by larger areas with T-bars and chairlifts. But large and small areas served different markets, and for a long time they coexisted. In the 1960s, when the number of chairlift areas doubled and their sizes increased greatly, the number of rope-tow areas only decreased slightly and the number of T-bar areas increased. Apparently, while the skiing was good, there were plenty of skiers for both large and small areas.

By the 1980s and 1990s, the skiing had stopped being good. Artificial snow, which serious skiers in the 1960s had thought dull and unsatisfying, now determined whether there was skiing at all. Many small ski areas and some of the middle-sized ones closed. The big ski areas that could afford snowmaking stayed open, but their costs increased. No new ski areas and few if any new trails were open. By 2000 there were only a third as many downhill areas as in 1970. Western New England had passed, in only a few decades, from being at the center of American skiing to being on its edge.

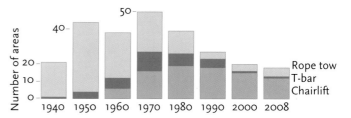

DOWNHILL SKI AREAS IN WESTERN NEW ENGLAND

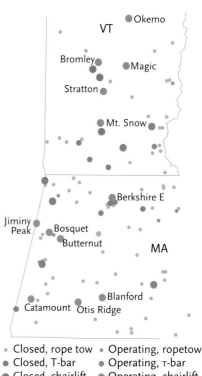

- Closed, rope tow · Operating, ropetow
- Closed, T-bar • Operating, T-bar
● Closed, chairlift ● Operating, chairlift

Hogback Mountain, Marlboro, Vermont

The High Peaks from Giant Ridge

7 ASSESSMENT: ADIRONDACK CARBON EMISSIONS

Part II of this book, An Adirondack Strategy, is an attempt to map out what a low-carbon future for the Adirondacks might look like. It is not a full map, both because this is a short book and because no one yet knows what a full map would look like. But it does try to determine where we are starting from, what tools we have available, and how much, given discipline, leadership, and passion, we might accomplish with them in the next 20 years. It does not say how we will do this. Once again, no one knows. But it does look hard at the fossil fuel problem—the mountain in our way, if you will—and says that there appears to be a route around the mountain, and that, based on what we know today, it is a good route and we should be able to travel it if we choose to. Knowing that there is a route is important; it doesn't give us a map or mile-by-mile directions, but it does give us the confidence we need to start out.

The fossil fuel problem is a big problem, and to solve it we will need an orderly approach. The one advocated here has four steps: assessment, reduction, replacement, and offsetting. Assessment, discussed in this chapter, estimates current carbon emissions. Reduction, in Chapters 8 and 9, lowers them by thrift and efficiency. Replacement, Chapter 10, reduces emissions further by replacing high-carbon fuels with low-carbon ones. And finally, offsetting, Chapter 11, balances the emissions we can't eliminate against the absorption of carbon, in our case in forests, to reduce our net carbon emissions to zero.

Why estimate emissions?

To reduce our carbon emissions we have to know what they are. If we don't know what we are emitting, we are, in effect, trying to balance the books for a business that doesn't have books. Thus, estimating for our emissions is an essential first step.

It may also be a mind-changing step. Almost no one in the Adirondacks, rich or poor, thrifty or profligate, climate believer or skeptic, knows their personal carbon budget. And further, as best I can determine, no Adirondack organization knows its organizational one. As a result, though we have lots of people and organizations that are concerned about carbon emissions in general, we have very few who are either aware of or concerned about their own emissions in particular.

Estimating our own carbon budgets can change this. When you figure out your own budget or your organization's, and see that it is coming out in tons and not pounds, you say, "This is not good. I really am a part of the problem I am talking about." At that moment you start to accept responsibility. From there it is only a short distance to thinking about reductions. And from there a short distance to an exciting point, a year or two down the road, when you say, "Well, 7% in two years is not a bad start. How about another 10% in the next two?"

When a hundred or two hundred people and a handful of businesses are thinking like this, we will have made a start. When that number increases ten times we will finally be on the right road. This chapter is about how we start.

Direct and Embedded Emissions

Carbon budgets contain two sorts of emissions, direct and embedded (pp. 18–19). Direct emissions are what we release when we burn fossil fuels ourselves or use electricity that comes from fossil fuels. They are easy to estimate, and you can learn all you need to know about them in a few pages.

Embedded emissions are the emissions that occur when someone does something on our behalf—refines petroleum, raises a steer, makes a board or a running shoe. In the case of the steer, for example, we have to account for emissions from making fertilizer, growing grain, raising the animal, processing the meat, shipping it here, and selling it. These are much harder to estimate than the direct emissions from fossil fuels, but still there are approximate estimates that are helpful.

Indirect emissions are also complicated because they include other greenhouse gases besides carbon dioxide. Fertilizers, for example, release nitrous oxide, a powerful greenhouse gas. Animals and manure release methane, trucks release nitrous oxide, and supermarket coolers release refrigerants. Taking account of these other gases is tricky. It is easy to compute the carbon dioxide output of a furnace, but much harder to compute the nitrous oxide output of a cornfield or the methane output of a cow. But again, it can be done, and useful approximations are available.

In this book, I will hide most of these details by talking about total greenhouse emissions, and measuring them in tons of $CO_2(e)$ (carbon dioxide equivalents), which means the amount of carbon dioxide that, if present by itself, would have the same effect as all the emissions put together.

Direct Emissions from Burning Fossil Fuels

These are the emissions that occur when we burn fossil fuel in a heater or an engine. The burning changes the carbon in the fuel to carbon dioxide, and it is the carbon dioxide that we usually measure.

For example: a gallon of gasoline weighs about 6.2 lbs and contains about 5.3 lbs of carbon. When it is burned, the carbon combines with oxygen and produces 19.5 lbs of carbon dioxide. For every pound of carbon we get 3.7 lbs of carbon dioxide, a useful figure to remember. If we burn 100 gallons of gasoline, we produce a little less than a ton of carbon dioxide, another useful figure.

The amount of carbon dioxide produced by a given amount of fuel is called the emission factor. The emission factors for some common fuels are:

LP gas	12.5 lbs/gal	Fuel oil	22.4 lbs/gal
Propane	12.7 lbs/gal	Natural gas	120 lbs/1,000 cu. ft
Gasoline	19.5 lbs/gal	Air-dried wood	1.8 lbs/lb
Kerosene	21.5 lbs/gal	Soft coal	2.5 lbs/lb
Diesel	22.4 lbs/gal	Hard coal	2.8 lbs/lb

Using these factors it is easy to calculate direct emissions. A household that used 500 gallons of fuel oil, 100 gallons of propane, and 500 gallons of gasoline in a year would have emissions of $500 \times 22.4 + 100 \times 12.7 + 500 \times 19.5 = 22{,}220$ lbs or 11.1 tons of carbon dioxide.

Fuels Compared

The emission factors tell us only about carbon, not energy. Diesel fuel releases more carbon per gallon than gas but also has more energy per gallon. Wood emits less carbon per pound than coal, but also produces less energy.

If we are trying to find the cleanest fuel, we need to look at the carbon emissions per unit energy. The graph shows this for some common fuels.

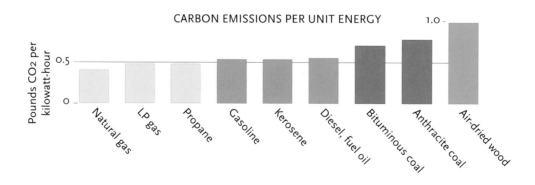

There are significant differences. Natural gas, at 0.4 lb of CO_2 per kilowatt-hour of energy, is clearly best. The other petroleum products, at 0.5 lb of CO_2 per kilowatt-hour, are second. Coal, at 0.7 to 0.8 lb of CO_2 per kilowatt-hour, is worst. Thus if you are going to heat with fossil fuels, you should try to use natural gas if you can get it. Propane is also a good choice, fuel oil a bit worse, coal much worse. The same house, heated with coal, would have about twice the CO_2 emissions that it would have with natural gas.

Wood is a special case. Because it has a lot of water in it, the useful energy content is low and the carbon-to-energy ratio high. If it were a fossil fuel it would be judged highly polluting and perhaps banned. But if it is harvested so that the forest reabsorbs the carbon at the same rate it is emitted, it is close to carbon-neutral, and is an excellent choice for a heating fuel (p. 123).

The emissions per unit energy are useful if we know the energy we need and want to estimate the carbon emissions. Conveniently, the common petroleum fuels emit about 0.5 lb carbon per kilowatt-hour. If a house needs 5,000 kilowatt-hours of heat per year, we can estimate (ignoring the efficiency of the furnace) that the emissions will be 2,500 lbs of CO_2. Or if we know we need an average power of 1,000 watts of heat, we can do a little arithmetic and find that supplying this power from petroleum fuels will result in emissions of a little over 2 tons of CO_2 per year.

ELECTRIC GENERATION IN THE UNITED STATES

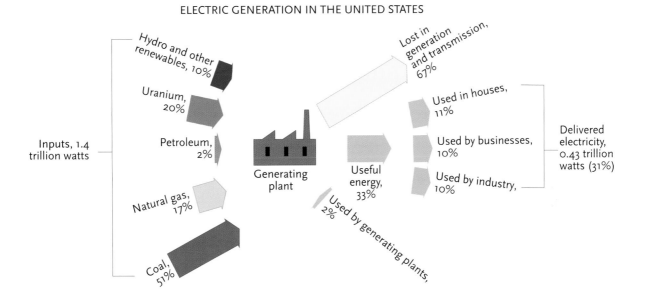

Emissions from Electricity

Electricity emits no carbon when used, but does, if made from fossil fuels, emit carbon when it is generated. This carbon is emitted on behalf of us, and if we use electricity it needs to go in our carbon budget.

The emissions depend on the fuel used to generate electricity. Uranium and the renewables emit no carbon dioxide. Natural gas is a relatively clean fuel, and coal, as always, a relatively dirty one.

The emissions also depend on the efficiency of the plant and of the transmission system. Coal plants are less efficient than gas plants. Long transmission lines are always less efficient than shorter ones.

The bottom line is that it takes, on average, 3 kilowatt-hours of fossil fuel energy to make 1 kilowatt-hour of electricity. Thus the carbon emissions per unit energy are about 3 times higher than they would be if the fuels were burned directly. Electrical emissions in the United States average 1.4 lbs of CO_2 per kilowatt-hour. For New York, which has relatively more nuclear power and hydro and less coal than the country as a whole, the average emissions are 0.85 lb per kilowatt-hour. For the midwestern states that get much of their electricity from coal, they may be over 2 lbs per kilowatt-hour.

Whether these emissions are justified depends on what we do with the electricity. Using it to operate a high-efficiency device like a heat pump (pp. 104–105) may be justified. But heating a room with it probably won't be. In New York State, electric space-heating emits 40% more carbon per unit heat than fuel oil, and 70% more carbon than gas heat.

This is a noteworthy result. *Electricity has a high carbon cost; we should use it for things like lighting and mechanical power that fossil fuels do inefficiently, and not for things like heat that fossil fuels do well.*

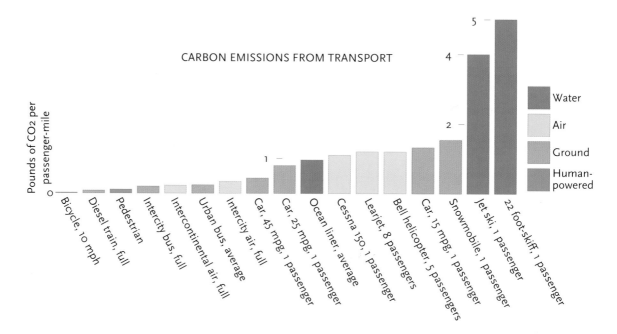

Emissions from Transportation

Emissions from transportation are measured in pounds of CO_2 per passenger-mile. The graph shows a range of values, from a cyclist at 0.02 lb CO_2 per mile, to a 22-foot outboard skiff that emits 5 lbs per mile, 2,500 times as much as the cyclist. Water travel emits the most, because boats make waves, and waves soak up a lot of energy. Air travel in small machines and individual travel in cars are not very good either. Driving alone in an SUV or big pick-up at 15 miles per gallon emits more carbon than taking a corporate jet with all its seats full.

Bus travel and air travel are better, and have similar emissions. Planes have to work hard to climb and cruise, but carry a lot more passengers and can save energy when they are descending. Both beat the best cars, but only if they are full and the cars are not. Put two people in a Prius or Civic, or three people in a small station wagon, and the emissions are as low or lower than a full bus or big aircraft on a long flight.

Rail of all sorts is better yet, mostly because trains are skinny compared to their length. Riding a full train is both the fastest and the least polluting form of commercial land travel yet developed.

Other Emissions from Petroleum and Transport

The emission factors given in the graphs on pp. 70 and 72 are the emissions released when fossil fuels are burned. But it takes energy to get energy and so there are emissions along the way when fuels are mined, refined, and transported. These emissions are, in effect, the carbon cost of supplying the fuel. For petroleum they are fairly well known: about 25% of the energy that comes out of the ground is used in mining, refining and shipping. Thus for every 75 gallons of petroleum we use, another 25 gallons have already been used to get it to us.

In carbon terms, this means that indirect emissions are about a third of the direct emissions. If we burn 100 gallons of gasoline and emit a ton of CO_2, we should add another third of a ton to account for the indirect emissions.

There are additional climate costs as well. Vehicles generate other greenhouse gases besides carbon dioxide: nitrogen oxides, ozone, water vapor, and, in the case of planes, particles that generate condensation trails. These emissions warm the climate, but just how significant they are, compared to carbon dioxide, is uncertain. For planes they may be very significant: David MacKay says that if you want to know the true greenhouse cost of a plane trip, you may want to take the carbon emissions and double or triple them.

GREENHOUSE GAS EMISSIONS FROM THE U.S. FOOD SUPPLY

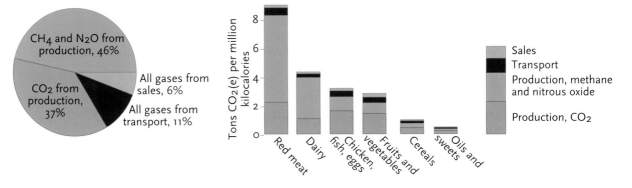

Indirect Emissions From Food

Large amounts of fossil fuel energy are used to grow, process, and transport food. This is partly because we have replaced human and animal power with fossil power and partly because we are supporting a growing population on a fixed land base and so have to farm more intensely (p. 19).

As a result, agriculture and its related industries are major greenhouse emitters. The companies that make fertilizer, farm equipment, and chemicals emit carbon dioxide, nitrous oxide (N_2O), and methane (CH_4). The farms that raise grains and vegetables emit carbon dioxide from machinery and nitrous oxide from fertilizer.

Meat and dairy animals emit methane directly and, when fed on grain, generate large indirect emissions from the farms that produce their feed. Trucking, processing, and retailing food emit yet more carbon dioxide.

The graphs on p. 73 show the average emissions from six different groups of foods. In every group, over 80% of the emissions are from farms and farm suppliers. Only about half of this is CO_2. The rest is methane from animals and nitrogen from fertilizers. Transport and retailing, the black and brown sectors in the graphs, are significant but not really large: overall they create about 17% of emissions. The really large emissions come from fertilizers, the animals and their manure, and the fossil fuels used on farms.

The emissions for different food groups differ significantly. Meat and dairy are the largest emitters. Producing 116 lbs of red meat results 1,800 lbs of greenhouse emissions, 15 times the weight of the food. About half of this come from the animals and the fertilizers used to raise the food that the animals eat. The rest come from the fossil fuels used along the production chain.

Emissions from food, then, are a consequence of both what we raise and how we raise it. If you want to cut down on your food emissions, buying locally will help, and buying locally from a farm that is not heavily mechanized will help more. But what will help most is buying vegetables fertilized by compost and meat and dairy products from animals raised on grass. Grain-fed animals and inorganic fertilizers are the big agricultural emitters, and only by avoiding them can we reduce the greenhouse impacts of agriculture.

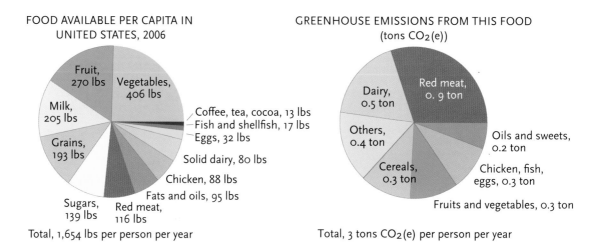

FOOD AVAILABLE PER CAPITA IN UNITED STATES, 2006

Fruit, 270 lbs
Vegetables, 406 lbs
Milk, 205 lbs
Coffee, tea, cocoa, 13 lbs
Fish and shellfish, 17 lbs
Eggs, 32 lbs
Grains, 193 lbs
Solid dairy, 80 lbs
Chicken, 88 lbs
Sugars, 139 lbs
Red meat, 116 lbs
Fats and oils, 95 lbs

Total, 1,654 lbs per person per year

GREENHOUSE EMISSIONS FROM THIS FOOD
(tons $CO_2(e)$)

Dairy, 0.5 ton
Red meat, 0.9 ton
Others, 0.4 ton
Oils and sweets, 0.2 ton
Cereals, 0.3 ton
Chicken, fish, eggs, 0.3 ton
Fruits and vegetables, 0.3 ton

Total, 3 tons $CO_2(e)$ per person per year

Because Americans eat a lot of meat and dairy products, they emit a lot of carbon. The United States produces or imports about 540 pounds of meat, eggs, and dairy product per capita. Should you eat your full share of this—which I don't recommend—you would be responsible for about 1.7 tons of carbon emissions. Should you eat your share of the rest of the food produced in or imported into the United States, you would be responsible for another 1.3 tons. The total would be an impressive 3 tons, comparable to the emissions from heat and light for a small house.

Much of the food produced in the United States is wasted and so the per capita food consumption is significantly less than the per capita food supply. But nonetheless, it is possible that in America as a whole the shopping cart carries as much energy as the oil truck, and that many American families emit as much carbon from their diets as they do from their houses.

Indirect Emissions from Goods and Services

On page 19 we suggested that the goods and services a family buys—their *stuff*—represent a significant energy flow, comparable to the other kinds of energy the family uses. If so, goods and services must represent carbon emissions as well. When we buy anything, someone has used energy to manufacture it, and this has released carbon. When we go to a dentist or a school, the office or campus is using supplies and energy, and this is releasing carbon.

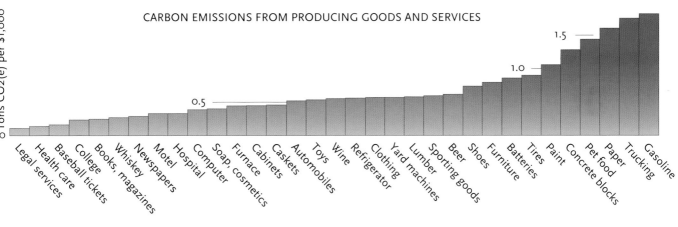

CARBON EMISSIONS FROM PRODUCING GOODS AND SERVICES

How do we estimate the greenhouse gases released from stuff and services? Tracking the exact emissions from making any particular object, say, a Schwinn bicycle, is difficult. But tracking the average emissions from making objects of a certain kind, bicycles in general, is easier. This method is called an *input-output analysis,* and is described in the notes. Its results tell you how much carbon, on average, each of several hundred economic sectors emits per $1,000 of product. We can call this the carbon costs of production. The results for 23 sectors are shown above, and some examples are given on p. 76.

Clearly there is a range of carbon costs. Services and labor-intensive industries like baseball and publishing spend more money on salaries than materials, and their carbon costs per thousand dollars of product are low. Material-intensive industries, like paper, petroleum, and paint, all have high carbon costs. But interestingly, over a broad range of industries as disparate as hospitals, wine-making, and shoe-making, carbon costs are generally similar and are somewhere in the neighborhood of 0.5 ton of $CO_2(e)$ per $1,000 dollars of product.

For those of us who are counting carbon and trying to reduce our carbon emissions, this is unwelcome information. We all knew that driving and heating houses and buying processed foods emitted carbon. But what the graphs say is that almost everything else you buy emits carbon too. *In general, for every $1,000 disposable income you spend, you will emit about a half ton of* $CO_2(e)$. If you keep a lot of dogs and buy batteries and cement blocks, you will do worse. If you go to ball games or send

CARBON COSTS OF LIFE
(in tons of CO$_2$(e))

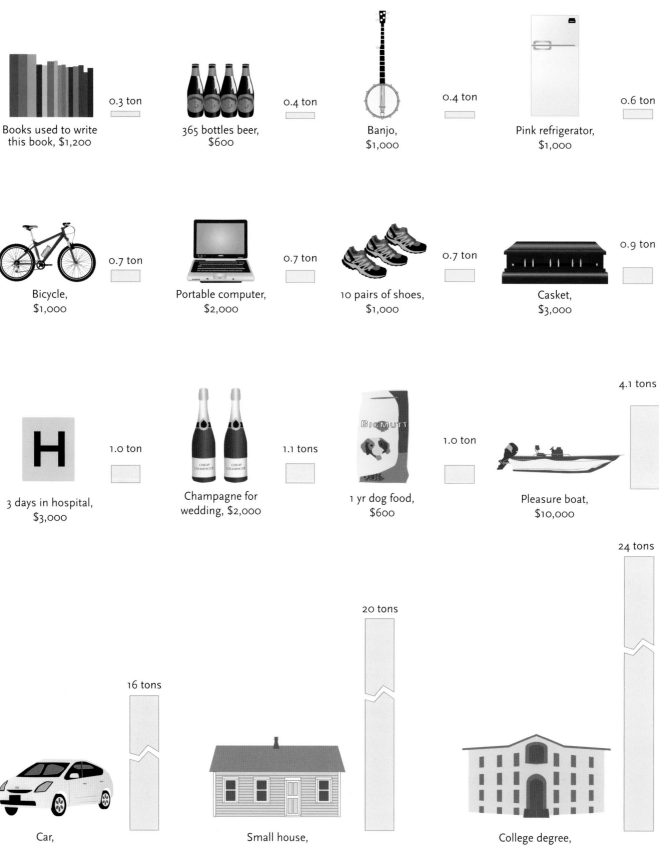

Books used to write this book, $1,200 — 0.3 ton

365 bottles beer, $600 — 0.4 ton

Banjo, $1,000 — 0.4 ton

Pink refrigerator, $1,000 — 0.6 ton

Bicycle, $1,000 — 0.7 ton

Portable computer, $2,000 — 0.7 ton

10 pairs of shoes, $1,000 — 0.7 ton

Casket, $3,000 — 0.9 ton

3 days in hospital, $3,000 — 1.0 ton

Champagne for wedding, $2,000 — 1.1 tons

1 yr dog food, $600 — 1.0 ton

Pleasure boat, $10,000 — 4.1 tons

Car, $30,000 — 16 tons

Small house, $100,000 — 20 tons

College degree, $100,000 — 24 tons

your kids to college, you will do better. But in general, because the world economy is fossil fuel based, we will not be able to truly decarbonize our own lives until we decarbonize the larger economy.

ENERGY AND CARBON BUDGETS OF AN ADIRONDACK HOUSEHOLD

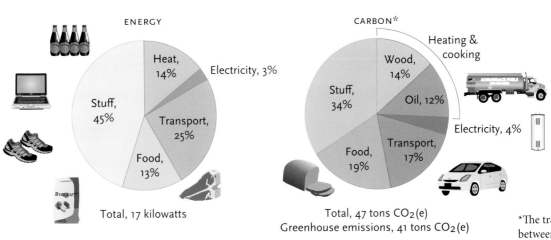

ENERGY

Heat, 14%
Electricity, 3%
Stuff, 45%
Transport, 25%
Food, 13%

Total, 17 kilowatts

CARBON*

Wood, 14%
Heating & cooking
Stuff, 34%
Oil, 12%
Electricity, 4%
Food, 19%
Transport, 17%

Total, 47 tons CO$_2$(e)
Greenhouse emissions, 41 tons CO$_2$(e)

*The translation between the energy and carbon embedded in stuff is approximate; no exact conversion is possible.

Estimating a Household Carbon Budget

Household carbon budgets are estimated by combining direct and embedded emissions. The left graph shows the energy budget for the Adirondack household introduced on p. 21. The household is imaginary, but based on some real ones described in the next section. It used about 7,000 watts of power directly and another 10,000 watts of embedded power. When this is translated into carbon emissions, we get the graph on the right. The total emissions of this household, direct and indirect, are 47 tons. Six tons of this comes from wood. If the wood is harvested sustainably it is carbon-neutral, and the greenhouse emissions are 41 tons or, since this was a three-person household, about 14 tons per person. Approximately 40% of the emissions come from direct energy use and 60% from embedded energy.

Real Adirondack Households

We have data on the direct carbon emissions, but not the embedded ones, of about 20 Adirondack households, and show 8 of them here. Remember that these are incomplete budgets and that if we included embedded emissions from food and stuff the totals might double.**

The graphs on p. 78 show my own energy and carbon budgets. I live in an old house that I have rebuilt with modern windows and thicker walls and ceilings. It still has mice and leaks. I heat with wood, cook with propane, get my electricity from solar panels, and travel to the forests and swamps where I work in a car that gets 25 miles per gallon.

My total power use is 5.2 kilowatts. About half, the gray portion of the graph, comes from fossil fuels. My total CO$_2$ emissions are 16.1 tons, of which 9.9 tons comes from

**To calculate the energy budget for your own household, see p. 169–170.

wood and 6.1 tons from fossil fuels. The carbon released from the wood is offset by carbon taken up by other trees on my farm and so is carbon-neutral. Thus my net carbon emissions are 6.1 tons.

DIRECT ENERGY USE & EMISSIONS OF AN OLD FARMHOUSE WITH GREEN HEAT AND POWER

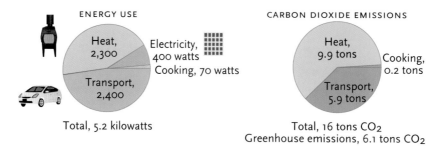

Like almost everyone else, I don't know my emissions from food and stuff. I buy about 80% of my food from organic producers within a hundred miles of where I live, and estimate that this might represent an emission of a ton of carbon dioxide. One of my current research projects is to track my food-and-stuff budget, and I hope to know more in a year or so.

The carbon budgets for 8 households are compared on p. 79. (My own is at the upper right.) They differ greatly in total emissions, but this is partly because there are different numbers of people in different households. On a per capita basis (graphed below) the emissions cluster more, and are mostly between 3 and 10 tons per capita. The lowest per capita emissions are from a family of two in a small, efficient, off-the-grid house. The largest, ironically, are from a single person who lives in a cabin of only 280 square feet but travels a lot.

PER CAPITA FOSSIL FUEL CO$_2$ EMISSIONS OF EIGHT HOUSEHOLDS

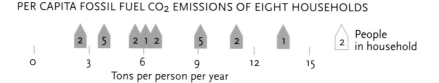

The budgets show several common features. Heating is significant in all budgets. Six out of eight have wood heat, and for five of these wood is the major source of heat, greatly reducing fossil fuel emissions. Electricity is less significant, and doesn't contribute more than an eighth of the carbon emissions in any budget. (This is partly because electricity in New York is relatively green.) Transportation is very significant, and accounts for over half of the fossil fuel carbon emissions in every household.

The median per capita carbon emissions of this small sample of households is about 6 tons. This is a lot smaller than the U.S. per capita average of 21 tons. It doesn't include stuff and food, which would likely double the emissions. But even when doubled, these are still thrifty Yankee households. The use of wood heat in six of the houses certainly contributes to that. If the energy derived from the wood

EMISSIONS FROM DIRECT ENERGY USE FOR EIGHT NORTHERN NEW YORK HOUSEHOLDS

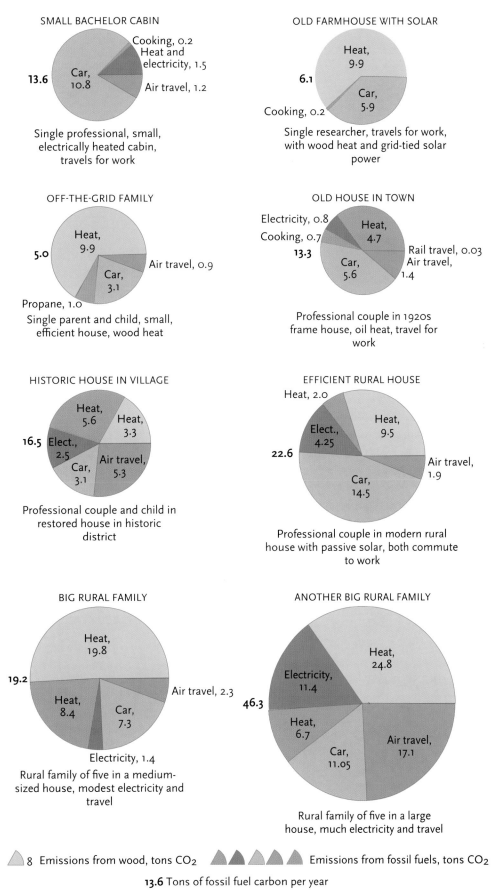

SMALL BACHELOR CABIN

13.6

Cooking, 0.2
Heat and electricity, 1.5
Car, 10.8
Air travel, 1.2

Single professional, small, electrically heated cabin, travels for work

OLD FARMHOUSE WITH SOLAR

6.1

Heat, 9.9
Car, 5.9
Cooking, 0.2

Single researcher, travels for work, with wood heat and grid-tied solar power

OFF-THE-GRID FAMILY

5.0

Heat, 9.9
Car, 3.1
Air travel, 0.9
Propane, 1.0

Single parent and child, small, efficient house, wood heat

OLD HOUSE IN TOWN

Electricity, 0.8
Cooking, 0.7
13.3
Heat, 4.7
Car, 5.6
Rail travel, 0.03
Air travel, 1.4

Professional couple in 1920s frame house, oil heat, travel for work

HISTORIC HOUSE IN VILLAGE

16.5

Heat, 5.6
Heat, 3.3
Elect., 2.5
Car, 3.1
Air travel, 5.3

Professional couple and child in restored house in historic district

EFFICIENT RURAL HOUSE

Heat, 2.0
Elect., 4.25
22.6
Heat, 9.5
Car, 14.5
Air travel, 1.9

Professional couple in modern rural house with passive solar, both commute to work

BIG RURAL FAMILY

19.2

Heat, 19.8
Heat, 8.4
Car, 7.3
Air travel, 2.3
Electricity, 1.4

Rural family of five in a medium-sized house, modest electricity and travel

ANOTHER BIG RURAL FAMILY

46.3

Heat, 24.8
Electricity, 11.4
Heat, 6.7
Car, 11.05
Air travel, 17.1

Rural family of five in a large house, much electricity and travel

8 Emissions from wood, tons CO_2 Emissions from fossil fuels, tons CO_2

13.6 Tons of fossil fuel carbon per year

had been supplied by fuel oil instead, the median emissions would have been about 5 tons greater.

The Town of Fine

A town is a collection of households, plus businesses, industries, and organizations. Its total emissions are the emissions from each of these, minus the emissions from forests that are storing carbon, plus the emissions from activities like logging and development that release it.

Here we look at the direct emissions from an Adirondack town. We have no data on embedded energy and forest storage, and so ignore them.

The best way to estimate the emissions for a town would be to take an energy census, polling sample households about how much fuel they used and what they bought and how far they drove. So far as we know, no one in our area has ever done this.

Lacking this kind of data, we took a more approximate approach. We got the numbers of households and business from census data and then walked around town and estimated the average size of a house and a business. We used regional data from the Department of Energy to estimate residential and business energy use per square foot of heated space. We calculated municipal emissions from figures on fuel use supplied by local officials.

Fine is a large, sparsely populated town that includes eight hamlets along the Oswegatchie and Little rivers in the northwest Adirondacks. Formerly it had large iron mines and was a busy industrial town. Now it is more of a seasonal and commuter town. The largest employer in the town is the Clifton-Fine School in Star Lake. The largest nearby employer is the Newton Falls Fine Papers in the town of Clifton.

The census and tax rolls say that Fine has 790 residents in 317 households, plus 370 seasonal houses and about 24 businesses and organizations. Only one of these, the Ranger

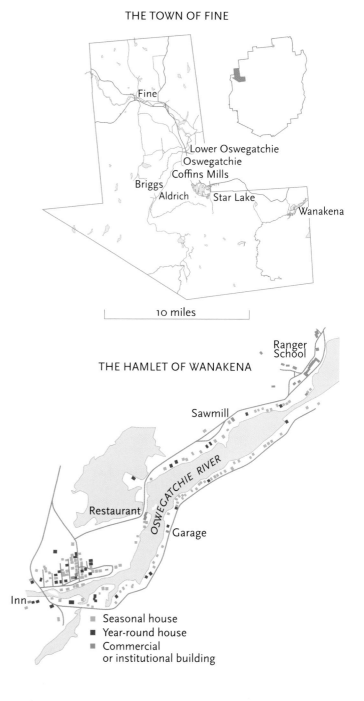

THE TOWN OF FINE

Fine
Lower Oswegatchie
Oswegatchie
Coffins Mills
Briggs
Aldrich Star Lake
Wanakena

10 miles

THE HAMLET OF WANAKENA

Ranger School
Sawmill
OSWEGATCHIE RIVER
Restaurant
Garage
Inn

■ Seasonal house
■ Year-round house
■ Commercial or institutional building

Wooden suspension bridge in Wanakena, built by Rich Lumber Company, ca. 1903.

School (a part of the forestry program at the SUNY College of Environmental Sciences and Forestry), is large.

From field data and regional averages, we estimated that the average year-around house was 1,700 square feet, used 2.6 watts of power per square foot, and emitted 12 lbs of carbon per square foot. We assumed, again using regional averages, that the average household drives 20,000 miles a year in a car that gets 23 miles per gallon. We had no idea what real emissions of the businesses and organizations were, but since most of the buildings were small, we assumed that they were at most twice the average emissions for a house. We estimated the Ranger School's emissions, crudely, from its size and number of students.

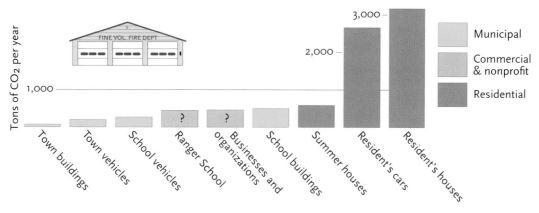

ESTIMATED CARBON EMISSIONS FOR THE TOWN OF FINE

Here are the results, which must be thought of as a quick, back-of-the-envelope estimates. The total emissions are about 8,500 tons of carbon dioxide. About 70% of this comes from the year-around residents' houses and cars. Another 13% comes from the central school. (Since this also serves the town of Clifton, in a more exact accounting some of the carbon would be assigned to them.) The remainder, which is not well known, comes from the summer residents, the businesses, and the organizations.

These results are likely to be typical of rural towns where the businesses are small and there is no heavy industry. In such towns, the emissions will be dominated by the emissions of the residents and visitors. The town and the businesses will contribute to the emissions, but will likely be a quarter or less of the total.

This will not be true in the more developed towns. The hospitality industry is energy intensive. Motels emit twice as much carbon per square foot as houses; restaurants four times as much. A resort town like Webb or Lake George could easily emit more carbon from its hotels and motels alone than does the whole town of Fine.

It will also not be true of towns with large industries or institutions. Whiteface Mountain, in Wilmington, and Sunmount Developmental Center, in Tupper Lake, emit almost as much carbon as the town of Fine. The paper mill in Newton Falls, a small mill in the days when paper was big, emits seven times as much.

Despite these exceptions, there is an important generalization here. In many rural towns, the total emissions will be dominated by houses and vehicles. *If we wish to reduce direct carbon emissions, we should start with houses and vehicles.*

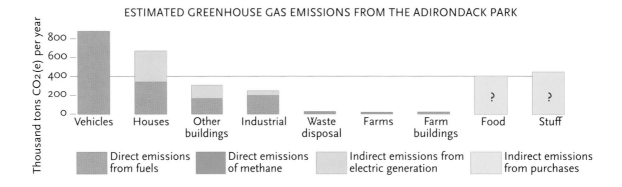

ESTIMATED GREENHOUSE GAS EMISSIONS FROM THE ADIRONDACK PARK

| Direct emissions from fuels | Direct emissions of methane | Indirect emissions from electric generation | Indirect emissions from purchases |

The Whole Park

Now what about the whole park? Its emissions will combine the residential emissions of the small towns like Fine and the industrial and commercial emissions of larger ones like Ticonderoga and Lake Placid. They will also include vehicle emissions from residents, visitors, and shipping.

Last year the Wild Center commissioned Energy and Environment, a consultancy dealing with energy issues, to estimate the carbon emissions of the park. They used a mixture of reported emissions and averages, similar to our estimates of the emissions for the town of Fine. The results have, as they acknowledge, significant uncertainties. But nonetheless they are our first picture of the emissions for any part of the Northeast and so are extremely interesting.

The graph above combines their estimates of direct emissions with my own crude estimates of embedded emissions from the residents' purchases of food and stuff. The total direct emissions are about 2.1 million tons per year. Residential and vehicle emissions are three-quarters of the total. Other buildings (including commercial, municipal, and nonprofit) and industry are most of the rest. Farms and waste are minor.

Petroleum is the largest energy source. The largest wilderness in the contiguous United States uses a startling 470,000 gallons of gasoline, propane, and fuel oil every day.

Carbon sources tend to be small and scattered. Most emit less than 50 tons a year. The larger buildings emit a few hundred tons of carbon a year. Ski areas, small industries, and prisons emit 1,000 to 10,000 tons each. The Dannemora Prison emits 20,000 tons, and the two paper mills 60,000 and 165,000 tons.

Embedded emissions from food and stuff are unknown but likely large. A minimum estimate for the residents totals 800,000 tons, comparable to vehicle emissions; an estimate including the visitors could easily be twice as large.

LARGE ADIRONDACK CARBON EMITTERS

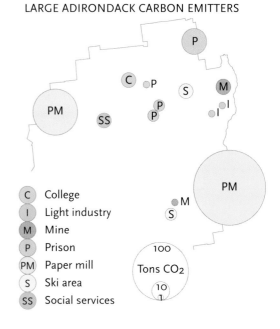

- C College
- I Light industry
- M Mine
- P Prison
- PM Paper mill
- S Ski area
- SS Social services

ADIRONDACK PETROLEUM USE AND CARBON EMISSIONS

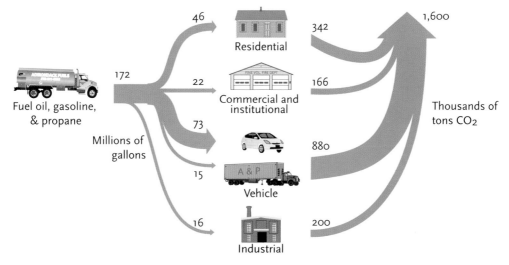

Fuel oil, gasoline, & propane

172 Millions of gallons

46 → Residential → 342

22 → Commercial and institutional → 166

73 → Vehicle → 880

15

16 → Industrial → 200

1,600 Thousands of tons CO_2

Summary

The Adirondacks are powered by two flows of energy and emit two flows of green-house gases. Petroleum products, fuel-wood, and electricity emit carbon directly. Food and goods emit carbon when they are produced.

The two flows are of comparable size and importance. The petroleum and electric flows are visible and, in principle, relatively easy to measure. The food and goods flows are more diffuse and harder to see and measure.

At all three levels, household, town, and park, vehicles and buildings are the largest direct emitters. If we wish to reduce emissions, they are where we should start.

Vehicles, in particular, dominate Adirondack petroleum use. A low-carbon Adirondack future will have to be one that is largely without petroleum-using ve-hicles. Is such a future possible?

Randy Hubbard and Mike Malbeuf on Paper Machine 3 at Newton Falls Fine Papers

Fuel tanks, town of Fine Highway Department

8 REDUCTION: LOW-CARBON TRANSPORT

The gas tank shown above holds about 400 gallons of gasoline, containing about 15,000 kilowatt-hours of energy. When used in vehicles it will produce about 4,000 kilowatt-hours of mechanical energy and 11,000 kilowatt-hours of heat.

The gasoline in the tank weighs about 2,400 lbs and is 87% carbon. When the carbon is burnt and combines with oxygen, it will produce a little less than 4 tons of carbon dioxide.

The tank is one of thousands in the park. Adirondack cars and trucks use approximately 88 million gallons of fuel a year and travel over a billion vehicle-miles a year. They are the biggest users of fossil fuels in the park, and hence the biggest emitters of carbon dioxide.

To reduce the park's carbon emissions, we will have to reduce its vehicle emissions. There are two strategies for doing this, thrift and efficiency. They work well together, and to get serious reductions we will have to use both.

Thrift, in the sense I use it here, means using vehicles less. Staying home, sharing vehicles, and using public transport (another form of sharing) are thrifty.

Thrift is an attractive strategy because it is cheap and effective. Staying home, for example, costs nothing, saves time, and reduces emissions 100%. Ride-sharing cuts emissions by 50% and costs by half. No other strategies we will discuss have these kind of benefit-cost ratios.

FOSSIL FUELS USED FOR TRANSPORT

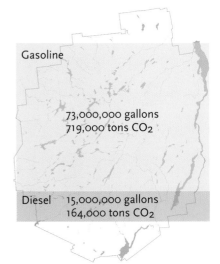

Gasoline

73,000,000 gallons
719,000 tons CO_2

Diesel   15,000,000 gallons
164,000 tons CO_2

THREE STRATEGIES TO EMIT LESS CARBON

	BUY A PRIUS	DRIVE 7,500 MILES LESS	CARPOOL 7,500 MILES
Miles in car	20,000	13,500	20,000
Time saved	0	166 hrs	0
Cost per year	$2,300	-$800	-$800
CO_2 saved	2.5 tons	2.5 tons	2.5 tons
Cost per ton	$920	-$320	-$320

The second and third strategies are behavioral. In the second you combine some trips and eliminate others and drive 7,500 miles less. This saves the same amount of carbon, plus $800 a year in gas, and 166 hours of driving time. This is equivalent to five 35-hour work weeks and so is a nice bonus.

In the third strategy you carpool 30 miles a day with a neighbor. This doesn't change your driving time, but it does generate at 2.5-ton savings of carbon dioxide, and an $800 savings on fuel, which you can split with your neighbor.

These are impressive numbers. Changing your driving behavior really works. If you can reduce your total mileage, you can save carbon and time, and get paid for doing it. If you can ride with someone else, you can make your car twice as efficient. With two people aboard, my old Subaru equals a new hybrid. With three it ties a good bus, and with four it equals an electric car.

Behavior, however, is famously hard to change. While driving less and increasing ridership are clearly good deals, they are also hard to do in an auto-centered culture. Strong increases in the price of fuel, like those we saw in 2008, have done it in the past, and may do it again. But, while there are clearly forces driving up the cost of petroleum, there are also powerful forces trying to keep it down. Thus, while price increases may be coming, we would be foolish to sit around and wait for them to solve our energy problems for us.

Further, no matter how thrifty we are, we are still going to need to drive. In fact, given the geography of the Adirondacks, we are going to need to drive a lot. To do so while reducing emissions, we need more efficient cars.

To find them, we need some basic engineering. Why do cars use so much energy? Can they be made to use less? How much less?

FORCES ON A MOVING VEHICLE

Inertia

Drag

Rolling resistance

The truck is a 1997 Chevrolet S10 EV, an all-electric pickup produced for fleet use but never offered for sale to the general public.

Where the Energy in the Gas Goes

The first question, why vehicles use so much energy, is simple. A moving vehicle is acted upon by forces that resist its motion and uses the energy in its fuel to overcome these forces. It uses a lot of energy because the forces are large, and because fossil fuel engines, like all heat engines, are inefficient.

The two principal forces are drag, the resistance of the air that the vehicle pushes out of its way, and inertia, the resistance that the vehicle's weight makes to being accelerated.

These forces come into play in different situations. When a vehicle is moving at constant speed, there are no inertial forces, and most of the mechanical power produced by the engine is used to overcome drag*. When I am driving 60 miles an hour in my Subaru, the fuel in the engine is generating about 76,000 watts of power.

*There are also inertial forces when a vehicle climbs or descends hills, but they cancel out over round trips.

ENERGY CONSUMPTION OF A SUBARU LEGACY AT 60 MILES PER HOUR

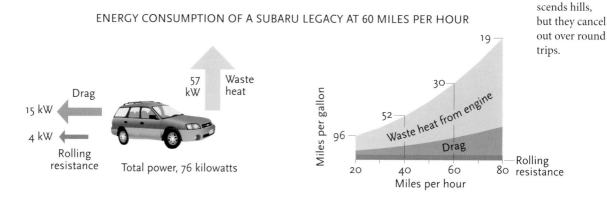

About 15,000 watts go to overcoming wind resistance and 4,000 watts to overcoming the resistance of the wheels and drive train. The rest is all waste heat.

The drag, which is the most important force on a car at cruise speed, depends on three, and only three, things: the frontal area, the streamlining, and the speed. Big cars push more air out of the way than small ones, and so use more energy per mile. Fast cars push the air harder than slow ones, and also use more energy per mile.

Note in the graph above that energy consumption increases roughly as the square of the vehicle's speed. Going 60 miles per hour takes 80% more energy per mile than going 40. Going 80 takes 50% more energy than going 60.

When a car is making frequent stops, the forces change. Drag is less important, and inertia more important. Every time the car accelerates, it uses energy from the fuel to increase its kinetic energy (energy of motion). Each time it slows down, this energy is lost as waste heat from the brakes.

ENERGY CONSUMPTION OF A SUBARU LEGACY MAKING FREQUENT STOPS

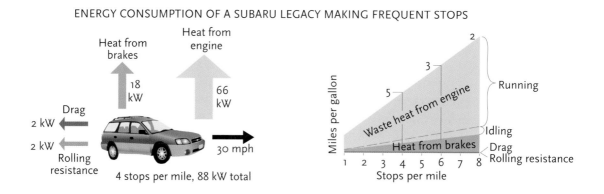

In the lower diagram on p. 88, I am driving at 30 miles per hour and making four 1-minute stops for traffic lights every mile. Almost all the mechanical power of the engine goes into accelerating the car, and then is dumped as waste heat from the brakes. My average speed, because of the stops, is only 10 miles per hour. Nonetheless, I am using 88,000 watts of power, more than I did at 60 miles per hour.

This is why cars overheat in start-stop driving. And it is also why, if we want to make them more efficient, we have to recapture the energy lost in braking.

HOW TO INCREASE ENERGY EFFICIENCY

Slow down   Reduce frontal area

Reduce weight   Increase engine efficiency

Capture energy from brakes

Making More Efficient Vehicles

Since there are only a few places that a vehicle's energy goes, there are only a few ways to make them more efficient. In particular:

1 For start-stop driving, we can reduce the weight (to reduce the inertial forces) and capture and reuse the energy released by braking.

2 At cruising speeds, we can reduce drag by making the car more streamlined and giving it a smaller frontal area.

3 In both kinds of operation we can reduce the waste heat by using more efficient engines and the total power consumed by driving more slowly.

Translated into design terms, what these rules say is that big, heavy, fast cars with internal combustion engines are inherently inefficient. A 100-mile-per-gallon gasoline-powered Hummer is physically impossible. If we want high efficiency, muscle and monster cars are out. Instead we are going to have to build small, light, low-power vehicles with nontraditional engines. Many such vehicles already exist, and more are being developed. They represent our best hope for low-carbon personal transport, and so are worth looking at carefully. They come in three basic flavors: hybrids, electric cars, and extended-range hybrids.

Hybrid Cars

Conventional hybrids combine a main gasoline engine that powers the vehicle with an electric engine that can capture and reuse the energy from the brakes and take over from the gas engine at low speeds.

Currently about ten manufacturers are making hybrids. The Toyota Prius, shown above and diagrammed on the next page, is a well-known example. Compared to my Subaru, the Prius is about 500 pounds lighter, has a third smaller main engine, and about a third less frontal area. It also has a regenerative breaking system that can recover about half the vehicle's kinetic energy when it slows down.

Drag, 8kW

Rolling resistance, 4 kW

2,932 lbs

32 kW Waste heat from engine

FOSSIL FUEL

Fuel
11 gal

Engine
98 hp

ELECTRIC

Motor-generator
80 hp

Battery
1.7 kWh

Energy consumption at 60 mph: 0.7 kWh per mile = 52 mpg

Overall the Prius uses about 45% less energy than my Subaru. On the highway, its advantage comes from its smaller size, better streamlining, and smaller and more efficient engine. In traffic, its main advantages are the regenerative braking system and the ability to shut down the gas engine and run on battery power for short distances.

The Prius, while an efficient gasoline car, is still a gasoline car. All of its energy comes from the gas tank, and, as in all cars with combustion engines, about 75% of that energy is lost as waste heat and does no work.

It may also be a member of the last generation of gasoline cars that we will see. Engineers have been tinkering with gasoline engines and aerodynamics for 100 years and have optimized them to a remarkable degree. The curve of improvements is pretty flat, and there may not be much left they can do. To do significantly better, a radical change is necessary: the fossil fuel engine has to go.

Electric Cars

Electric cars do just this: they get rid of the gasoline engine and run on an electric motor and a battery. This has advantages and disadvantages, both significant.

The advantages are in simplicity, weight, torque, and efficiency. Electric motors are simpler and lighter than the gas motors that they replace, and have better torque at low speeds. They have regenerative braking built in and are 90% efficient. No gasoline automotive engine is more than about 28% efficient.

The main disadvantage is that it is hard to carry electricity in a car. The best lithium-ion batteries store about 5 kilowatt-hours per hundred pounds. Small electric cars can carry at most a few hundred pounds of batteries, and so store only 10 to 20 kilowatt-hours of electricity—less than the energy (37 kWh) in a gallon of gasoline.

The low energy capacity limits how far electric cars can go between charges, which is bad. But it also forces them to be very efficient, which is good. Carrying 600 kWh of fossil fuel energy in your car is certainly a convenience, but it starts to look less desirable when you realize that 430 kWh of it will be lost as heat and do no useful work. Buying and burning energy that we couldn't use was a badge of honor in the fossil fuel age. It will not be in the low-carbon age.

Electric cars have a long but episodic history. Electric carriages were popular in the late 1890s and early 1900s, and in fact outsold gasoline carriages until about 1910. They then vanished from commercial production for 80 years.

In the 1990s they returned, but in a noncommittal way. In response to clean-air regulations, automakers produced some excellent designs—the Ford Ranger EV pickup and the Chevy EV1 coupe are classics—but refused to promote them. They leased the vehicles rather than sold them and, despite an enthusiastic reception by

HIGH-EFFICIENCY HYBRID AND ELECTRIC VEHICLES

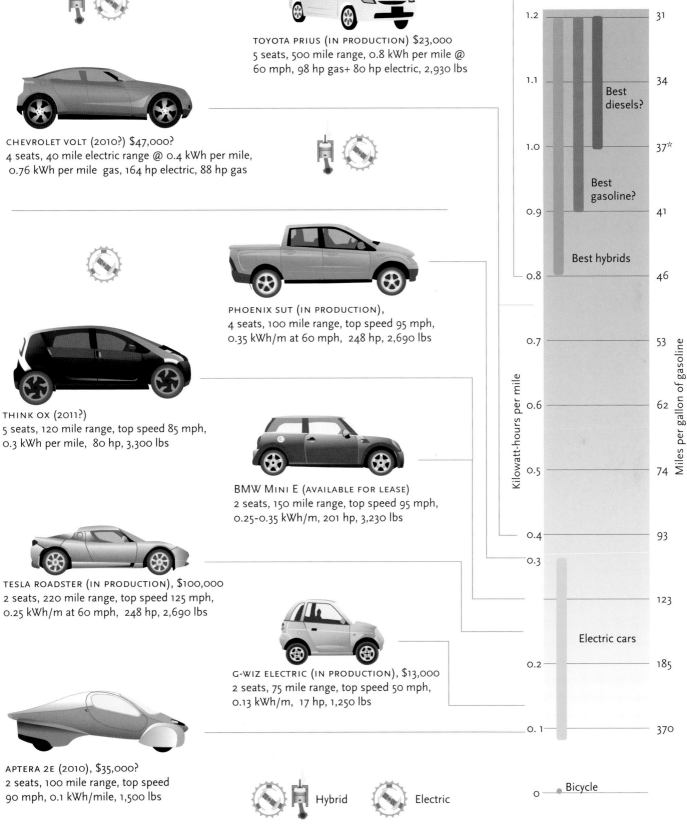

ENERGY COST OF TRANSPORTATION

TOYOTA PRIUS (IN PRODUCTION) $23,000
5 seats, 500 mile range, 0.8 kWh per mile @
60 mph, 98 hp gas+ 80 hp electric, 2,930 lbs

CHEVROLET VOLT (2010?) $47,000?
4 seats, 40 mile electric range @ 0.4 kWh per mile,
0.76 kWh per mile gas, 164 hp electric, 88 hp gas

PHOENIX SUT (IN PRODUCTION),
4 seats, 100 mile range, top speed 95 mph,
0.35 kWh/m at 60 mph, 248 hp, 2,690 lbs

THINK OX (2011?)
5 seats, 120 mile range, top speed 85 mph,
0.3 kWh per mile, 80 hp, 3,300 lbs

BMW MINI E (AVAILABLE FOR LEASE)
2 seats, 150 mile range, top speed 95 mph,
0.25-0.35 kWh/m, 201 hp, 3,230 lbs

TESLA ROADSTER (IN PRODUCTION), $100,000
2 seats, 220 mile range, top speed 125 mph,
0.25 kWh/m at 60 mph, 248 hp, 2,690 lbs

G-WIZ ELECTRIC (IN PRODUCTION), $13,000
2 seats, 75 mile range, top speed 50 mph,
0.13 kWh/m, 17 hp, 1,250 lbs

APTERA 2E (2010), $35,000?
2 seats, 100 mile range, top speed
90 mph, 0.1 kWh/mile, 1,500 lbs

Hybrid   Electric

Best diesels?

Best gasoline?

Best hybrids

Electric cars

Bicycle

Kilowatt-hours per mile

Miles per gallon of gasoline

* Diesel fuel has about 10% more energy per gallon than gasoline, and so 37 miles per gallon
of gasoline and 40 miles per gallon of diesel are both equivalent to about 0.9 kWh per mile.

91

users, discontinued production and confiscated and crushed the vehicles they had made when the regulations were rescinded.

Now electric cars are appearing again, and within three years there should be 20 to 30 models in commercial production. The 6 shown on p. 91 differ greatly in size and concept. The Phoenix, like its famous 1990s predecessor, the Chevy S10 EV (illustrated on p. 87), is an ordinary small pickup truck with electric power. The Ox, the Mini, and the MIEV are small four-seaters for general use. The Tesla Roadster is a high-powered, high-end sports car. The G-Wiz is a "city car"—a tiny two-seater with limited speed and range that is intended for low-speed use in traffic.

Also striking is the number of electrics coming from small companies and start-ups. The major manufacturers are also involved, but their main interest at present seems to be gasoline-electric hybrids rather than pure electrics. After its great hundred-year run, the combustion engine still has many friends in the big auto towns.

Here are two examples, as a quick preview of the low-carbon auto world we may be entering.

MITSUBISHI MIEV: FULL ELECTRIC

Energy consumption at 60 mph: 0.16 kWh per mile = 230 mpg

The Mitsubishi MIEV is a conventional four-seater minicar redesigned as an electric. It is smaller than the Prius and 500 lbs lighter. It has lithium-ion batteries that store 16 kilowatt-hours of energy and is powered by a 63 horsepower electric engine with a maximum speed of 80 miles per hour. The average energy consumption is 0.16 kilowatt-hour per mile, and the range on a 16 kilowatt-hour charge is about a hundred miles. As with all electric cars, 90% of this energy is used to move the car and hence the loss in waste heat is tiny.

Even for a small vehicle, these are remarkable numbers. This is a vehicle that goes 100 miles on the energy of three pints of gas. Its overall efficiency will be about five times that of the best gasoline cars, and hence comparable to that of the most efficient urban bus or electric-rail systems. From the point of view of our transportation options this is radical: in a few years we could have individual vehicles that are as efficient as any public transportation system we could build.

The Aptera 2E, in contrast, is a high-tech two-seater that may be near the limits of what a small passenger vehicle can achieve.

APTERA 2E: TWO-SEATER, AERODYNAMIC ELECTRIC

Energy consumption at 60 mph: 0.1 kWh per mile = 370 mpg

As its name suggests, the Aptera is built like a wingless aircraft. It has a slender, highly streamlined body, built using the composite technology used in advanced aircraft, and so is both light and extremely strong. Its coefficient of drag, a measure of streamlining, is lower than that of any other production car. As a result, its energy consumption at 60 miles per hour is about 0.1 kilowatt-hour per mile, equivalent to 370 miles per gallon. It carries only 10 kilowatt-hours of electricity—equivalent to 9 ounces of gasoline—but can go 100 miles on that power.

What all of the cars shown on p. 91 have in common is their high efficiency. When running on electricity, the least efficient of them, the Volt, is still twice as efficient as a Prius. The most efficient of them, the Aptera, is thirteen times as efficient as my Subaru, and twenty-five times as efficient as a Hummer.

CHEVROLET VOLT, EXTENDED-RANGE ELECTRIC VEHICLE

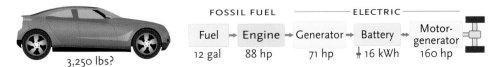

Energy consumption: battery power, 0.4 kWh/mi (90 mpg); gas power, 0.76 kwh/mile (50 mpg)

Extended-Range Hybrids

None of the first-generation electrics, it must be said quickly, will do everything we need in the Adirondacks. Most of them cannot cross the park and come back without a charge. The MIEV does not look like it would be very good at pulling a trailer; the Aptera was designed in southern California by people who have never seen mud or snow and has only 5 inches of clearance between the ground and the nacelles. None of them have all-wheel drive and none except the Phoenix have significant cargo capacity.

Nonetheless, they have considerable potential. Electrics already can do many of the things we need to do, like commute, run errands, and carry loads over a short range. They may enter our fleet, as hybrids did, as the summer or short-trip cars of two-car households. Then, 10 years down the road, they may have become tough enough or versatile enough to be our winter cars and all-around cars.

In the meantime, extended-range hybrids may be a useful interim solution. They are basically electric cars that have a small gasoline engine to charge their batteries. You can charge them electrically and run them at high efficiency for short trips, or run them on gasoline, at lower but still attractive efficiencies, on longer ones.

The Chevrolet Volt may be one of the first on the market. The driving power comes from a 160 hp electric engine and a 16 kWh battery that allows a range of 40 miles. The battery can be recharged by a small constant-speed gasoline engine, allowing the car to go several hundred miles on the gas in its tank. It is projected to get about 90 miles per gallon as an electric and 50 miles per gallon as a hybrid.

The Volt is still in development and at this point no one is sure how it will turn out or what its real mileage will be. Viewed optimistically, it may be a brilliant way of adding range to electric vehicles. Viewed more pessimistically it may Detroit's last attempt to keep the gasoline engine in the game. Either way, it is the first of a new class of vehicles, and many of us are eager to see how it performs.

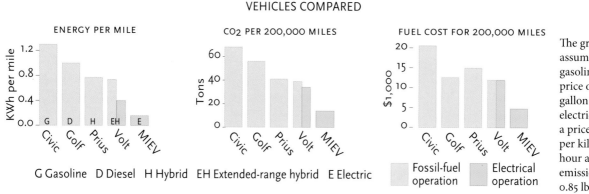

VEHICLES COMPARED

ENERGY PER MILE · CO2 PER 200,000 MILES · FUEL COST FOR 200,000 MILES

G Gasoline D Diesel H Hybrid EH Extended-range hybrid E Electric

Fossil-fuel operation   Electrical operation

The graphs assume that gasoline has a price of $3 per gallon and that electricity has a price of $0.15 per kilowatt-hour and emissions of 0.85 lb CO_2 per kilowatt-hour.

The Bottom Lines: Carbon and Costs

To solve our carbon problem we need affordable, low-emission vehicles. Electric vehicles may or may not be the answer. We know they are efficient, but until we know where they will get their electricity, we won't know what they will emit. And until we know what they will cost, we won't know whether people will buy them.

As I write this in 2009, with at most a few thousand electric vehicles in the United States, it is too early to answer either of these questions. But so far the numbers look promising.

Carbon first. Electric cars emit no carbon themselves. But they need electricity, and electrical generation does release carbon. Just how much carbon depends on the balance of fossil fuels and renewables in the electricity supply.

In New York, generating stations release on average 0.85 lb of CO_2 for each kilowatt-hour they deliver to the customers. If we used this power to charge an electric vehicle with an energy consumption of 0.2 kilowatt-hour per mile, we would emit 0.17 lb of CO_2 per mile.

This is a pretty good number. For comparison, a Prius uses 0.8 kilowatt-hour of fossil fuel energy per mile and emits 0.4 lb CO_2 per mile, over twice as much.

But not all electricity is as green as New York's. If the electricity was generated from coal, the dirtiest of the fossil fuels, the emissions would be 0.42 lb per mile, about the same as the Prius.

Thus electric cars are clean only if we have clean electricity to power them. If we can provide enough clean electricity—a serious *if*—they can save a lot of carbon.

How much is a lot? The graphs compare five cars, a gasoline car, a hybrid, a diesel, an extended-range electric, and a pure electric. The energy per mile ranges from 1.3 kilowatt-hours for the gasoline Civic to 0.16 kilowatt-hour for the electric MIEV. The carbon emissions closely parallel the energy use. The Civic will release 68 tons of CO_2 over 200,000 miles. The MIEV, powered from the New York grid, will emit 14 tons, a reduction of 79%. If the MIEV were powered by green electricity from sun or wind, the emissions would be zero and the savings 100%.

How much will it cost to get these savings? It is hard to know because only a few electric cars are currently in production, but manufacturers are suggesting prices in the $40,000 to $50,000 range for four-seaters. These costs are high—twice that of a hybrid, three times that of a conventional four-seater—but remember that there are compensations. Electric cars are eligible for a $7,500 federal tax credit. Gasoline cars, over 200,000 miles, cost more to fuel than they do to buy, which may explain why the fossil fuel industry is so loyal to them.

In five years or so, as the market for electric cars increases, they will likely come down in price. But suppose you are impressed by the carbon savings and determined to have one as soon as possible. What will it cost you to buy it and run it?

LIFETIME COSTS AND CARBON EMISSIONS OF THREE VEHICLES

	CIVIC	PRIUS	EV FROM GRID	EV+SOLAR
Purchase price	$17,000	$23,000	$40,000	$48,500
Fuel cost 200,000 mi	$22,000	$13,000	$8,000	$0
Car+fuel	$39,000	$36,000	$48,000	$48,500
Additional lifetime cost	$0	-$3,000	$9,000	$9,500
CO_2 saved	0	26 tons	52 tons	69 tons
Cost per ton CO_2 saved	-	-$115	$173	$138

The table assumes that an electric car with a fuel consumption of 0.2 kWh per mile will be available for $40,000 after tax credits, that a 3.6 kW solar system to power it costs $8,500 after incentives and tax credits, and that the average cost of grid electricity will be $0.20 and of gasoline $3.10 over the next 10 years.

The table shows a simple accounting of the purchase and fuel costs for three vehicles over a 200,000-mile lifetime. It neglects finance costs, and does not discount future savings. It suggests that when you account for gas costs, hybrids may be cheaper than conventional cars, and electric cars not that much more expensive.

The Civic owner pays $17,000 up front to buy the car and another $22,000 over 10 years for gas. His total cost is $39,000.

The Prius owner pays $23,000 up front and $13,000 for fuel for at total cost of $36,000. She saves $3,000 over the Civic, and avoids emitting 26 tons of CO_2.

The owner of the first electric vehicle spends $40,000, after tax credits, for the vehicle and $8,000 for electricity from the New York State grid. His total costs are $48,000. This is $9,000 more than the Civic owner, but saves 52 tons of CO_2.

The owner of the second electrical vehicle notices that, with incentives and rebates, she can buy a photovoltaic system for herself for $8,500 and pay for it out of $8,000 savings in gas. She spends the largest amount, $48,500, up front. But she saves 69 tons of carbon and has free power for her next car as well.

All of these numbers assume $3.10 per gallon of gas. If gas were to go to $5 per gallon, the lifetime cost of the Civic would be $54,000 and the Prius $44,000. At these prices the electric car would be highly competitive.

Heavy Vehicles: Trucks, Buses, and Planes

If the numbers in the previous sections of this chapter are right, there are good, cost-effective ways of reducing the emissions from light passenger vehicles. Unfortunately, there do not seem to be any comparable ways to reduce the emissions of trucks, buses, and planes.

The main problem is the quantities of energy involved. A truck carrying 50 gallons of diesel fuel is carrying 2,000 kilowatt-hours of energy. To replace this with electricity would require 20 tons of batteries, half of the legal maximum weight. Transport systems make money because they carry freight, not fuel, and trucks or buses with 20 tons of batteries would not be competitive.

The problem is even more difficult for airplanes, because planes have to use energy to stay up in the air. As a result, their energy needs are high compared to comparable forms of transportation. Batteries are out of the question because they don't contain enough energy to support their own weight. Increases in engine efficiency and flight performance are possible, but commercial planes have already been carefully optimized and so further progress will be slow. Barring some radical advance in design or propulsion, the planes of 20 years from now may only be 10% or 20% more efficient than those of today.

It thus appears that, within the 20-year window this book is considering, heavy vehicles will continue to use liquid fuels and so continue to have significant carbon

HEAVY VEHICLES

emissions. We will be able to reduce these emissions by reducing the amount we use heavy vehicles, and offset them by using biologically derived fuels when they become available. But we will not, in the near future, be able to eliminate them.

The continued presence of heavy vehicles and liquid fuels will influence the Adirondack carbon budget. Currently diesel vehicles, most of them heavy, emit about 164,000 tons of CO_2 per year, about a fifth of the vehicle emissions in the park. The amount Adirondackers fly is unknown. If 150,000 Adirondackers took one cross-country trip a year, the direct CO_2 emissions would be 150,000 tons, roughly equal to that of all the diesel vehicles in the park.

Summary

This chapter has a simple story. Vehicles are the largest source of direct carbon emissions in the Adirondacks. We can change this by changing how the vehicles are made and how we use them.

The key elements to making more efficient passenger vehicles are to make them smaller and lighter and to power them with green electricity rather than petroleum. Such vehicles already exist, but none are yet suitable for all-around Adirondack use. In the meantime, hybrids and extended-range hybrids may be our best alternatives.

The key elements to using passenger vehicles more efficiently are to drive them less, drive them slower, and drive them with more people in them.

Unfortunately, no similar options exist for heavy commercial vehicles. In the near future our only options seem to be to use them less if we can and offset their emissions by using biofuels when they become available.

Old Forge, 2009

9 REDUCTION: LOW-CARBON BUILDINGS

The Adirondack Park contains about 80,000 private houses and a smaller but still significant number of commercial and institutional buildings. These buildings require 455 megawatts of power. They emit about 400 tons of carbon dioxide directly from their furnaces, and another 470 tons indirectly through the electricity they use. Clearly, if we want to do something about Adirondack carbon emissions, we must do something about buildings.

This chapter is about what we can do. It has both good news and bad news. The good news is that most houses use far more energy than is necessary. The main components of their energy use—heating, hot water, lighting, general electricity—can all be cut by 50%. In some cases they can be cut by 75% or more.

The bad news is that getting these kinds of savings will not be easy or cheap. Serious increases in efficiency will require significant investment—removing siding, replacing windows, reinsulating, replacing heating systems, and so on.

Rebuilding houses at the scale necessary will take capital and incentives. The capital requirements, though large, can potentially be met. The Adirondacks spend over $400 million per year on energy for buildings. At least half of this could be saved by investing in energy efficiency. It should be possible to borrow against potential savings to get the capital needed. Many investments in energy efficiency pay for themselves in less than 10 years, which means they have a return of over 10%, an attractive rate in almost any market.

ENERGY USED IN BUILDINGS

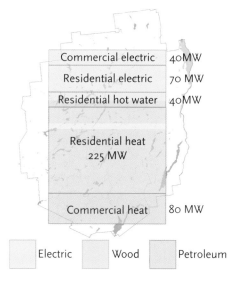

Commercial electric   40MW

Residential electric   70 MW

Residential hot water   40MW

Residential heat
225 MW

Commercial heat   80 MW

Electric   Wood   Petroleum

97

The incentive problem is harder. Many owners and most landlords are more or less satisfied with their buildings. The last thing they are about to do is to spend a lot of money to retrofit and rebuild them. If we want them to do this, we need some powerful way to provide money and create dissatisfaction. Right now, no one really knows how to do this. But if we are to reduce residential energy use, someone will have to find a way.

I return to costs and incentives in Chapter 13. Here the problem is much simpler. We need to know why buildings use so much energy, and how they can use less. We start by asking where the energy goes.

What do households use energy for?

Since there are far more houses than commercial buildings in the park, I focus on them for the remainder of the chapter. Everything I will say is true of commercial and institutional buildings as well; the differences are mostly ones of scale.

Regional energy surveys say that an average northeastern household uses about 4,100 watts of power. About sixty percent of this is used for space heating, 18% for heating water, and the rest for general electricity—appliances, lights, and gadgets.

We have no specifically Adirondack data. The overall pattern is probably similar but with more space heating because of the colder climate.

Since space heating is the largest energy use in most households, it is where we should start if we want to reduce carbon emissions. To make a serious dent in carbon emissions we will need to cut household energy use in half. We are not going to do this by changing shower heads or buying better toasters.

ENERGY USE BY AN
AVERAGE HOUSEHOLD

Space heating, 58%

Hot water, 18%

Appliances and light, 24%

Total power 4,100 W

How much energy does it take to heat a house?

The energy required, called the heating load, varies greatly. In our survey of a dozen Adirondack households, heating loads ranged from 1,000 watts to over 10,000 watts. This is probably a typical range for modern single-family houses in our climate. Had we included exceptionally large houses, we might have gone to 20,000 watts. Had we included some of the grand and barely insulated castles that the Adirondack gentry built a century ago, we might have gone to 30,000 watts or beyond.

To put these numbers in context, the thrifty home with a heating load of 1,000 watts could be heated with 200 gallons of fuel oil a year. The lavish one with a load of 10,000 watts would take 2,000 gallons, and the old-style castle 6,000 gallons. Thrift clearly makes a difference.

The variation in heating from house to house comes from five factors: the temperature difference between the inside of the house and the outside, the size of the house, the heat loss, the solar gain, and the efficiency of the heater.

All are important, and in a truly thrifty house all will have been optimized to decrease the heating load. We look at them one by one.

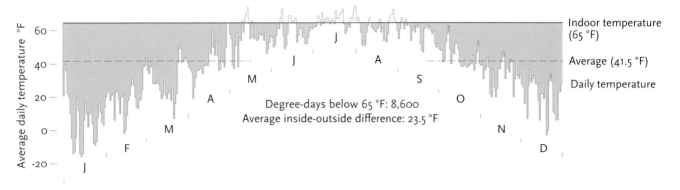

THE HEATING DEMAND IN LAKE PLACID, 2004

Indoor temperature (65 °F)

Average (41.5 °F)

Daily temperature

Average daily temperature °F

Degree-days below 65 °F: 8,600
Average inside-outside difference: 23.5 °F

Inside and Outside Temperatures

The rate at which heat leaks out of a house depends on the difference between the inside and outside temperatures. The residents control the first, the climate the second. Together, they determine how much energy the house uses. Other things being equal, a house kept 20 degrees warmer than the outside will use twice as much energy for space heating as one kept 10 degrees warmer.

The cumulative difference between the inside and outside temperatures is called the heating demand and measured in degree-days. The graph above shows the demand for a house in Lake Placid kept at 65 degrees. The distance between the top and the bottom lines is the average indoor-outdoor temperature difference on any given day. The shaded area between them is the total heating demand, in this case 8,600 degree-days.

Note that most of the area of the shaded figure is near the top, in the 20 to 60 degree range. The subzero days that make the Adirondack climate memorable are relatively rare and don't influence the heating demand that much. The average temperatures do. A cold April, with temperatures nearer 30 than 40, will have a big effect on heating demand: a few super-cold January nights won't.

Each town has its own temperature curve. The differences in these curves can generate small differences in heating demand. The coldest Adirondack towns have about 5% more heating demand than Lake Placid. The warmest ones have about 10% less demand.

Each house, of course, has its own average indoor temperature, and these differences generate large differences in heating demand. Higher indoor temperatures—more wood in the stove or a higher thermostat setting—move the red line at the top of the graph up and generate increases in heating demand. Lower indoor temperatures move it down and generate reduction.

As shown in the graph on p. 100, small changes in the indoor temperature make big changes in the heating demand. Raising the indoor temperature from 65 degrees to 75 degrees uses 40% more energy. Dropping it from 65 degrees to 50 degrees uses 45% less energy.

Households that heat with wood often monitor their daily energy use and generally know that hot houses need a lot more wood than cold ones. Households with central heating systems often do not. Leaving the thermostat set high overnight or when you are out of the house seems like a small thing and unlikely to influence your overall energy consumption.

HEATING DEGREE-DAYS

+10

● Tupper Lake
● Old Forge

o-● Lake Placid

● Dannemora
● Plattsburgh
● Watertown
● Binghamton
● Albany
● Rochester

HDD relative to Lake Placid, %

-10

-20

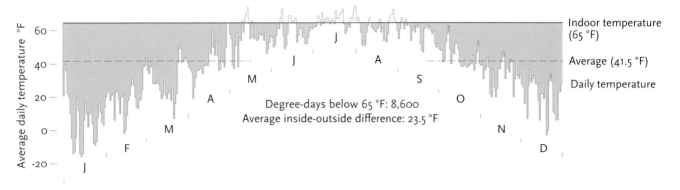

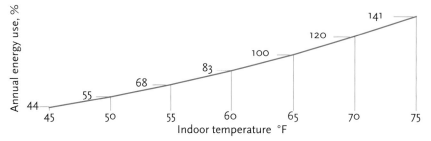
ENERGY CONSUMPTION FOR DIFFERENT INDOOR TEMPERATURES

The numbers, however, say otherwise, and this leads to our first rule for saving energy. *The thermostat is an energy control and a very sensitive one. Keep it as low as possible, and only turn it up when you need to.*

The key to keeping the thermostat low is not using heat that you don't need. With programmable thermostats, the house can be cold when you are not in it or when you are asleep. With zoned heating, rooms you are not using can be colder than the ones you do use. With auxiliary stoves and space heaters, the parts of the rooms that you actually use can be warmer than the parts that you don't.

Because the curve of energy consumption versus temperature is steep, the savings involved are not trivial. If you can get the average temperature of your house down from 68 degrees to 60 degrees, you can save 30% on your fuel costs, and cut your carbon emissions as well.

The fuel companies, of course, have long recommended the opposite strategy. Set the whole house to a "comfortable level," they say, and keep it there day and night, whether you are in it or not. Tinkering with the thermostat, we are advised, costs more energy than it saves.

This turns out to be nonsense. Cool rooms always use less energy than warm ones, even when you count the energy needed to heat them up again. Fussing with the thermostat takes effort but saves energy. If you have an inefficient house, and if you can't afford to rebuild it, rationing your energy use by adjusting the thermostat is probably the single most effective way of reducing your energy consumption.

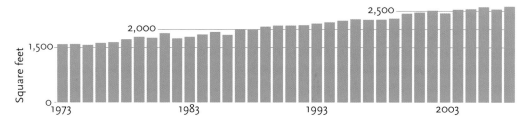
AVERAGE SIZE OF NEW SINGLE-FAMILY HOUSES IN NORTHEAST

Size of Houses

Grown humans are all roughly the same size. The houses they live in are not. A tiny cabin or caravan might have 100 square feet of floor area. An average contemporary home for a couple or small family might have 2,000 square feet. A second-tier mansion might run 5,000 or 10,000 square feet, a high-end one 20,000 square feet or more.

The size of houses is directly related to their energy consumption. Houses lose energy through their surfaces. Since the surface area is roughly proportional to the floor space, a house that has twice as much floor space will use approximately twice as much energy.

The size of houses has long been a measure of the wealth of their occupants, and as America has become more wealthy, its houses have become larger. The three-bedroom house that I grew up in the 1950s was under 1,000 square feet. By 1975 the average new house in the Northeast was over 1,600 feet. By 2005 it was over 2,500 square feet, more than 50% larger.

All of this is good news for the building and fuel industries but bad news for energy and carbon. Big houses are big energy users and carbon producers. The houses being built today are considerably more efficient than those built 30 years ago. But they are also considerably bigger, and the increase in size has tended to cancel the gains in efficiency. As with car travel and air travel, having a more efficient machine is useless if you turn around and use it more.

Thus the second rule for saving household energy. *If you want to lower your household energy consumption, live in the smallest house you can and then make it smaller by leaving parts of it unheated in the winter.*

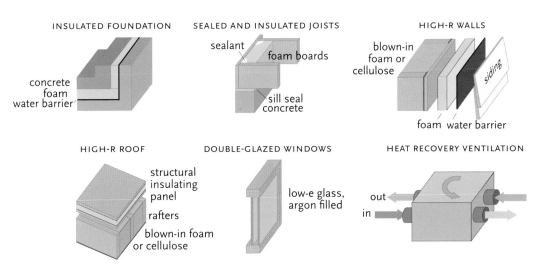

STOPPING HEAT LOSS

Heat Loss

Heat that is put into houses leaks out again. The leakage rate depends on tightness and insulation. An uninsulated house with leaky sills and windows can cool from 70 degrees to freezing overnight. A tight, well-insulated house might cool less than 10 degrees in the same period. The first step in making a house, old or new, more efficient is to make it tighter.

Since the rate at which heat leaks out determines the rate at which heat must be put in, all efficient houses are designed to reduce thermal leakage. This can be done

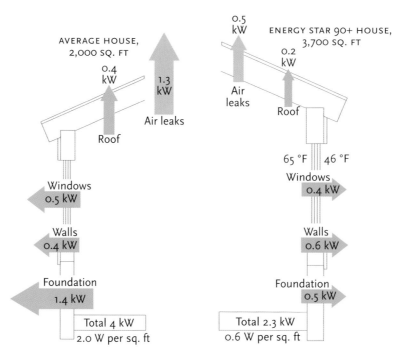

HEAT LOSSES FROM TWO NEW HOUSES

in many different ways. The goal is to eliminate air leaks and create a continuous sheet of insulation. Common approaches are insulating the foundation and the shell with foam boards or structural insulating panels, filling cavities with high-density foam or cellulose, using double-glazed or triple-glazed windows, and sealing the shell and all the openings for pipes and wires with foam. A less common but highly effective approach is to use the outgoing air to heat the incoming air.

The combined effects of insulating and sealing can be impressive. The diagram compares the heat losses of two houses, one with average and one with exceptional construction. The house on the left, an average contemporary house, has reasonably thick walls and ceilings but is not well sealed and uses fiberglass insulation, which is notoriously leaky. As a result, its heat loss is dominated by air leaks and heat leaking through the foundation. It is not a bad house, and, in fact, would have been considered excellent 30 years ago. But it is far from the best that can be done today.

The house on the right of the diagram has been certified by the Energy Star program and has received an energy efficiency rating of over 90. This is near the top of what is routinely available today. The house has a continuous insulating skin, efficient windows and doors, excellent sealing, and mechanical ventilation. It is also, as high-efficiency houses often are, nearly twice as large as an average house.

Despite its size, the Energy Star house is very efficient. Air exchange and leakage through the foundation have been greatly reduced; leakage through the windows and roof is less, even though the window and door area is greater. Overall the house is 40% more efficient than the average house. Had it been the same size as the average house it would have been 70% more efficient.

The potential 70% efficiency gain is impressive, and leads to our third rule. *If you are building or rebuilding a house and want high energy efficiency, build a small, leak-free house with a continuous insulating skin and heat recovery ventilation.*

Solar Gain and Solar Design

All houses are heated by the sun and so have some solar gain. In most houses, even highly efficient ones, the gain is small. An average house might receive only 10% or 20% of its winter heat from the sun, and might lose much of that at night through the same windows it gained it by in the day.

If, however, a house is specifically designed to collect and store solar heat, the numbers can be higher. Good solar houses in our climate can get 40% to 50% of their energy from the sun. Exceptional ones can go over 60%.

The ways of doing this have had an interesting evolution. Thirty years ago, solar houses were thought of as ordinary houses to which an active solar heating system had been added. The active solar system had collectors and pipes and pumps and controllers. It collected heat at high temperature, moved it to rock piles for storage, and then pumped it back when it was needed. Such systems could work well, but even the best of them were expensive, complicated, and prone to failure.

Solar houses today are quite different. Most contemporary solar houses are passive. Rather than using special collectors, they just let the light come in the windows; rather than using pumps and ducts to move heat to special storage areas, they use natural convection and store it in floors and walls. Such houses don't look very different from ordinary houses, and don't do anything that a normal house doesn't do. The big difference is how well they do it.

Despite differences in detail, most passive solar designs in our climate have several features in common. They tend to be oriented with the long axis of the house facing south and most of the window area on the south side; they have an open floor plan that allows air to circulate; they are built on a thick concrete slab that stores heat; they use overhangs to exclude sunlight in the summer, and often insulated shutters or shades to retain heat in the winter; and they are extremely well insulated and well sealed. The best of them use only small stoves or heaters for backup heat. This is extremely cost-effective, because the additional costs of the insulation and heat-storing slab are offset by omitting the basement and central heating system.

Well-designed passive solar houses are among the simplest and most comfortable houses we have. They have even, radiant heat, and little temperature variation between day and night. They use very little fuel. They have no complicated mechanical systems to maintain, and are among the quietest and safest of all houses. They are freeze-proof in the winter, and as evenly cool in the summer as they are warm in the winter.

And this leads us to our fourth rule. *If you are building a new house or rebuilding an old one and want comfort and high efficiency, incorporate solar gain, thermal storage, and natural air circulation in your design.*

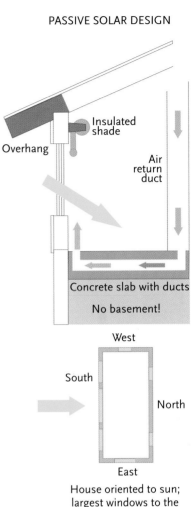

PASSIVE SOLAR DESIGN

Overhang
Insulated shade
Air return duct
Concrete slab with ducts
No basement!

West
South
North
East

House oriented to sun; largest windows to the south and east

Open fireplace, 10% | Parlor stove, 30%? | Airtight stove, 50%? | Secondary combustion, stove, 65% | Catalytic stove, 70% | Boiler with forced draft, 85%

Efficient Heaters

Houses are heated by the sun on the outside and by various combinations of fire and machinery on the inside. Sunlight is free and has no carbon emissions, and so the efficiency with which we capture it is not too important. Other fuels cost money and emit carbon, and the efficiency with which we use them is very important.

Recall (p. xiii) that the efficiency of a heater is the ratio of the energy it uses to the heat it produces. The efficiencies of heaters vary greatly, and have a correspondingly great effect on energy consumption. The diagram shows this for wood heaters.

All stove and furnaces send heat up the chimney and so have efficiencies less than 100%. Open wood fireplaces send 90% of their heat up the chimney and have an efficiency of only 10%. Iron stoves do better, and may reach 70% efficiency with catalytic converters. Wood boilers with forced drafts and two-stage combustion can do even better, and are comparable to good oil burners (p. 123). Condensing gas boilers in which the waste heat is used to preheat the incoming water are even better, and can reach efficiencies of 95%.

Ninety-five percent is probably the practical limit to the efficiency of a combustion heater. There will always be some waste gases, and, beyond a point, the things that you have to do with pumps and blowers to recover that heat in those gases start consuming more energy than you recover.

Electric heaters produce no waste gases and so their efficiency, measured at the place where they are being used, is 100%. But there is a catch: the electricity the heater uses has been generated somewhere else, and generating it and moving it often wastes energy (p. 71). When we include the energy used to make the electricity, their efficiency is lower. If the electricity is made nearby from renewables, then the efficiency may still be near 100%. But if it comes from fossil fuels and has been moved long distances over power lines, two-thirds of the energy in the fuel will be lost before it gets to your house, and the efficiency will be under 30%.

Heat Pumps

Heat pumps are machines that use compressors and heat-absorbing gases to take heat from one place at one temperature and deliver it to another place at another temperature. Refrigerators and air conditioners, which take heat from inside something and dump it outside, are common examples. Geothermal heating systems, which pump heat the ground from ground into a house, are less familiar examples.

In a few more years they may be much more familiar. Heat pumps are the most efficient space-heating systems currently available, and are being used in many high-efficiency houses and commercial buildings. Skidmore College, for example, heats all of its new buildings with heat pumps, and has plans to convert many of its older buildings as well.

The diagram below shows how they work. The heat source is either the soil or the water in a well. In the closed-loop system shown in the diagram, a pump circulates water and antifreeze through pipes in a trench or in a loop inside a well. The heat pump extracts heat from the circulating water and uses it to heat air, which is then circulated through the house. The cold water goes back to the ground loop, picks up more heat, and then returns again.

GROUND-SOURCE HEATING SYSTEM

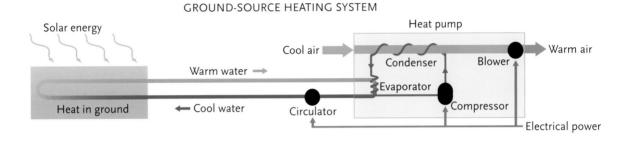

The heat that the heat pump delivers to the house is actually solar heat. The ground is, in effect, a large, solar-charged battery (p. 125). The sun heats it in the summer. The ground holds the heat, only gradually losing it in the winter. When we use the heat, we cool the ground, discharging the battery. The sun recharges it the next summer, and we can tap it again the following winter. As long as we don't take more heat from the ground than the sun can supply in the summer, we can do this for as long as we want.

Heat pumps run on electricity. What makes them both attractive and a little spooky is that a little electricity can move a lot of heat. The typical heat pumps used in ground-source heating systems can move about 3 kilowatts of heat for each kilowatt of electricity. Since the electricity is turned into heat in the process, the pump delivers 4 kilowatts of heat for every kilowatt of electricity, and the potential efficiency is a startling 400%.*

* This is the efficiency of the heat pump itself. When the energy for the circulator pump and the blower is included, the overall system efficiency is 300–350%.

THE ENERGY BALANCE OF A HEAT PUMP

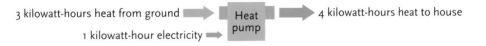

As with electric heaters (p. 104), to get this efficiency we need renewable electricity produced nearby. If we use grid electricity from fossil fuels, much energy is wasted, and the overall efficiency drops to somewhere between 100% and 120%. This is significant but not crippling. Heat pumps powered with renewables seem to be the cleanest and most efficient heating systems we have. Heat pumps powered by grid electricity are not nearly as good, but, as we will see in a moment, may still be more efficient than electrical or combustion heaters.

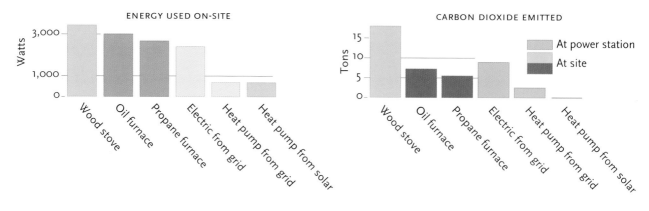

SPACE-HEATING SYSTEMS COMPARED

Space-heating Systems Compared

The overall efficiency of a heater is only part of the story. The bottom-line numbers for building owners are the fuel consumed on-site and the carbon emitted. The first predicts the operating cost, the second the climate impact.

The graphs show the on-site energy use and total carbon emissions for six heating systems. I assume that the household, like average one on p. 98, needs 2,400 watts of heat. The wood heating system is assumed to be 70% efficient, the oil system 80%, the propane system 90%, and the electrical system 100%. The heat pump system, which includes circulator pumps and blowers as well as the heat pump itself, is assumed to be 350% efficient. The energy in the left graph is the energy used on-site. The emissions in the right graph are the total emissions, both from the house and from the power station.

The systems fall into three groups. Grid electricity, oil, and propane are generally similar, differing mostly in the efficiencies of the heaters and the greater carbon emissions from generating and moving electricity (p. 71). All emit over five tons of carbon dioxide per year, an unacceptably large amount if we want to do our part in reducing world carbon emissions.

Heat pumps are much better. Here they use 700 watts of electricity to deliver 2,400 watts of heat, an excellent bargain. If the electricity comes from the grid, producing it emits 2.6 tons of carbon dioxide, an improvement but probably still not good enough. If the electricity for the pumps comes from solar power, no carbon is emitted at all, which definitely is good enough.

The wood stove is a special case. Wood stoves are only moderately efficient, and wood emits more carbon per kilowatt-hour of energy than any other fuel we use. But wood is also cheap and local, and if it is harvested at less than the growth rate (p. 123) the forest can remove the carbon as fast as it is emitted. So we can consider it green (and have colored it green on the graph) but with the caution that it is a green fuel only when it comes from a green forest, and some forests are greener than others.

Summing up the discussion of heating, we have the fifth rule. *If you want to make a serious reduction in your household's carbon emissions, heat either with wood or with a heat pump. If you want the lowest possible emissions, the best choice is a heat pump powered by renewable energy.*

How efficient can a house be?

The preceding sections suggest that the standard northern New York house is an energy hog. It is too large, too hot inside, and too leaky. It has an inefficient heating system and little solar gain.

In theory at least, we should be able to do much better. By piling up small improvements in size and construction, and adding some big ones in solar gain and efficient heating, we should be able to end up with a house that is several times more efficient than usual.

Surprisingly, at least for those of us who distrust theory, this seems to be true. The graph on the right compares the heat required by different houses in northern New York. It shows that the best high-efficiency houses without passive solar are two to three times as efficient as conventional houses, and the best high-efficiency houses with passive solar are eight times or more as efficient as conventional houses.

These numbers come with a serious caveat; data on house performance tend to be incomplete, scattered, and often difficult to compare. Computer models showing how houses are supposed to perform are common. Real data showing how they actually do are much rarer.

But if the numbers are even approximately true, they say something important. Good modern houses use only a quarter or a fifth of the energy per square foot of average houses. Add a passive solar heating system or a ground source heat pump, and they may use only an eighth of the energy of an average house.

These numbers are exciting. Like electric cars, efficient houses could make a real difference in our carbon emissions.

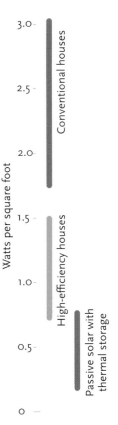

ENERGY NEEDED TO
HEAT HOUSES

Rebuilding Old Houses

Houses, however, last longer than cars. Most of the cars in the Adirondacks today will be gone in 10 years. Most of the houses will still be here. And thus, while it is nice that we know how to make new houses highly efficient, this is not really our problem. We have to deal with existing houses, many of them leaky and inefficient. What can be done with them, and how hard will it be to do it?

Surprisingly, given all the old houses and all the repairs that are done on them, this question doesn't have a clear answer. There is a lot of information about patching them with caulking and rock wool and getting 10% or 20% energy savings. But patchwork by itself won't produce serious carbon reductions. What we need to know is how to get the kind of 50% and 80% savings we get from new ones. If we can do this, we can preserve our fine old buildings and, in the process, avoid the carbon emissions associated with building new ones (pp. 139-140). If we can't, we are going to have to think about tearing them down and building new ones.

Thus far, I have not been able to find a systematic account of the costs of rebuilding an old house and the energy gains that resulted. Lacking anything better, I will describe my own experiences.

I live in a house that was built some time before 1850, got plumbing and its first coat of paint in 1968, and its first (inadequate) insulation in 1973. It was cold, drafty, and never really warm, no matter how much wood I burned. Over the next 30 years I made small changes and did some patching, without much effect. In 2004, I started

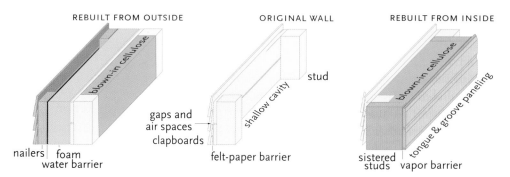

TWO WAYS OF REBUILDING AN OLD HOUSE

REBUILT FROM OUTSIDE · ORIGINAL WALL · REBUILT FROM INSIDE

blown-in cellulose

stud

gaps and
air spaces
clapboards

shallow cavity

blown-in cellulose

tongue & groove paneling

nailers | foam
water barrier

felt-paper barrier

sistered | vapor barrier
studs

on a systematic rebuilding. The job is about two-thirds complete, with some major work still to come.

All 19th-century houses have three basic problems: the wall and rafter cavities are too narrow to hold enough insulation, the windows are single-glazed, and there are air leaks everywhere. To get anywhere you have to address all three problems. You must thicken the walls, replace the windows, and seal everything you can get to. This is serious work and goes deep in the house. Walls have to be opened, floors taken up, sills replaced, windows and doors reframed, and so on. It is heavy, dirty, exciting work and requires an interesting mixture of stubbornness and daring.

The work can be done either from the outside or the inside. Working from outside you remove the siding and add a new foam skin. Working from the inside, you thicken the walls and then fill them with a high-density insulation. In many ways working from the outside is easier, and would be the best way to approach a house with an interior that you want to preserve.

In my case, the interior was a mess and so I chose to work from the inside. I started from the bottom: removed the floors and walls, sealed the foundation, and put down a vapor barrier. I then built a new frame inside the old one: sistered the studs and rafters, put in new windows, and sealed the cracks. A contractor then put a retaining membrane over the beams and blew high-density cellulose insulation into the cavities. I added another vapor barrier, built new doors, and finished the walls and ceilings with wood paneling.

The process was in many ways like building a second house inside the first. The results seem to have been good. Even though the work is not finished, the house is easier to heat and much more comfortable. The finished parts are now draft-free and hold their temperature within 8 degrees on cold nights.

The energy use is also much improved. I now heat with about 3.5 cords of wood. This delivers about 1,500 watts of heat to the living space and so represents a power density of a bit over 1 watt per square foot, quite comparable to many well-built modern houses. I hope to get it still lower, but, considering that I started with an uninsulated, tumble-down farmhouse that was almost unheatable, this is a long way to have come.

The total cost for materials and the insulation contractors so far has been $22,000, or about $10 per square foot of shell. The new windows, which were essential, were $9,000, and the insulating $6,000.

Since the house was not heated with fossil fuels before the renovation, it is not really possible to say how much fuel and carbon I have saved. A rough calculation

Rebuilding the east wing of my house, 2006. New floor and windows, sistered studs.

that suggests that similar renovations on an oil-heated house might save 800 gallons of oil and 9 tons of CO_2 per year. At \$3 per gallon this would be a savings of \$2,400, for a payback period of 9 years.

What I conclude from my experience is that it is possible to rebuild an old house and reduce energy consumption by over 50%. To do this you have to do a complete rebuild, foundation to roof, with significant investments in materials and labor. In my case, doing almost all the work myself, the payback period was under 10 years. Had I hired people to do it, the costs would have been higher and the payback longer.

Hot Water

Besides space heating, houses use energy to heat water and power appliances, lights, and gadgets. Most of the uses are small and intermittent, but they still add up. On average a northeastern household uses 1,700 watts—over a third of its energy—for hot water and miscellaneous electricity. The Adirondacks as a whole are estimated to use 110 megawatts. Since 110 megawatts is a lot of power, and since much of this power is electricity and hence carbon intensive, we need to reduce this significantly if we are going to reduce carbon emissions.

The place to start is with hot water. Our average northeastern household with a gas hot water heater uses 740 watts of power, produces 60 gallons of hot water a day, and emits two tons of carbon a year. To those of us who have lived in places where we carried water and heated it on the stove, this seems like an enormous amount of hot water. But a family that took long showers and ran their washing machine and dishwasher every day could easily use that much or more.

Once again, the quickest and cheapest way to save energy is by thrift. Take shorter showers, wash clothes in cold water, run the dishwasher only when it is full. Put insulation around heaters with tanks so they won't leak heat. Put switches on them and only turn them on when you need hot water.

REBUILDING MY HOUSE

New 12-inch rafters filled with cellulose

Tongue and groove paneling

Double-glazed, casement windows

New 6-inch walls filled with cellulose

New floor

cellulose — foam

Crawl space

vapor barrier   mortar

Vedder-Weber, Johnsburg, 1980, 1,700 sq. ft, ground-source heat and photovoltaic electricity. 1.4 watts per sq. ft for heat and hot water.

Jenkins, White Creek, ca. 1840, 1,400 sq. ft heated space, wood heat, photovoltaic electricity, ca. 1.1 watts per sq. ft for heat.

Muehsam, White Creek, 2000, 1,000 sq. ft, stucco over hay-bale, solar hot water heat with propane backup, photovoltaic electricity.

McIntosh, Cambridge, 1976, 1,300 sq. ft, passive solar with wood heat, photovoltaic electricity, ca. 0.7 watt per sq. ft.

Black Kettle Farm, Essex, ca. 1820, 2,100 sq. ft, wood and oil heat with solar hot water.

Nevulis, Lake Placid, 5,800 sq. ft, passive solar with wood heat, less than 0.2 watt per sq. ft.

How much energy you can save depends on how much you were using in the first place and how thrifty you become. I would guess that for many households a 25% savings would be easy, and a 50% one possible but hard.

The second, and more costly, way of saving energy is to install a more efficient water heater. Conventional heaters with tanks are relatively inefficient because they leak heat from the tank and, if fired by oil or gas, send lots of energy up the chimney. Condensing gas heaters reduce the chimney losses and tankless heaters eliminate the tank losses. Both are about 25% to 30% more efficient than conventional gas heaters. Solar heaters are more efficient still, and can reduce energy and emissions by 60% or more.

A solar system supplying 70% of the hot water for our average house might cost $5,000 to $7,000 retail. State and federal incentives will reduce this by several thousand dollars. The energy savings will pay for the system in 5 to 10 years at current fuel prices.

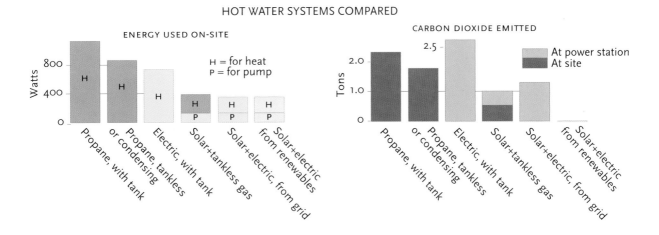

HOT WATER SYSTEMS COMPARED

As with space heaters, to compare hot water systems we have to look at both energy use and carbon emissions. The graphs show these for six different systems. The standard propane heater is assumed to be 65% efficient, the tankless and condensing heaters 85% efficient, and the electric heater 100% efficient. The solar systems have either a tankless gas or an electric heater for auxiliary heat.

The results clearly favor the solar systems. Using either gas or grid electricity for the backup, they cut both energy use and carbon emissions to about half that of the best conventional heaters. Using renewable power for the backup, they cut emissions by 100%.

Electricity and Appliances

The remaining household energy use is the electricity for gadgets, lights, and appliances—what I call general electrical use. This is about a fifth of all residential energy consumption and a fourth or a third of all residential carbon emissions. Our average household uses 900 watts of power from the New York grid for electrical devices, pays $1,300 a year for the electricity, and emits 3.4 tons of carbon dioxide as a result.

The strategy for reducing this is simple. Replace the light bulbs, the refrigerator, and possibly other major appliances. Then use everything else as little as possible.

The light bulbs are important because there are a lot of them. My house has 37 light fixtures. I use compact fluorescents in all of them, typically 13-watt bulbs for general lighting and 15-watt or 23-watt floods over workspaces and in places where I need bright light. I buy them from mail-order houses to get the shapes and colors I want, and equip them with reflectors or track-light housings to eliminate glare and get the light where I want it. I also have a lot of individual switches so I can turn on one light or one bank of lights at a time.

The savings are consequential. I have a total 550 watts of compact fluorescent lighting in the house. This gives me the same amount of light as about 2,200 watts of incandescent bulbs, a savings of 75%.

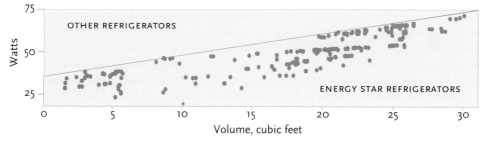

Refrigerators are important because they have big motors and run for several hours a day. A big inefficient refrigerator may use 100 watts of average power, 10% or more of total household electricity. A smaller, more efficient one, like my Vestfrost, may use under 30 watts, and a very small one under 20 watts.

With refrigerators, smaller is almost always better. You can certainly save money by buying a certified Energy Star refrigerator instead of an average one, but you can save even more energy by buying a small Energy Star refrigerator rather than a big one.

This is a point that we have already made, but it is important and deserves emphasis. Big appliances, like big houses and big cars, are energy hogs. Increasing the volume of a refrigerator from 10 to 20 cubic feet increases the energy consumption by 25%. With some appliances this might be justified. If you need a large freezer to store a winter's worth of vegetables, or if a large washing machine lets you wash less often, this makes sense. But if you use a large refrigerator mostly for storing moldy preserves and empty bottles of ketchup, it makes no sense at all.

Replacing other appliances may or may not gain you much. Unless the appliance is used a lot, and uses a lot of power, replacing it probably doesn't make sense. Replacing a washing machine that is used every day may be important. Looking for a high-efficiency answering machine or coffee pot is meaningless.

After lights and appliances, everything else is thrift and increment. You try to use appliances less or more efficiently. You turn lights and electronics off when you are not using them. You get a power meter, identify the gadgets that continue to draw current after they are turned off, and make sure they have a real switch between them and the wall socket.

Just how much you can save by doing this will depend, as always, on how unthrifty you are now. If you run a permissive house where switches stay on for weeks at a time and electronic devices are allowed to draw power whenever they please, you may save a lot. If you run a more disciplined one where switches stay off on principle and only the water pump and the refrigerator are allowed to draw power whenever they please, there will be less to save.

Either way, because grid electricity is carbon intense, small savings matter. Every watt of average power you use costs $1.50 a year, and emits 7.5 pounds of CO_2. If you can trim 300 watts in usage, you will save $450, and emit a little over a ton less carbon. This is enough to make a dent in a household energy and carbon budget. And, because the Adirondacks are made up of households, if enough of us do it, it will make a dent in the Adirondack budget as well.

Summary

Adirondack houses use more energy than they need to. They use the energy because they are too big, too leaky, too inefficiently heated, and too inefficiently managed. New ones can be made better by building them smaller and tighter and by incorporating passive solar design. Old ones can be retrofitted or rebuilt. Any house can be heated more efficiently by replacing fossil fuel heaters with wood heaters or heat pumps, and by heating water with solar collectors. And any house can be operated more thriftily by turning the heat down and the gadgets off.

Because most existing houses are not very efficient, the scope for improvement is great. A savings of 50% should be a start, not a target.

Except for turning things off, none of this is cheap. But energy isn't cheap either. At current energy prices many improvements will pay for themselves in 10 years or less, which makes them respectable investments. If energy prices rise, they will pay for themselves faster. Either way, the owners that undertake them have the benefit of carbon savings while they are being paid for, and continued energy savings after they are paid for.

Still, houses will always need energy. After we have made them as efficient as we can, our next step is to find carbon-free energy for them. How we can do that is the subject of the next chapter.

Osgood River, August, 2009

My 4.2 kW photovoltaic system in my 2 kW meadow

10 REPLACEMENT: LOW-CARBON ENERGY

Cars and buildings are our largest energy users today and, no matter how efficient we make them, will probably still be our largest energy users 50 years from now. If we supply this energy in conventional ways, with a lot of fossil fuels and a few renewables, we will emit a lot of carbon. This chapter is about how we can reduce those emissions by supplying energy in unconventional ways.

Our choices are limited. We can switch fuels–use more propane and natural gas, for example–but this will produce only small reductions in emissions (p. 70). We can try to capture the carbon from fossil fuels and put it back in the ground. Thus far, this has never been done on a commercial scale. It may be an option in 10 or 20 years, but it is not one now. If we want emission reductions today, our only option is to use a low-carbon energy source.

On the planet as a whole there are only four low-carbon sources of energy: sunlight, tidal energy, deep geothermal energy, and nuclear energy. Tidal energy and deep geothermal energy are not available here. Solar energy, in both direct and indirect forms, is. Nuclear energy is produced near the Adirondacks and could be available here. Thus we really have only two choices: the various forms of solar energy (photovoltaic, thermal, wind, hydro, shallow geothermal, biomass) and nuclear energy.

This chapter compares these choices. It is, by necessity, a short summary of a large subject. The sources given in the notes, and particularly the general books by Gipe, Goodall, MacKay, and Smil, were essential in putting it together and worth reading by anyone who wants to know more.

Be aware that while the costs and productivity of renewables are of key importance, they are also highly variable. Costs depend on markets, manufacturing techniques, and subsidies. All change frequently. Productivity depends on resource availability–sunniness and windiness and so on–and this varies greatly from site to site. The numbers given here are averages and educated guesses, and should be used with appropriate caution.

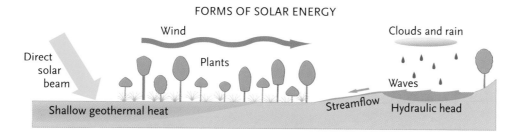

FORMS OF SOLAR ENERGY

How much solar energy is there?

Solar energy comes in direct and indirect forms. The direct form is the *solar beam*. Its strength is measured as the power per unit area and varies with the month and the weather. For rough Adirondack calculations we can use a yearly average of 150 watts per square meter on a flat surface, like a solar collector, tipped at 45 degrees, and 100 watts per square meter on the ground.*

This is a lot of energy–400,000 watts per acre, or 2.4 trillion watts for the entire park. Could we convert even a thousandth of it into useful energy, we would have more than enough power for the whole park.

Unfortunately, our conversion efficiencies are low. Solar heating and hot water systems, which can capture 30% or more of the energy in the solar beam, are the best. This is why passive solar houses (p. 103) work well. The photovoltaic panels in common use capture 10% of the energy in the solar beam. Forests are much lower. Ours probably capture about 0.1% or less of the energy in the solar beam.

The indirect forms of solar energy include wind, hydropower, shallow geothermal, and biomass. Hydropower and wind are relatively concentrated, which is why they can be used commercially for large-scale power generation. A 15-mile-per-hour wind has a power of about 300 watts per square meter of vertical area. A large wind turbine can capture about 33% of this power, a small one 20%.

Shallow geothermal heat and biomass energy are more dilute and correspondingly harder to capture. Heat from the sun flows into the surface of the ground at a rate of somewhere around 10 watts per square meter, and this drops to 5 watts per square meter at the depths where we collect it. This is only a thirtieth of the power in the direct solar beam, which is why shallow geothermal systems need a collecting area much larger than the house they are heating. Forests store energy at even lower rates: 0.1 watt per square meter may be a reasonable average for the Adirondacks. This is a fiftieth of the rate at which the ground stores energy, suggesting that it will take 50 times as much land to heat a house with wood as it will to heat one with geothermal heat.

The low power densities of renewables and low conversion efficiencies of our collectors are the facts of life of the renewable energy world. They are not reasons why we shouldn't use renewables. But they will be controlling factors in how we use them and how much it will cost us to do it.

Direct Solar Power: Photovoltaics

Photovoltaics–solar panels–generate electricity directly from the sun by using thin films or slices of a semiconductor, commonly silicon. Photovoltaic installations are

AVERAGE SOLAR ENERGY IN THE ADIRONDACKS

*Metric units are almost always used for power densities; 1 watt per square meter = 0.93 watt per square yard = 4.0 kW per acre = 2.6 MW per square mile.

simple and reliable and achieve high power densities. Their chief drawback is their high cost: currently solar panels cost about $3 per watt of capacity (peak power) wholesale, and $8 per watt installed. Much research is aimed at lowering their cost, and there are processes currently under development which could produce them for as little as $1 per watt wholesale. If this is achieved they will be competitive with other forms of power, and we may see them incorporated into the skins of buildings and vehicles and used on a large scale.

The diagram shows a typical residential installation. This is a grid-tied system, without batteries, which is the commonest sort of system in our area. The panels are mounted in a rack on a pole or on the roof of a building. They produce direct current, which is converted to alternating current by the inverter and fed into the grid through the main service box in the house. The PV meter reads the power produced by the solar system; the net meter reads the power drawn from the grid. When the system is producing more than the house uses, the net meter runs backwards, allowing the house to build up a credit that it then can draw on at night or on dark days.

How much photovoltaic power would a family need to replace grid electricity altogether? The average northeastern household described on p. 98 uses about 940 watts of electrical power. In our area the average power produced by a PV system (its capacity factor) is about 13% of its peak capacity. To produce 940 watts of average power, the system needs a peak capacity of 7,200 watts. The retail cost of this, including installation, would be $58,000. About 40% of this cost is the panels themselves. The rest is the mountings, electrical components, and installation. The system would need about 700 square feet of panels, which might be most or all of the south-facing roof space of a 2,000-square-foot house.

As with cameras and cars, nobody buys PV systems retail. In order to build the demand for PV systems and get the cost of panels down, governments around the world are subsidizing PV installations. The subsidies take the form of direct payments to certified installers, tax credits for purchasers, and, in many countries and a few states, guaranteed rates that the utilities pay the producers of PV power. World-wide, guaranteed rates have proved the most effective means of financing renewable power, and we discuss them in more detail in Chapter 13.

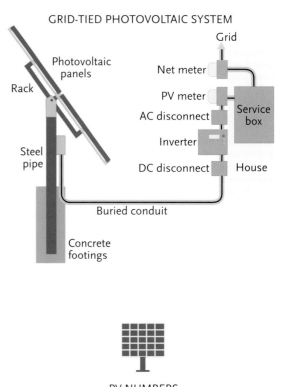

GRID-TIED PHOTOVOLTAIC SYSTEM

Grid

Photovoltaic panels

Rack

Net meter

PV meter

AC disconnect

Service box

Inverter

Steel pipe

DC disconnect

House

Buried conduit

Concrete footings

PV NUMBERS
10%-15% capacity factor
$8,000 per kilowatt capacity, installed
$2,400 per kilowatt capacity after incentives
15 watts production per square meter of panels
10 watts production per square meter of ground

Setting poles for a PV installation. Six feet of 6-inch steel pipe above ground, eight feet below.

New York does not have guaranteed rates but it does have a liberal program of incentives. Between state incentives and state and federal tax credits, residential solar installations receive a 72% subsidy.

With this subsidy, the cost of a 7.2 kW PV system comes down to $17,000. This is not cheap, but it is definitely affordable. It will pay for itself in about 10 years at current electric rates, and less if rates rise.

If our household followed the strategy recommended here and reduced its electric use by efficiency and thrift, the costs would be lower. If they were able get to their power consumption down to 500 watts, they could use a 4,000-watt capacity PV system. After incentives, this would cost $8,400.

At this price PV electricity is a pretty good deal. For the price of a used car that will last you 5 years, you can reduce your electrical bills and electric carbon emissions to zero for the rest of your life.

Good deal or not, because of the high up-front cost, the number of residential solar installations is low. In 2009, New York had less than a thousand grid-tied, residential PV systems, with a total peak capacity of about 5 million watts. Their average output is probably around 700,000 watts, okay for a start, but a very small part of the 18 billion watts of electricity used in the state.

Nevertheless, photovoltaic electricity is growing. New York has approved applications for another 10 million watts of residential PV systems, which will triple the installed capacity.

INCENTIVES FOR PV SYSTEMS
IN NEW YORK

Direct payment from state, 38%

State tax credit, 15%

Federal tax credit, 19%

Paid by owner, 28%

SOLAR HOT WATER SYSTEM

Pressure relief valve

Cold water supply

Hot water out

Sensor

Controller

Propane or electricity

Tankless auxilliary heater

Solar collectors, 60 sq. ft total

Circulating pump

Electric supply

Expansion tank

Check valve

Storage tank with heat exchanger, 60 gallons

Closed circuit with antifreeze   Open circuit with water

Direct Solar Power: Solar Hot Water

The other common use of the sun's direct beam is to heat water. This is a hybrid technique that uses sunlight for heat, electricity to run the circulating pumps, and gas or electricity for a backup heater for cloudy days. Its efficiency and carbon balance were discussed on p. 111. Here we give a brief description and some overall numbers, for comparison with photovoltaics.

The diagram shows a medium-sized solar hot water system. The collectors may be either flat panels or vacuum tubes. There are arguments for both. The collectors heat a freezeproofed mixture of water and antifreeze. This circulates through a storage tank where it heats water. The water passes through an auxiliary heater that is used on cloudy days.

It is considerably easier to turn sunlight into heat than it is to turn it into electricity. The solar panels commonly used in residential PV installations use high-tech materials and turn about 10% to 20% of the incident sunlight into electricity. The panels used to heat water use copper and glass, and turn 30% or more of the incident sunlight into heat.

As a result, solar hot water collectors can be smaller and cheaper than PV panels. A family using 60 gallons of hot water a day might use a 60-square-foot collector with a peak power of 3,000 watts. Such a system currently costs under $5,000, including piping, storage tank, circulator, controller, and installation. State and federal tax credits are available that will bring the cost to around $2,200. At this price, the system will pay for itself in under eight years if it replaces a gas hot water heater, or in under five years if it replaces an electric one.

SOLAR HOT WATER
8%-10% capacity factor
$1,300 per kW capacity
$600 per kW capacity after incentives
50 watts production per square meter of panels

HYDROELECTRIC PLANT WITH PENSTOCK

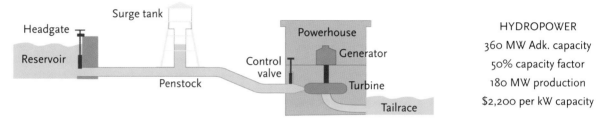

HYDROPOWER
360 MW Adk. capacity
50% capacity factor
180 MW production
$2,200 per kW capacity

Hydropower

Hydroelectric power stations generate electricity from the differences in pressure of water at different heights. In the diagram above, a penstock brings water, under pressure, from a reservoir to a powerhouse. The pressure of the water spins a turbine, whose shaft turns an electric generator. The generator makes electric power which is fed into the grid.

Hydroelectric power is one of the oldest and most reliable forms of sustainable energy. The first Adirondack plants were built over a century ago. Plants similar to the one shown above were being built by the 1920s and 1930s. Some of the original turbines and generators in these plants are still in service today and have hundreds of thousands of operating hours.

The Adirondacks have 23 hydroelectric stations with peak capacities of a million watts (a megawatt) or more. The total capacity is 360 million watts, a significant amount of hydro, but only 8% of the 4.6 billion watts of hydro capacity in New York as a whole.

Most of the Adirondack stations were originally built by utilities. Many have since been sold to investment groups specializing in electric power. Since they require little maintenance and no fuel, they make excellent investments. As a result, almost all the hydro stations in the park are now owned by national and international companies, and almost all the profits from operating those stations are exported from the park.

I have found no authoritative figures for how much hydropower is generated in the Adirondacks. The capacity factor–the ratio of the average power to the peak capacity–for New York as a whole is a bit over 50%. If we assume a 50% capacity factor for the Adirondack stations, then the total generation is 180 million watts. This is 30 million watts more power than Adirondacks are estimated to use, and puts the Adirondacks on the short list of places that generate all the electricity they use from green sources.

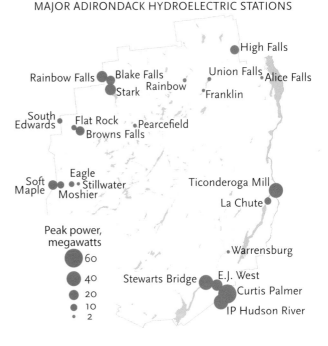

An important question in the next few years will be whether they could generate more. It seems unlikely that any new hydro dams will be built in the park. But there are existing dams, especially toward the center of the park, without hydro power. How much power could we generate if we built hydroplants at these dams?

No one at present knows the answer and a careful study is badly needed. My personal guess is that the amount of power that we are likely to get will be small. The reason is that the places where there are really good opportunities for hydropower already have it. The dams without hydropower tend to be on headwaters lakes, where flows and gradients are low. Note on the map that there are no hydro plants on any of the big lakes in the center of the park. This is because they are in relatively flat country. The water is there but the energy isn't.

This doesn't mean that there aren't opportunities for getting power from existing dams. There certainly are, and they should be explored. But I think that most of them will yield at most a few megawatts.

The recent history of hydro development supports this: in the last 20 years there have been only two new hydro projects, totaling 3 megawatts, in the park.

Big Wind

Wind power has been around for over a thousand years, and wind-generated electricity for over a hundred. But it was only in the 1980s, with the development of large wind farms in Europe and California, that wind electricity became commercial. And it is only in the last 10 years, with the development of reliable machines in the 1-megawatt range, that commercial wind generation has become competitive with other energy sources and started to grow rapidly.

Currently wind power provides 20% of the electricity in Denmark and 7% in Germany. In the United States, a much bigger country, it supplies only about 0.4%. But the United States' current wind capacity of 25 billion watts is now slightly larger than Germany's, and the United States is adding capacity at the rate of 5 billion watts a year.

The reason for the rapid growth is that wind farms are excellent investments. While they cost more to build than fossil fuel generating stations, they receive federal subsidies and, in some states, guaranteed wholesale rates. They can be built quickly because little on-site construction is involved. A hundred-turbine wind farm can be operating a year after the contracts are signed, something impossible with any other kind of power, and can pay for itself in five years or less.

As a long-term investment, wind farms are even more attractive. They are reliable and cheap to run. Their fuel costs are zero. They require no wells, pipelines, terminals, or refineries to support them. There are no wind power cartels and no wars over wind. They use no fuel and will never have to pay for their carbon emissions. They are cheap to decommission and have no wastes to store. It is quite possible that if we look at the total costs, direct and indirect, over the lifetime of a generating station, wind is the cheapest way of generating electricity currently available.

Because wind farms are good investments, recent growth in wind power has been impressive. In 2000, New York had no large-scale commercial wind energy. It now has 830 megawatts. Northern New York got its first commercial wind farm in 2004. It now has 450 wind turbines with 700 megawatts of capacity. This is about a third of its hydroelectric capacity. The hydroelectric capacity was built over 100 years, the wind capacity in 4 years.

Wind however has its own limits and problems, and this may slow its expansion. Commercial wind farms involve big machines spaced fairly widely apart. A 100-megawatt farm with 65 turbines might need 6 square miles of land or more. The site needs to be windy enough for the turbines to function efficiently, developed enough that there are roads and power lines nearby, and yet not so developed that public opposition will stop the project. Ridge-top farm country is ideal, and that is where all the New York wind farms have thus far been built. How many more open windy ridges we have, and how many of them will welcome wind developments, is unknown.

WIND
TURBINES

390 ft

265 ft

GE 1.5
MW

111 ft

Bergey
10 kW

WIND FARMS IN NORTHERN NEW YORK

Vespas 1.65 MW turbines at Maple Ridge

Chateaugay
Clinton
Ellenburg   •Altona

Adirondack
Park
● Maple Ridge

● 360 megawatts •100 megawatts

COMMERCIAL
WIND

30%-40%
capacity factor

$2,000 per
kW capacity

3 W/sq.m of
ground area

300 W/sq.m
of rotor area

Small Wind and Community Wind

It seems unlikely that we will see large wind farms within the Adirondack Park in the near future. The steep terrain and lack of power lines near many potential sites present technical problems. The regulatory climate and extent of public opposition to large developments present political ones.

Wind development, however, needn't always be measured in megawatts and square miles. Single small or medium-sized turbines might be acceptable in many places where large wind farms wouldn't be, and this might be where the future of wind within the Adirondacks lies.

This could happen in several ways. One is with local ownership. A town might form a wind district, similar to a water district, raise money, erect one or two turbines, and distribute the power to residents. For a million dollars, comparable to building a new municipal building or putting a wing on the school, a town could install a 0.5 megawatt turbine and generate 150,000 or 200,000 watts of power. This would be enough, say, to power the school and the town buildings and 150 houses. The turbine could pay for itself in well under 10 years, or less if New York adopts the kind of guaranteed wholesale power rates now used in Ontario and Vermont (p. 156).

A town wind project would differ from the large commercial wind farms around the edges of the park in both scale and ownership. It would be smaller and less visible: a single 200-foot turbine rather than a fleet of 400-foot ones, a single hilltop rather than a 5,000-acre development. And it would be locally rather than corporately owned, and so the profits would flow back to the residents in the form of reduced taxes or electrical rates.

Both features would build support for wind power. Once word got around that a town had cut its utility bills or school taxes by installing a wind turbine, other towns' feelings about putting a turbine on the hill above the school might start to be very different.

A second path to wind development in the Adirondacks is through residential installations. Small wind turbines can only be used at good sites, usually hilltops where the average wind speed 100 feet above the ground is 10 miles per hour or more. This much wind is uncommon here because most Adirondack settlements are in valleys. But where it is available, it is an excellent source of residential electricity, particularly in winter when there is not enough sun for photovoltaic systems.

The Bergey 10-kilowatt turbine shown here is one of the most widely used small wind generators in the world. It has three 11-foot carbon-fiber blades. The blades turn a ring-shaped permanent magnet which surrounds a fixed set of coils. The turbine has only a few moving parts, and has proven to be highly reliable.

Residential wind turbines need to be mounted on towers, typically about a 100 feet high, that get them out of the turbulence that occurs near the ground. The Bergey starts generating power at wind velocities of 7 miles per hour and furls (turns itself at right angles to the wind) when the wind speed reaches 35 miles per hour. In a grid-tied operation the electricity is fed from the tower to an inverter and then to the grid, much as in the PV system on p. 116.

With state and federal incentives, the economics of small wind are reasonably attractive. A 10-kilowatt system with a Bergey generator and tower currently costs $50,000 retail, but only $16,000 after incentives and tax credits. Its average production is

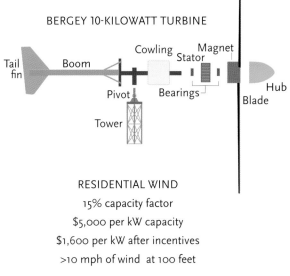

BERGEY 10-KILOWATT TURBINE

RESIDENTIAL WIND

15% capacity factor

$5,000 per kW capacity

$1,600 per kW after incentives

>10 mph of wind at 100 feet

1,500 watts, more than enough for the electricity for an average house. The electricity it produces is currently worth about $2,200 a year. The payback is 7 years at today's prices.

HEAT AND ELECTRICITY FROM WOOD

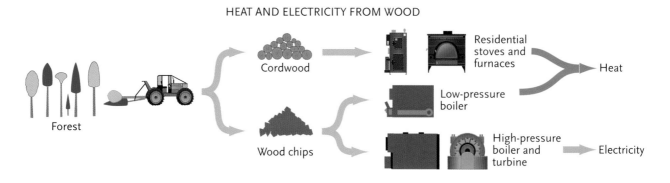

Woody Biomass

Woody biomass–forest products that are burned for fuel–is both our oldest source of renewable energy and, after hydro, our second most important contemporary one. In New York State, about 7% of all energy consumed is from hydro and 3% from wood. The other renewables are about 1%.

Biomass energy is currently used at three different scales. Home heating systems, using cordwood or pellets, are typically in the 1 kilowatt to 20 kilowatt range. Commercial heating systems, burning wood chips in automated low-pressure boilers, range from 100 kilowatts to a few megawatts. Wood-fired power stations, burning chips in high-pressure boilers, range from 15 megawatts to 50 megawatts or more.

Biomass energy has long been attractive because biomass is cheap. But it has also long been considered a second-class power source because biomass burning was labor intensive, inefficient, and dirty.

Technical innovations have changed this. Wood stoves now incorporate either catalytic converters or secondary combustion to increase efficiency and reduce emissions. Wood furnaces use multi-stage combustion controlled by stack blowers. The most advanced ones are computer-controlled and can run with flue temperatures as low as 220 degrees and reach efficiencies of nearly 90 percent.

A new generation of gasifying burners, currently restricted to wood-fired power stations and combined heat and power plants, are even more efficient. They turn wood into a combustible gas by heating it under low-oxygen conditions and then use the gas to fire a boiler. The best of these systems remove fly ash and particulates with filters and cyclonic separators and emit little besides carbon dioxide and water.

The combination of technical advances and rising fossil fuel prices have made wood energy increasingly competitive with fossil fuels. A ton of green wood chips currently sells for around $50 and generates enough energy to replace about 60 gallons of fuel oil. If oil costs $2 per gallon this is a savings of around 60%. If it costs $4 per gallon, this is a savings of 80%.

The chief barriers to wood heat are the capital costs. An efficient wood boiler for a house might cost $8,000 or $10,000. A boiler for a central school might cost $500,000, and facilities for storing and delivering the chips to it might cost another

$500,000. A modern 20-megawatt power station, with gasifiers, boilers, turbines, and fly-ash separators, could be over $60 million. At current fuel prices, these prices result in fairly long payback times, mostly over 10 years.

As with other renewables, there are incentives that reduce the prices and payback times. Currently Vermont underwrites 70% of the costs of school biomass projects. As a result, Vermont now has 44 schools with biomass heating systems. The federal government offers tax credits for producing renewable electricity, and some states have additional production credits for each unit of electricity produced. The total capacity for biomass electricity in New York and New England is now about 500 megawatts; if the incentives remain in place and the regulatory climate remains favorable, that capacity could double in 10 years.

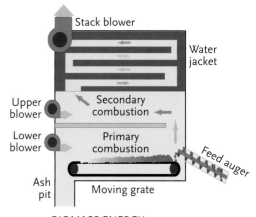

COMMERCIAL WOOD CHIP BOILER

BIOMASS ENERGY

Dry wood: 0.1 W per sq. m

Green wood: 0.07 W per sq. m

Electricity: 0.02 W per sq. m

Wood Stoves: $150 per kW

Residential furnaces: $400 per kW

Commercial furnaces: $1,250 per kW

Wood-chip electricity: $3,300 per kW

How sustainable is biomass energy?

Wood energy is widely assumed to be sustainable, carbon-neutral, and beneficial to local economies. It has a potential to be all of these things, but it is not guaranteed to be any of them.

The problems are not with how the wood is burned but with how it is produced. For wood energy to be sustainable and carbon-neutral, the forests have to be healthy and capable of removing as much new carbon from the air each year as is released by harvesting them (Chapter 11). This requires that the forests supplying biomass be harvested in a way that maintains their average carbon stocks and preserves their nutrient supply.

Because biomass is a low value product, lands used for biomass production are vulnerable to over-harvesting. The temptation is for managers to squeeze as much wood as possible out of the forest by whole-tree chipping, or by chipping and selling the residues from ordinary harvests as biomass. The results are unsustainable removals of wood and nutrients that end up depleting the forest–much of the forest's mineral supply is in the logging residues–and releasing more carbon than the forest can reabsorb.

To guard against this, responsible biomass energy producers either have their own forestry standards, or require that their biomass come from certified forests. This seems an important safeguard, and I would urge that it be made a condition of any large-scale biomass development in the Adirondacks.

The economic benefits of biomass harvests are uncertain. The critical question is whether biomass will supplement or displace higher-value products. Biomass provides a market for low-value wood. Since we have a lot of low-value wood, in principle this is a good thing. But biomass is also land-intensive, requiring 3,000 acres of land for every megawatt of heat. If the demand for biomass energy rises, we could see large amounts of forest treated as biomass plantations and not producing any other products. This might not be a good thing.

To get a sense of the amount of land involved, note that the annual growth from an acre of Adirondack forest harvested sustainably at 80% of the growth rate will produce somewhere around 300 watts per acre of dry wood, or 250 watts per acre of green wood.

Suppose that an Adirondack town, say the town of Fine (pp. 80–81), wants to convert to biomass heat. Between the houses, a few businesses, the municipal buildings, and the school, the town uses about 2 million watts of heat. To supply this from biomass could be done from 8,000 acres or less. Since the town has over 50,000 acres of private forests, biomass heat would not likely displace other forest products and is certainly a reasonable possibility.

Biomass electricity might not be. Suppose the town decided to build a 10-megawatt biomass generating station to supply power for the residents and the paper mill in the next town. Biomass electric plants burning green wood are about 30% efficient, and thus 250 watts of green wood per acre would produce 75 watts of electricity–one light bulb's worth. A 10-megawatt plant would then require about 130,000 acres–twice the amount of private land in the town. This would preclude other potentially better paying uses of forest products and might make neither economic nor environmental sense.

The conclusion from this quick survey is that biomass burning is only carbon-neutral if the forests the biomass comes from are carbon-neutral, and is most economically beneficial if biomass production is integrated with lumber production rather than displacing it. Achieving the first will require careful attention to harvest rates and nutrient loss. Achieving the second will require careful attention to the scale of biomass projects and the existing uses of the forests that supply them.

Liquid fuel from wood?

About a third of the fossil fuel used in the United States is used in vehicles. There would be great environmental benefits if we could replace this with a carbon-neutral biofuel, and great economic rewards to anyone who figured out a good way of doing it.

There is, as a result, a well-funded movement to research and develop biofuels that can be used in conventional engines. The movement goes back to the early days of the internal combustion engine–both Rudolf Diesel and Henry Ford expected that biofuels would be widely used as energy sources–and has continued in a quiet way ever since. But it is only in the last 10 years, with rising oil prices and increased concern about carbon emissions, that it has attracted large-scale research and investment.

Thus far the biofuels industry has had two small-scale successes, biodiesel and biomethane, and a large-scale failure, corn-derived ethanol. None of them are likely to be produced in large quantities in our area, though they could become important as imports. As explained in Chapter 8, diesel trucks are likely to be with us for some time, and right now biodiesel is the greenest truck fuel available.

The great hope of the biofuels industry is cellulosic ethanol, ethanol made from grasses and wood. We have a lot of wood and so cellulosic ethanol concerns us directly.

Cellulosic ethanol is made by breaking the cellulose and lignin in the wood into smaller organic compounds and then converting these into ethanol. This has not yet been done on a commercial scale. The big problems are cost and efficiency. Turning cellulose into ethanol is not that difficult. Turning it into ethanol in an energy-efficient way and at a price that can compete with fossil fuels is much harder. Many companies around the world are trying to, and hundreds of millions of dollars are currently being invested in research and pilot plants. Thus far, no one has succeeded, and no one knows whether success is a year away or 20 years away.

If it becomes possible to make cellulosic ethanol here, it may be a mixed blessing. It could give us a local source of carbon-neutral liquid fuels, and that would be good, especially while we still have a lot of conventional vehicles on the road. But it would not give us all that much fuel. If we assume wood energy could be turned into ethanol with 33% efficiency–a generous assumption–then the 2.5 million acres of private forests in the Adirondacks might be able to support 200 million watts of ethanol-based transportation. This is a lot of transportation, but only half of the 400 million watts of petroleum-based transportation we now have.

Neglecting the question of whether there are better things to do with our cellulose, it is not clear whether this would be a step forward or a step back. Cellulosic ethanol is intended, almost exclusively, as a fuel for combustion engines. Combustion engines are a low-efficiency technology from the energy-wasting 19th and 20th centuries. They have little place in the high-efficiency century we need to build.

THE GROUND AS A STORAGE BATTERY

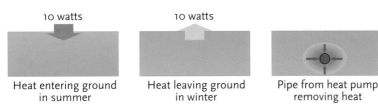

10 watts

Heat entering ground in summer

10 watts

Heat leaving ground in winter

Pipe from heat pump removing heat

SHALLOW GEOTHERMAL

20%-30% capacity factor

$1,500 to $3,000 per kW capacity

$900 to $1,800 per kW after incentives

5 W/sq. m of ground

Shallow Geothermal Energy

Shallow geothermal energy is solar heat that is stored near the surface of the ground. It is distinct from the deep geothermal energy that comes from radioactive decay in the earth's interior. Deep geothermal heat is used as an energy source in volcanically active places like Iceland and Alaska but is not important in the Adirondacks. Shallow geothermal heat, on the other hand, is one of our cheapest and most plentiful forms of renewable heat.

Shallow geothermal heat is collected with heat pumps, which use a chilled fluid to pick up energy from the ground and a compressor and a refrigerant gas to transfer the energy to hot air or hot water. Heat pumps were described on p. 105. Here we give a few more numbers, to compare them to other renewables.

Heat pumps work by removing solar energy from the ground and, over the long term, can't remove energy faster than the sun can replenish it. In our area, the average rate of flow of heat at the depths where heat pump collectors work is about 5 watts per square meter, or 20,000 watts per acre (p. 115). This is a useful number because it gives a sense of how much land is needed for a heat pump system. Our average reference house (p. 98) needs about 2,400 watts of heat. At 20,000 watts an acre, this should require about an eighth of an acre of land, or 5,000 square feet. Typically this might be configured as an elongate trench, carrying perhaps 1,000 feet of pipe, but other configurations would work too. The important thing is that there be enough ground surface to recharge the heat; the best collector in the world can't do much if there is not enough energy for it to collect.

Geothermal systems vary greatly in cost depending on whether they have trenches or wells, and on whether they are new installations or conversions of existing systems. A small, efficient house of 1,500 square feet might need a system with 10 kilowatts of peak power. Depending on the complexity of the installation, such a system could cost anywhere from $15,000 to $30,000. Tax credits and incentives would reduce this by 40%, to somewhere between $9,000 and $18,000.

Geothermal systems reduce heating fuel expenditures but increase electrical ones. At today's prices, residential systems typically pay off in 10 to 20 years (p. 106). If oil prices rose relative to electric prices, or if geothermal was combined with a solar or wind system that produced the electricity, the payoff would be faster.

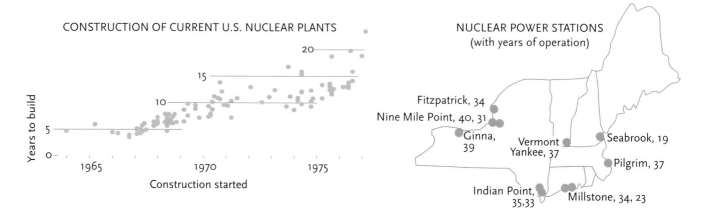

Nuclear Energy

The future of nuclear energy is a large subject and a controversial national issue. Because it is unlikely to be important in the Adirondacks, I treat it simply here, giving a few facts and two contrasting views of its future importance.

The facts are these. There are 104 nuclear plants currently operating in the United States. Together, they generate 20% of all the electricity in the United States and 29% of the electricity in New York. The technology and the plants are old: the designs were developed in the 1960s and 1970s and the plants mostly constructed between 1965 and 1985, though in some cases construction stretched into the 1990s. Construction of the earlier plants took about 5 years; construction of the later ones was much slower, and took from 10 to 20 years. Up to the 1979 accident at the Three-Mile Island plant in Pennsylvania, the nuclear industry was growing, and several new plants began construction every year. Since then, none have been started in the United States, and relatively few have anywhere in the world.

The U.S. nuclear plants were originally licensed for 40 years, and many are approaching that age. Half of the 104 plants currently operating, and 9 of the 11 plants operating in New York and New England, are in the last 10 years of their design lifetimes.

In the first 30 years of nuclear power there were seven major civilian reactor accidents, four in North America, one in Switzerland, one in Russia, and one in England. Six out of the seven involved experimental or relatively primitive reactors. In only two of them, Chernobyl (Russia, 1986) and Windscale (England, 1957), was highly radioactive material released to the atmosphere.

For the last 30 years, since Three-Mile Island, there have been no major reactor accidents in North America; for the last 23, since Chernobyl, there have been none in the world. In this period, European and American nuclear plants have evolved into high-reliability, environmentally benign power sources that provide the base load for many electrical grids. Nuclear plants emit no sulfur, nitrogen, mercury, or carbon. In the United States they are our largest source of low-carbon power, producing almost twice as much electricity as hydro and the other renewables put together.

Despite their usefulness and excellent operating records, it has been 32 years since any U.S. utility began the construction of a nuclear plant. This is in part a political decision, reflecting the determined public opposition to nuclear power. But it is also an economic one. By the 1980s nuclear plants had become very slow and expensive to build. Construction delays and cost overruns were universal, and investors had no way of knowing how long a project would take or what it would cost. Given that gas generators and wind farms could be built much more quickly than nuclear plants, and given further that existing nuclear plants face unknown future costs for waste disposal and decommissioning, it is not surprising that utilities and their investors turned away from nuclear power, and that much of the new generating capacity installed in the last 20 years uses natural gas or wind.

The result is that today both the United States and Europe have aging fleets of nuclear power plants which are their principle sources of low-carbon electricity. As the plants reach the end of their design lifetimes, none of their owners have chosen to replace them with new nuclear plants. The Europeans have been replacing their plants with wind farms. Germany, for example, now has 21 gigawatts of nuclear capacity and 24 gigawatts of wind. The United States has been taking the more questionable course of extending the licences of its plants. Since 2000, the Nuclear Regulatory Commission has extended the licenses of 52 nuclear plants from 40 to 60 years, and allowed some of them to increase their power as well.

These license changes are taking the U.S. nuclear industry, as well as all of us who live downwind of nuclear plants, into unknown and potentially dangerous territory. Nuclear reactors are complicated collections of tanks and pipes that contain dangerous chemicals and operate under stressful conditions. As reactors age, cracks, corrosion, and structural failures are constant problems. Thus far there has not been a major loss-of-coolant accident at an aging plant, but that may be only because there have not been many aging plants. The potential is there and there have already been some near misses.

If you ask what the future of nuclear energy is, you get two contrasting visions. The nuclear optimists say that nuclear power is an essential part of the low-carbon future. They point to new designs that will be safer, cheaper, faster to build, and perhaps located underground. They mention new fuel cycles that cannot be subverted to supply plutonium to terrorists or aspiring nuclear states. And they note a recent renewal of commercial interest: since 2007, when the government announced new subsidies, 17 companies have applied for licenses to build 26 new U.S. reactors.

The nuclear pessimists see a different future. They note that most of the new designs exist only inside computers, that none have ever been tested on a commercial scale, and that none of them are truly "passively safe" and thus able to remain intact in a major accident. They note that the long-term waste disposal problem has not been solved, that safeguarding nuclear fuels from terrorists is a major issue, and that safety issues and decommissioning still discourage investors. And finally they note, tellingly I think, that an industry that has been idle for the last 30 years, and which even in its prime couldn't build plants on time or on budget, may have a tough time convincing investors it can do so now.

Which of these two futures will prevail is unknown. If the nuclear engineers can deliver on their promises of safe, cheap, clean energy, nuclear energy could be an important part of the low-carbon world. Unfortunately, nuclear engineers have a long history of not delivering on their promises.

It will be 20 years or more–the length of time it will take to develop and test a new generation of reactors–before we know who is right. In the meantime, while the nuclear industry is trying to survive, renewables are flourishing. If we want to see the future of Adirondack energy, it is to them we should look.

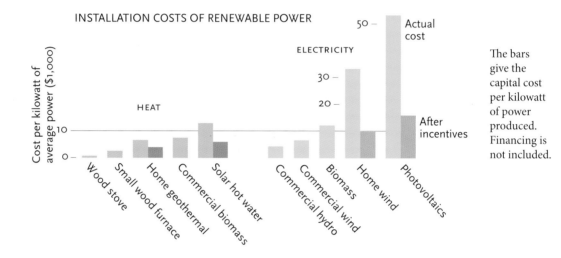

INSTALLATION COSTS OF RENEWABLE POWER

The bars give the capital cost per kilowatt of power produced. Financing is not included.

Summary: Renewables Compared

All the renewables discussed in this chapter have the capacity to provide energy and replace fossil fuels. How do their costs and land requirements compare, and which is best for what?

Of the direct uses of solar energy, photovoltaic electricity has the greatest potential importance because it is the simplest and most compact way available of producing renewable electricity, and the only one that can be incorporated into the surfaces of buildings and vehicles. Its current limitation is its cost. If the cost of solar panels continues to drop, as many expect, they will become very widely used.

Solar hot water is much cheaper than solar electricity and is one of the more cost-effective ways of producing hot water. Solar water heaters are also more compact than photovoltaic panels and hence easier to install on existing buildings.

Wind is the fastest growing form of renewable energy in the United States. It needs truly windy sites, and is most efficiently generated by large turbines high off the ground. When these conditions are met, it is an excellent investment, and, with current federal and state incentives, can compete economically with most other ways of generating electricity.

Wind generation currently exists at two scales: in home installations of a single small machine, and in commercial wind farms of fifty or a hundred machines. Both have disadvantages. Small wind machines are more costly and less efficient than big ones. Big wind farms must use a lot of land–on the order of 100 acres or more for each machine–and so generate public opposition.

In Europe an intermediate scale of wind power, involving medium-sized machines placed singly or in small groups, has been very successful. In this kind of medium-sized wind development the turbines are spread out, and the visual impacts and land requirements are less. Medium wind is well adapted to cooperative ownership; other things being equal, a medium-sized machine with ten owners will generate more power and make more money than ten small machines. Cooperative ownership has been successful in Europe and a few places in the United States. Given the right incentives (p. 156), it might work well here.

Woody biomass is well adapted to producing heat, both residentially and commercially. The equipment and fuel costs are relatively low; after passive solar heating (p. 103), it is probably the cheapest way of providing renewable heat. The land requirements–several acres per kilowatt–are significant, but can easily be met in many Adirondack towns.

Biomass electricity is more of a mixed bag. It is considerably more costly than wind, and requires large acres of forest to supply fuel. But it is greener and cheaper than fossil fuels. It is clearly useful in combined heat-and-power situations and may be valuable where the wind resource is limited. It comes with a caveat: the harvest rate must be carefully controlled. Otherwise it is neither carbon-neutral nor sustainable.

Shallow geothermal heat is potentially one of the most valuable alternate sources of heat. It is more costly to install than biomass, but runs automatically and frees forest land for carbon storage or producing other forest products. It produces modest carbon savings when used with grid electricity, and larger ones when used with renewables (p. 106).

These, then, are the renewables: five recruits who, we hope, will in time become our energy warriors. In Chapter 12 we talk about what they might accomplish if we turned them loose and told them to build us a low-carbon economy. But before that we have one more question to look at. The Adirondacks are one of the most densely forested places in the United States. Forests are giant pools of carbon. What does our pool of forest carbon have to do with climate and energy?

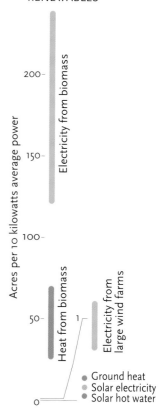

LAND NEEDED FOR
RENEWABLES

Acres per 10 kilowatts average power

Electricity from biomass

Heat from biomass

Electricity from large wind farms

● Ground heat
● Solar electricity
● Solar hot water

Zond 550-kilowatt turbines, Searsburg, Vermont

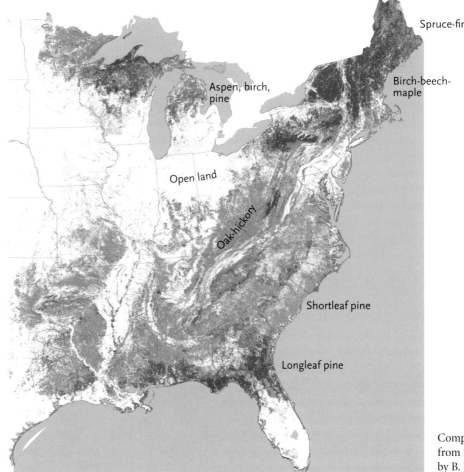

Spruce-fir

Birch-beech-maple

Aspen, birch, pine

Open land

Oak-hickory

Shortleaf pine

Longleaf pine

Computer-generated map from forest inventory data by B. Ruefenacht et al.

11 OFFSETS: CARBON IN ADIRONDACK FORESTS

Thus far in this book we have talked entirely about carbon emissions. But there is another column to the ledger; carbon also leaves the air and enters forests, soils, and the sea. By doing so it offsets carbon emissions. In forested areas, these offsets are an important part of the carbon balance. The Adirondacks, as the map shows, are densely and continuously forested. This chapter is about the carbon their forests contain. How much stored carbon is there, how fast is it increasing, and how can we be sure it continues to increase?

First some background. In the climate change century, forests are both assets and liabilities. They absorb carbon from the atmosphere and slow the rate of global warming, which is good. But they also release carbon when they die, are harvested, or are cleared. Because they have a lot of carbon, that is not good.

Currently, the world balance sheet is negative, which is what a carbon balance sheet should be. World forests absorb 3 billion tons of carbon a year. The clearing of forests releases of 1.6 billion tons. The balance is 1.4 billion tons of carbon absorbed, enough to offset 22% of the world's fossil fuel emissions.

This is good, but not as good as it could be. If we were not clearing tropical forests and turning them into farms, the net storage could be the full 3 billion tons, enough to offset 47% of all fossil fuel emissions. That would be an ecosystem service that really meant something.

Besides storing carbon, forests are harvested for wood, fiber, and fuels. The harvests also affect the carbon balance. Forest products are renewable resources, again good. But they are not necessarily carbon-neutral resources. Harvesting a forest uses fossil fuels and releases carbon from soils and logging residue. Making forest products uses more fossil fuels—in the case of paper, a lot more fossil fuels. Burning wood releases additional carbon. As the forest regrows, it will remove the carbon again. But even though the carbon is eventually removed, while it is in the air it is causing global warming.

This doesn't mean that we shouldn't burn wood or use forest products. Quite the contrary. Wood fuels, if harvested sustainably, can replace fossil fuels and reduce total carbon emissions. Forest products, if produced efficiently, can replace more energy-intensive products like plastics and also reduce total emissions.

But it does mean we have to be careful about our accounting. Forest products appear on both sides of the carbon ledger—they have both carbon costs and carbon benefits. The carbon benefits are potentially important and will figure prominently in the energy independence plan in Chapter 12. But if we are going to claim the benefits, we need to be honest about accounting for the costs.

A Large Carbon Bank

The map shows the forests of the eastern United States. These forests, along with the adjacent ones in southeastern Canada, make up one of the largest temperate deciduous forests in the world (map, p. xi) and one of the great carbon banks on the planet.

The bank has had serious losses. All the white areas east of the Mississippi River were once forests. Their carbon is now in the air and is a climate liability.

Current growth is offsetting past losses. Most eastern forests are young and many are expanding. If they are allowed to mature, they will remove much of the carbon from the atmosphere that was released when the forests were originally cleared or cut.

There is, however, no guarantee that these forests will be allowed to mature. Many will be harvested before they mature. Others will be cleared for development. All will be subject to climate change. In the coming century these factors could combine and tip the balance from storage to release. The eastern deciduous forest is a big bank, and if it starts releasing carbon there will be world-scale consequences.

The Adirondacks are one of the branches of this bank. They are part of the forest region, colored dark blue, that is variously called the northern hardwood forest or northern deciduous forest. It is a cold-climate forest that extends from southern Canada to the northern edge of Pennsylvania, with an outlier in the mountains of West Virginia. Most of its trees and many of its other plants and animals are adapted to cool climates. How they will fare as the climate warms is not known. Simple climate-habitat models (p. 31) suggest that the trees will decline. More complicated physiological models (p. 136) say that we don't know.

All that can be said for certain at this point is that the Adirondack carbon bank matters and that we know some things about it but not enough. Here we summarize what we know, emphasizing that this is a preliminary account with many gaps.

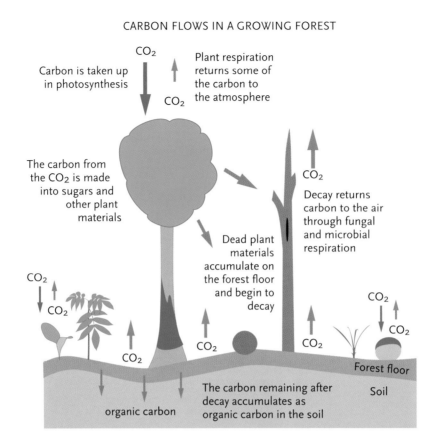

How Forests Absorb Carbon

We start by looking at when carbon is absorbed and when it isn't. The key idea is that forests have two simultaneous carbon flows, one incoming and one outgoing. The balance between these flows determines whether the forest is storing or releasing carbon. The balance is quite sensitive to environmental factors and can easily be shifted by small changes in light or moisture.

The incoming flow is driven by photosynthesis. Carbon enters the leaves and is converted into sugars and other plant materials, which are then moved to other parts of the tree. Leaves and branches die, fall, and decay; some of the carbon in them is released by decay, and some is incorporated into the forest floor and soil.

The outgoing flow is driven by respiration, which breaks plant materials down and releases CO_2. Respiration is universal: plants, animals, decay fungi, and soil microbes all respire and release carbon.

The rate at which the forest is storing or releasing carbon can be determined by measuring air movements and CO_2 concentrations at different heights within the forest. The graph on p. 133 shows the estimated flows for an old-growth hemlock stand in eastern Massachusetts. On most days from April through mid-November, the net carbon flow was into the forest (green dots). On most days from late November through March, the net carbon flow was into the air (red dots). The rate of flow in the winter was quite low: respiration was occurring but limited by temperature.

Carbon also flowed out of the forest on cloudy days in the summer and fall. The temperature was greater then and the outflow rates several times higher.

CARBON FLOWS IN A HEMLOCK STAND AT HARVARD FOREST, 2000-2001

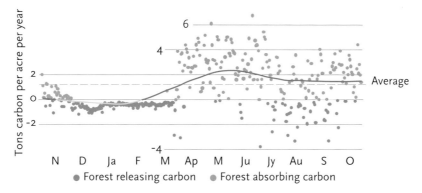

The average carbon storage, shown by the solid line, peaked in May and June when the days were long and the forest was moist, and decreased in summer as the days got shorter and the forest got drier. The annual accumulation was 1.4 tons of carbon per acre per year, a high but not unprecedented rate for an old-growth stand.

CARBON STORAGE IN A NORTHEASTERN MAPLE-BIRCH-BEECH FOREST

In most undisturbed forests, photosynthesis exceeds respiration and carbon accumulates. The graph, from U.S. Forest Service inventory data, shows this process in a northern hardwood forest recovering from a clear-cut. For the first 10 years the forest loses carbon because there is lots of respiration from the litter and dead wood and almost no photosynthesis to balance it. Gradually the trees regrow, and the carbon balance becomes positive again. The maximum rate of carbon storage occurs at 30 years, when the young forest is densest. After that, growth slows. At 125 years, when the Forest Service data end, it is still storing carbon, though at a third of the rate it did when it was younger.

Just how much carbon it will eventually store is uncertain. As the forest gets older, the death of old trees starts to balance the growth of the younger ones. At this point the living biomass—the amount of leaves and wood in the forest—will stay constant or only increase slowly. But the dead trees will still be adding carbon to the soil, and so the total amount of carbon in the forest may continue to increase.

We have no Adirondack data on carbon in older forests. But recent review of carbon storage in old-growth temperate and boreal forests from around the world showed that this pattern—living biomass staying constant, soil carbon increasing—is common, and that many old-growth forests are storing carbon at surprisingly high rates. The diagram below illustrates their findings. The average rate of carbon storage for temperate forests 200 years old and older was 0.9 ton per acre per year. Most of the carbon was stored in dead wood and the soil. The net storage in live biomass was 0.15 ton per acre; in dead wood and the soil it was 0.75 ton per acre.

ANNUAL FLOW OF CARBON IN TWO-HUNDRED-YEAR-OLD TEMPERATE AND BOREAL FORESTS

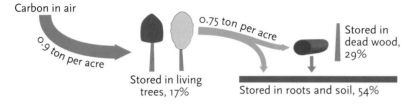

How much carbon is in Adirondack forests?

If we neglect water and moderately or intensely developed lands, the Adirondacks have about 2.6 million acres of forested private land and 2.5 million acres of forested state land. The 2000 Forest Service inventory (FIA) data give 29 tons per acre of carbon in living trees and snags on private lands and 40 tons per acre on state lands. The graphs on p. 133 suggest that there may be an additional 50 to 55 tons per acre of carbon in the forest floor and soils. Multiplying out, this gives about 205 million tons of carbon on private lands and 225 million tons on state lands, or 430 million tons overall. This is an average of 85 tons of carbon per acre for the forested parts of the park, or 70 tons per acre for the park as a whole.

This is an impressive amount of carbon. Regarded as an energy source, it would fuel the park for 350 years. Regarded as carbon removed from the air, it is equal to 750 years of the park's carbon emissions.

It is also carbon that could cause significant warming if it were released in the atmosphere. If, through unsustainable logging or land clearance (pp. 143–144), 1% of the stored carbon was released in the air in a year's time, this would be the same as a seven-fold increase in fossil fuel use. If the great fires that burned a sixth of the Adirondacks between 1895 and 1915 were to recur, they would release as much carbon as 100 years of fossil fuel emissions.

The Adirondack carbon stores thus represent a rich source of energy, but in a dangerous form. If we use the stored energy carefully, it can make our economy greener. But if we use it carelessly, the carbon released will be as damaging or more damaging than the carbon released by our current fossil fuel use.

How much carbon do Adirondack forests store each year?

The FIA data suggest that between 1990 and 2000 the private forests in the Adirondacks stored about 0.4 ton of carbon per acre per year in living trees. If we assume, based on the carbon accumulation curves shown on p. 133, that carbon storage in the forest floor and soil is about 0.1 ton per acre per year, this gives us a total accumulation rate of 0.5 ton of carbon per acre per year.

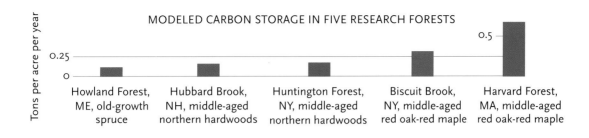

MODELED CARBON STORAGE IN FIVE RESEARCH FORESTS

Tons per acre per year

| 0.25 | | | | 0.5 |

| Howland Forest, ME, old-growth spruce | Hubbard Brook, NH, middle-aged northern hardwoods | Huntington Forest, NY, middle-aged northern hardwoods | Biscuit Brook, NY, middle-aged red oak-red maple | Harvard Forest, MA, middle-aged red oak-red maple |

This estimate is reasonably consistent with other estimates for our area. The accumulation curve on p. 133 suggests that 50-year-old northern hardwood forests in the Northeast store 0.6 ton of carbon per acre per year and 100-year-old ones 0.4 ton. These values bracket our value, and are consistent with the range of ages that we see on private lands. An analysis of the FIA data for New York, Vermont, New Hampshire, and Maine by Charlie Canham and Nicole Rogers gave 0.32 ton of carbon in living trees per acre per year, slightly smaller than our value of 0.4 ton. A growth model developed by Scott Ollinger and his collaborators, shown above, gave values of 0.2 to 0.6 ton per acre per year for five research forests. These average lower than our value, perhaps because the research forests were older and less disturbed.

We have, unfortunately, no comparable data for the state lands, and the best we can do is guess. The trees on the state lands are older than those on the private lands and presumably slower growing. But, unlike the private lands, the state lands are not logged. Balancing the losses from aging against the gains from eliminating logging, a total accumulation rate of 0.4 ton of carbon per acre per year on state lands might be reasonable.

Using these numbers—0.5 ton per acre per year on private lands, 0.4 on state lands—as a first approximation, the Adirondacks store 1.3 million tons of carbon per year on private lands and 1.0 million tons of carbon per year on state lands, for a total of 2.3 million tons of carbon per year.

ESTIMATED ADIRONDACK FOREST CARBON

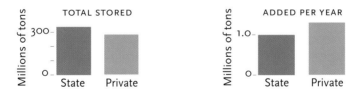

Carbon warrior or carbon wimp ?

How significant is the 0.4 to 0.5 ton of carbon per acre per year that Adirondack forests store every year? Here are several ways of looking at it.

Looked at as a photovoltaic system with carbon-based batteries, each acre captures and stores 300 to 400 watts of solar energy or about 0.1 % of the solar energy received.

Looked at as part of the energy and carbon balance of the park, the total storage of 2.3 million tons of carbon a year is about four times the estimated carbon emissions from fossil fuels. The total power production is between 1.5 and 2 billion watts, equal to that of 3,000 windmills or several nuclear plants.

Looked at practically, it appears that Adirondackers and Adirondack towns could get a significant amount of their heat from forests (pp. 124, 149–150). A family in a moderate-sized house that needed 4,000 watts of heat a year could get this from 10 acres of young forests. A town that needed a few million watts of heat for its residents and public buildings could get this from 5,000 to 10,000 acres.

These results are both encouraging and cautionary. They say that Adirondackers can reduce their carbon emissions significantly by using biomass energy from private forests. But they also say this is only possible because the Adirondacks have a lot of land per resident. Any region with a greater population density—and most settled regions in the Northeast have greater densities—is going to need more than 400 watts per acre for its energy needs, and will not be able to live on forest energy alone.

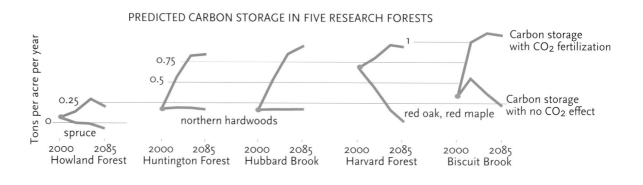

How will climate change affect Adirondack carbon storage?

A century from now, Adirondack forests will be warmer and have more carbon dioxide available to them. They may also be drier in the summer. The warmth will give them faster decay rates. The dryness may decrease their summer photosynthesis. The increased CO_2 levels will fertilize the trees and should, if enough water and mineral nutrients are available, increase their photosynthesis.

Which of these effects will predominate we do not know. If CO_2 fertilization increases the photosynthesis of the whole ecosystem, the rate of carbon storage may increase. But if growth slows down or decay increases, then the rate of carbon storage will decrease.

The habitat-suitability model shown on p. 31 concluded that most northern trees will decline in abundance. A carbon storage model developed by Scott Ollinger and his colleagues, shown above, couldn't decide. If it was told to assume that photosynthetic rates would increase as CO_2 concentrations rose, then carbon storage rates went up. If it was told that carbon fertilization would have at most a temporary effect, then storage rates remained constant in the northern hardwood forests and declined rapidly in the more drought-prone red oak-red maple forests.

At present, no one knows which future we will get. Many ecologists think, and some long-term experiments suggest, that scarcities of water and nutrients will offset the fertilizing effect of CO_2. For what it's worth, I agree with them. If we are right, the future may lie closer to the lower curves than the upper, and Adirondack carbon storage may stay constant or decline.

If so, this will be bad news. Forest carbon storage and forest products are significant assets in the fight to control global warming. Without their help, the task will be all that much harder.

CARBON FLOWS FROM A CLEAR-CUT HARVEST

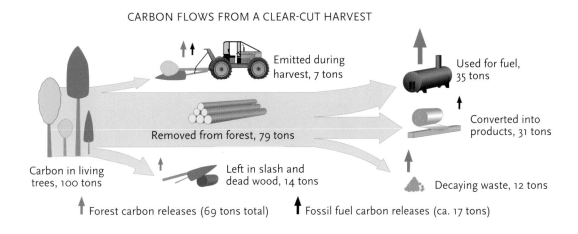

Emitted during harvest, 7 tons

Used for fuel, 35 tons

Converted into products, 31 tons

Removed from forest, 79 tons

Carbon in living trees, 100 tons

Left in slash and dead wood, 14 tons

Decaying waste, 12 tons

Forest carbon releases (69 tons total)   Fossil fuel carbon releases (ca. 17 tons)

Carbon Releases from Logging and Forest Products

There are two ways of getting climate benefits from a forest. We can simply leave the forest alone and let it store carbon (p. 141). Or we can harvest it, and get renewable energy and materials that can decrease our fossil use (p. 142).

Harvests, however, release carbon, and we have to account for this carbon if we want to know the true balance of carbon benefits against carbon costs.

The largest carbon releases come from logging and mill wastes. Logging leaves wood and debris in the forest. Mills discard or burn bark, scrap, and sawdust. As a result, only about a third of the carbon in the harvested trees makes its way into wood products. The rest decays or is burnt. The carbon in it returns to the air, often relatively quickly.

Besides generating waste, harvesting and processing require fossil fuels. Many wood products are energy intensive—rough lumber the least, fancy paper the most—and so this flow is significant. The harvest shown above, based on Forest Service averages for the Northeast, stores 31 tons of carbon in wood products and emits 69 tons of forest carbon and 17 tons of fossil fuel carbon.

POST-HARVEST EMISSIONS FROM FOREST DISTURBANCE

CO_2 More carbon released than stored
CO_2

Slash, bark, tops decaying

Forest floor decaying

5 years after cutting

CO_2 High rate of carbon storage
CO_2

Dead wood and litter beginning to accumulate, decay rate low

20 years after cutting

Another source of carbon is the forest itself. After harvest, growth is slow because there are fewer trees, and decay fast because the forest floor is warmer and the pool of dead organic matter larger. Decay exceeds growth, and the forest loses carbon. This period lasts until the canopy closes, the decay rate drops, and the growth of the new trees exceeds decay. After a heavy cut this may take 10 to 20 years.

The last source of carbon is the gradual decay of forest products. Most forest products don't last very long. The average lifetime for paper products and cardboard is less than a year. Books are thrown out, pallets and forms discarded, cheap furniture scrapped, houses razed. Some of the carbon is released into the air, some winds up in landfills. The result is that 50 years after harvest, less than half the carbon made into forest products is still in storage. The rest is in the air.

The diagram, again from Forest Service data, shows how the pools of carbon change after a clear-cut. The cut removes 50 tons of carbon from the pool of living biomass. About 20 tons of this goes into products or remains as dead wood on the forest floor. The rest, along with 8 tons of fossil fuel carbon, goes into the air.

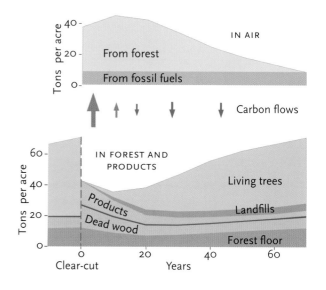

CARBON POOLS AFTER A CLEAR-CUT

In the first 10 years after harvest, another 8 tons of carbon is emitted from the forest and from the decay of short-lived products. Then, as growth accelerates, the forest carbon is gradually removed from the air and stored in new growth. At the end of 65 years, of the 50 tons of forest carbon initially harvested, only 7 are still in forest products. This is a climate benefit, but it has been offset by the emission of 8 tons of fossil fuel carbon that is still in the air.

This is a complicated story with a simple conclusion. *Making forest products contributes little to carbon storage.* When all the carbon flows are accounted for, most forest products are carbon-positive. Making them, as noted on p. 131, may still be an environmentally sound strategy, because in many cases they are the least harmful way of getting the materials that we need. But producing them still has climate consequences, and hence the more thriftily we can make and use them the better.

This might not be true in an artisanal society that harvested wood by hand and made books and houses that lasted for 500 years. But in our present high-energy, short-lifetime environment, the conclusion stands: *most forest products generate carbon emissions rather than abating them.*

Carbon Emissions from Industrial Materials

The last section had good news and bad news. The bad news was that forest products are carbon-positive, and that a carbon-removal strategy based on making a lot of forest products simply will not work.

The good news was that many forest products aren't *very* carbon-positive. This makes them good choices for construction: a wood building will use less fossil fuels and release less energy than building one of concrete or steel.

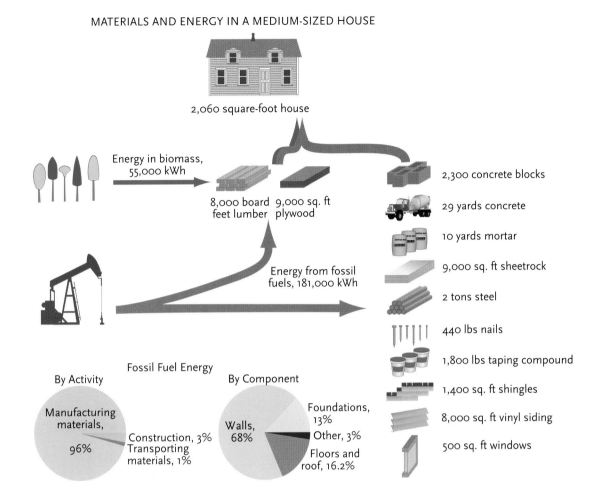

2,060 square-foot house

Energy in biomass, 55,000 kWh

8,000 board feet lumber   9,000 sq. ft plywood

Energy from fossil fuels, 181,000 kWh

2,300 concrete blocks

29 yards concrete

10 yards mortar

9,000 sq. ft sheetrock

2 tons steel

440 lbs nails

1,800 lbs taping compound

1,400 sq. ft shingles

8,000 sq. ft vinyl siding

500 sq. ft windows

Fossil Fuel Energy

By Activity

Manufacturing materials, 96%

Construction, 3%
Transporting materials, 1%

By Component

Walls, 68%

Foundations, 13%

Other, 3%

Floors and roof, 16.2%

There is, however, a further caveat. While wood products are fairly clean, like old-time politicians they often have business associates who are not.

The problem is that contemporary wood construction uses a lot of other materials besides wood, and many of these materials are energy intensive. When we build a modern house we set the wood on concrete or steel, fill it with wires and pipes and insulation, and cover it with paint, sheet-rock, or shingles. The result is that, from an energy and carbon perspective, what we call a wooden house is really a manufactured house with a wood skeleton. And that is something quite different.

The diagram illustrates this for a house of 2,060 square feet, built with conventional construction methods and materials. The house contains approximately 10 tons of wood and so stores 5 tons of forest carbon. Producing and transporting the other materials releases 9 tons of fossil fuel carbon. The net carbon balance, after accounting for storage, is a release of 4 tons.

The lesson is simple: *new wood houses with manufactured materials come with carbon debts.* If we are thinking about building a new house, or trying to decide, as a matter of climate policy, whether to rebuild or replace old houses, we need to think about these carbon debts as well.

This is especially true when building requires clearing land. The diagram at the top of p. 140 shows an example. To compare with emission figures in other chapters, the

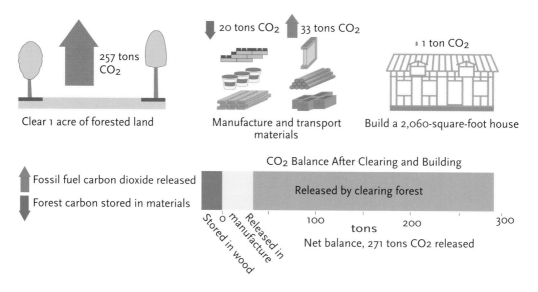

THE CARBON DEBT OF A MEDIUM-SIZED HOUSE

numbers are in tons of CO_2. Building the house creates a carbon debt of 14 tons of CO_2, after the carbon stored in the lumber has been accounted for. Clearing an acre of forest creates a debt of 257 tons. The total debt is 271 tons of CO_2. If the residents were environmentally conscious and saved 8 tons of CO_2 a year by installing solar panels and geothermal heat, it would take them 35 years to pay off the carbon debt they had contracted by clearing the land and building the house.

Managing Forest Carbon

The Adirondacks contain approximately 2.6 million acres of private land, much of which is forested. The owners of this land are the custodians of a pool of 200 million tons of carbon (p. 134). This is a 300 times larger than the estimated annual carbon emissions (0.6 million tons of carbon) of the park (p. 82). How these owners manage their forests can thus have large effect on the carbon balance of the park. This section looks at their options, and explains, in a deliberately simplified way, the carbon consequences of different forestry strategies.

Before we explain these, we need to emphasize that owners have multiple responsibilities. Carbon storage is one of those responsibilities. But it is far from being the only responsibility. And, even from a climate change perspective, it may not be the most important responsibility.

To make this concrete, imagine that you are the owner of several thousand acres of Adirondack land. It was bought by your great-grandfather and has been passed down in the family. Your great-grandfather logged it for big spruce in the last days of the river drives. Your grandmother cut it heavily for virgin hardwoods in the railroad days. Your father cut several times with trucks and skidders and, after the manner of his times, left less timber for your generation than you would like.

You and other family members are trying to plan for the next 50 years. You expect to continue harvesting and are also considering limited development, perhaps only for family members. You also want to take carbon into account. You have read about climate change, and want your forests to continue to store carbon and so remain carbon-negative.

Carbon is not, of course, your only consideration. Economics are equally or more important. The forest pays the taxes and the upkeep on the land, and is a traditional part of your family's income. The harvesting employs local foresters and loggers. Their jobs are fairly green because they use renewable resources and relatively little fossil fuel. You believe that the Adirondacks need green jobs and want your forest to continue to supply them.

Ecology matters too. The forest has been impacted by acid deposition and beech disease in your lifetime. You are tempted to make a heavy salvage cut and remove diseased trees. But you are worried about nutrient depletion, and no one can guarantee that the young trees you release will be healthier than the ones you harvest.

How you can balance these responsibilities—which, interestingly, range from familial to global—is beyond the purview of this book. What I can tell you is that, from the perspective of forest carbon, there are really only four different management strategies. Any thing you do will be either one of the four or a mixture of them.

The next four sections describe the strategies in order of decreasing greenness, from carbon-negative to carbon-positive. The greenness of a strategy is determined by a simple rule:

The goal of forest carbon management is to keep carbon out of the atmosphere. Anything that increases the average amount of carbon stored in the forest is carbon-negative and hence good. Anything that increases the average amount of carbon in the atmosphere is carbon-positive and hence bad.

When applying this rule, note that it is the average carbon that counts, and not the carbon at the end of the cutting cycle. If you want to be a good carbon steward, you are not allowed to clear-cut a thousand acres, wait 60 years for it to grow back, and claim that this is a carbon-neutral strategy because the forest is back to where it started from. The forest may be back to where it started, but, because the carbon you released spent 60 years in the air, the climate is not. But you are allowed to make small clear-cuts at frequent intervals, as long as the forest can reabsorb the carbon the cuts release in the year following the cut.*

*This is the principle of "harvesting at less than the growth rate" mentioned in the discussion of sustainability on p. 123.

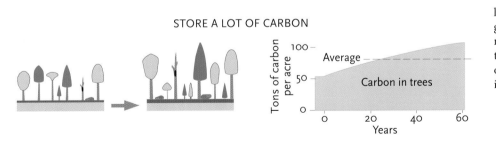

STORE A LOT OF CARBON

Strategy 1: Emphasize Storage

The first strategy focuses on storage. The forest is either left uncut or harvested selectively at much less than the growth rate. It either produces no forest products, or a little fuel and some high-grade trees. Either way the trees get bigger, and the average amount of carbon stored increases. This strategy is strongly carbon-negative and is in fact the most carbon-negative strategy possible. In the example in the graph, the forest starts with 50 tons per acre of carbon in the trees (typical for an Adirondack forest that is mature enough to cut) and then adds to it, doubling its carbon stores in about 60 years.

This is an excellent strategy for storing carbon, and is the *de facto* strategy being used on the New York State Forest Preserve and other conservation lands. It also might be a good strategy for restoring an ecologically damaged forest that needed to rest, or for an individual who had large carbon emissions—a taste for air travel, a large house, a heated swimming pool—that he wished to offset. But it produces no forest products or green jobs, and, unless prices for carbon storage improve, very little income (p. 153). And it may, forest economists remind us, have perverse side effects: the forest products not produced here may be produced somewhere else with greater carbon emissions, and the people not employed in green jobs here may find browner jobs elsewhere.

HARVEST IN SMALL YEARLY CUTS

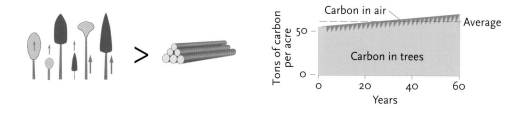

Strategy 2: Harvest below the Annual Growth Rate and Produce Green Products

This strategy focuses on products and income. We take the same forest and cut a portion of it every year. The cutting rate is below the growth rate, meaning that every year the forest grows more than we cut. Only a small amount of carbon is released into the air, and it is removed by next year's growth. Since growth exceeds harvest, the average carbon in the forest increases, and the forest's overall carbon balance is carbon-negative. It is not as carbon-negative as the storage forest of Strategy 1, but it still has climate benefits.

We then add to these climate benefits by producing biomass or long-lived products. Cordwood and wood chips can be used to replace gasoline or oil (p. 122). A thousand acres of forest might produce a thousand tons of wood a year. When burned for heat this could replace about 80,000 gallons of fuel oil. If harvested sustainably (p. 123), there will be a significant greenhouse benefit: biomass fuels may be the greenest products that we can produce in our forests.

Alternately we can produce forest products. As explained on p. 137, this is a carbon-positive strategy because we probably release more fossil fuel carbon than we store forest carbon. But it still may be a desirable strategy. If, for example, we are producing wood for energy-efficient houses, the long-term benefits of a low-emission house may exceed the short-term costs of making the materials for it.

By harvesting sustainably and emphasizing products that reduce fossil use, we both generate income and produce greenhouse benefits. This is an attractive combination, and is likely to be one that many carbon-conscious landowners use.

Both Strategy 1 and Strategy 2 have significant climate benefits. They are the only strategies that do.

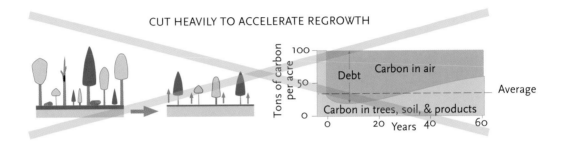

CUT HEAVILY TO ACCELERATE REGROWTH

Strategy 3: Stimulate an Old Forest by Cutting

Standard forestry practice regards old forests as nonperforming assets because they contain slow-growing trees that may die before they can be sold. The orthodox remedy is usually a heavy cut, to get the old trees to the mill before they rot and to accelerate the growth of the young ones.

Sometimes, mostly in informal discussions, this is suggested as a way of increasing carbon storage as well. "The old trees are not storing much carbon," the argument (falsely!) runs, "and so we should cut them down and transfer their carbon to forest products so that the young trees can store more."

Rejuvenating a forest in this way may be good timber management, but it is poor carbon management. As explained on p. 138, when we make a heavy cut, most of the carbon ends up in the air and not in forest products. The carbon in the air represents a carbon debt; this carbon has to be removed from the air before there are any benefits from the increased growth. Removing it takes time because old forests start with a lot of carbon and lose a lot of it when they are cut. Thus it may be a century or more before the debt is paid; all this time the forest carbon is in the air, and all the time it is in the air it is doing harm.

Based on what we know about how older forests continue to store carbon (p. 134), attempting to rejuvenate them with heavy cuts is a bad strategy based on a bad premise. It takes forests that were storing carbon fairly well already and, in the name of increasing storage, releases their carbon into the atmosphere where it remains for many years. Whatever its forestry benefits, this strategy has no merit as a serious attempt to manage atmospheric carbon.

Strategy 4: Scattered Development

Low-density development is permitted in private Adirondack forests. It is currently happening at fairly low rates, perhaps several hundred houses a year. This may seem unimportant compared to the size of the park, but in fact it has significant carbon consequences.

Like cutting old forests, development creates carbon debts. If we clear an acre of 60-year-old commercial forest, we release 60 tons of carbon. If we build a small house and heat it with fossil fuels, we add 5 tons to the carbon debt from the manufactured materials in the house, and an additional 8 tons a year from the emissions from fossil fuels and electricity. Thus the debt starts large and continues to climb.

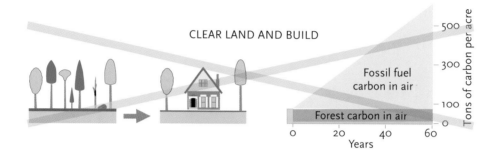

Suppose the acre is part of a larger holding and the owners, as good carbon managers, wish to offset the carbon emissions by taking other land out of production. To pay off the initial carbon debt they would have to increase the carbon storage elsewhere by 65 tons—say, by raising the minimum allowable carbon stock on 65 acres of their land from 60 to 61 tons, effectively putting the next two years of growth on that land permanently off limits. To offset the carbon emissions from heat and electricity, they would have to devote an additional 18 acres of land to permanent carbon storage. Thus the carbon debt from adding even a few houses to a forest ownership can change the carbon balance of the ownership, and require significant reductions in harvesting if the owners wish to keep the property carbon-negative.

Summary

The results of our audit of the Adirondack carbon bank are simple and important. The bank is large by world standards. It holds a lot of carbon and is adding to its stores. We can use those stores as a source of energy and green materials; potentially they could replace some of the fossil fuels we use in the park and in doing so support a green economy.

Our use of carbon from the bank is, however, subject to a stringent condition. If we want the forests to remain carbon-negative, we must harvest less than the growth rate, so that the total amount of carbon stored in the bank increases or stays the same.

This condition—that we may tap the bank's interest but not touch its principal—leads to a straightforward definition of carbon storage forestry. Managers who wish to protect their carbon stores will cut at a rate less than the annual growth, and emphasize long-lived products and biomass energy. They will avoid strategies (like heavy cuts in old-growth) that reduce the average carbon stores of the forest. And they will be cautious of development, recognizing that a even a small amount of development can create large carbon debts.

Indigenous energy: maple-oak forests on Paintball Hill, Johnsburg, July, 2009

12 CAN THE ADIRONDACKS BECOME ENERGY INDEPENDENT?

The last four chapters described a set of tools for reducing energy use and carbon emissions. The tools are used in a three-stage process that I call the thrift-efficiency-replacement cycle. Thrift eliminates unnecessary uses. Efficiency reduces the energy needed for necessary uses. Replacement supplies this energy from low-carbon sources and so decarbonizes our energy supply.

The previous chapters looked at the tools themselves and asked how good they were. The quick answer was that many were valuable and some–electric cars, passive solar houses, wind turbines, heat pumps–looked very good indeed. If we fail to build a low-carbon future, it won't be because we lack the tools.

This chapter asks what it will be required to build that future.

Suppose we were, over the next 20 years, to make a determined effort to use these tools to reduce our carbon emissions. What would it take to deploy them at serious levels? How much land would be needed? How fast could we do it?

And, most important of all, just how much could we do? Could we cut emissions by 50% and aim ourselves toward a low-carbon future? Could we go further and get 80%? Or 100% and become carbon-neutral?

To answer these questions, we start by making a picture of our energy use.

Setting a Goal

In Chapter 7 we summarized the carbon emissions of the park, based on work by Josh Wilson and his colleagues. If we calculate backwards from their emission figures to get energy use, the result is the energy stack shown on page 146. The total use is about 1,200 megawatts. The lower 980 megawatts of the stack, in brown and yellow, is the energy used within the park. Wood heat, which we assume to be roughly carbon-neutral, is not included. I will call this our direct energy use.

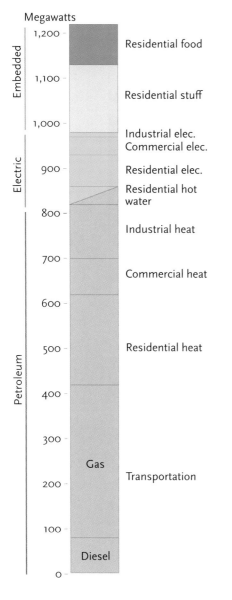

THE ADIRONDACK ENERGY STACK

Megawatts

Embedded	Residential food
	Residential stuff
Electric	Industrial elec.
	Commercial elec.
	Residential elec.
	Residential hot water
Petroleum	Industrial heat
	Commercial heat
	Residential heat
Gas	Transportation
Diesel	

1,200
1,100
1,000
900
800
700
600
500
400
300
200
100
0

The upper 250 megawatts of the stack, in green and gray, is my rough estimate of the energy embedded in our food and goods. It is the amount that people in other places–farms in Idaho, factories in China–emit while growing and making the things we buy from them.

The true amount of embedded use is unknown. My estimate is minimal, and it could be much larger.

To reduce our carbon emissions we have to reduce and decarbonize this stack. Unfortunately, only the lower part, our direct use, is under our direct control. The embedded use is not. We can affect it by buying fewer pairs of shoes and growing food locally. But our own agricultural capacity is limited and we will still need shoes, so in the near future we are not going to be able to change the flow of embedded energy very much.

That doesn't mean it is not a problem, or that people shouldn't be working to change it. But it is a problem that will need to be tackled on a world and national scale and not an Adirondack scale.

Our direct use, on the other hand, is very much an Adirondack problem. We use a total of 980 megawatts of local power, and much of this comes from fossil fuels. If we could replace the fossil fuels with locally generated low-carbon energy, we would have achieved energy independence. We would not be carbon-neutral, because there would still be the flows of embedded energy. But we still would have done something remarkable, and gone a long way toward carbon neutrality in the process.

In carbon reduction the achievable will always trump the perfect, and so I focus on our direct use here. The question then becomes: *Can the Adirondacks generate enough renewable energy to eliminate our local fossil fuel use and become energy independent?*

Reducing the Stack: Thrift and Efficiency

Much of the energy in the Adirondack stack is wasted or unnecessary. We want to eliminate this use, not waste our valuable renewables replacing it. So the first steps toward energy independence will be thrift and efficiency–cutting use and using what we have better.

How far can these steps take us? Chapters 10 and 11 suggested that electric cars can be made to use a quarter of the energy of conventional ones, and that old buildings can be rebuilt to use a half or a third of the energy they did before. So in theory, if we replaced all the cars and rebuilt all the buildings, we could reduce our energy consumption by 60%.

This is unlikely to happen. In the next 20 years, most of the passenger cars in the park will be replaced at least once, and many twice. But it will be a while before many of these are replaced by fully electric vehicles. In the meantime we will see more hybrids. We will see little change in the fleet of large diesel trucks, though more of them may use biodiesel. And, because America loves its big machines, we will still see many low-mileage, gas-powered trucks and SUVs.

My hope is that rising fuel prices and maybe carbon taxes will gradually increase vehicle efficiency and that by 2029 we will be using 30% less energy overall. This seems achievable, especially if the incentives are right. If all that mattered was efficiency, we could easily be using 60% less energy in 2029. But when thinking about people and their machines, efficiency is never all that matters.

Unlike cars, very few buildings will be replaced in the next 20 years. If we want them to use less energy, we will have to retrofit and rebuild them. Even with rising fuel prices and financial incentives, this will be slow. Old cars wear out and have to be replaced. Old buildings do not have to be rebuilt, and right now they only rarely are.

I hope that this changes. I can imagine increased energy costs becoming the driver, and local firms specializing in energy-saving rebuilding being created to meet the demand. I can also imagine a mix of tax incentives and low-interest loans, perhaps from local nonprofit energy trusts, that will make it affordable. But all this will take time. I am going to be conservative here, and assume that we can reduce residential and commercial energy by 30% in 20 years. Given the number of old leaky buildings in the Adirondacks, that will still be a big job. But with a mix of rebuilds and repairs–for example rebuilding a third of the buildings to high standards, and doing more limited retrofits on the remainder–it certainly could be done.

REDUCING THE ENERGY STACK

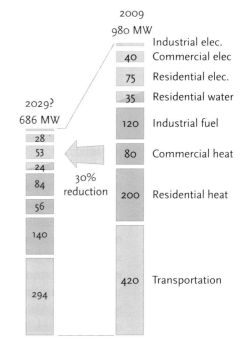

The last type of energy use in the stack is industrial. Each industry uses energy in its own way, and so it is hard to generalize about how efficient industries are and how much they might change. But two principles stand out. On the one hand, much of the energy is essential: the stone has to be crushed, the logs sawn, the water driven out of the paper. On the other hand, energy is costly, and any industry that wants to stay competitive has to minimize its energy use.

How these will play out I am not sure. I am going to be optimistic and assume that some mixture of market and government forces and the normal replacement of machinery will allow overall gains similar to those in housing and transport, and that industrial energy use will fall by 30%.

Under these assumptions, our need for local energy will fall by 30% across the board, from 960 megawatts to 686 megawatts. This is the amount of renewable energy that we will need to find to eliminate fossil fuel use and become energy independent.

The first place to look for this energy is right in front of us. How much renewable energy is currently produced within the park?

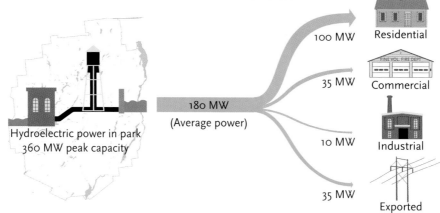

ADIRONDACK HYDROPOWER

Hydroelectric power in park
360 MW peak capacity

180 MW
(Average power)

100 MW → Residential

35 MW → Commercial

10 MW → Industrial

35 MW → Exported

Existing Renewables

The answer is not known exactly, because there are no public records of how much power dams and wind turbines produce. But there are records of the installed capacity and the average capacity factors for our area. Local hydro plants produce, on average, about 50% of their installed capacity. Wind turbines produce around 30% of their installed capacity and photovoltaic installations about 12%.

Using these numbers, we can get rough but useful estimates of renewable power production. Northern New York as a whole probably produces about 940 megawatts of hydropower and 250 megawatts of wind power, for an impressive total of 1.2 billion watts of renewable energy. The Adirondacks, with 360 megawatts of installed hydroelectric capacity, probably produce 180 megawatts of hydropower. Thus far they have no commercial wind.

Photovoltaic power is a distant third, probably totaling less that 0.02 megawatt of average power, and so adding little to the renewable energy total.

The 180 megawatts of Adirondack hydropower represents renewable power that we are already producing and that can be deducted from the power we need to reach energy independence. If we do this, our target becomes 506 megawatts. Thus, always assuming that we can reduce our present demand by 30%, *finding another 506 megawatts of renewable power in the next 20 years will allow us to eliminate fossil fuels and become energy independent.*

Potential Costs and Areas

This is good news, and in fact exciting news. Half a billion watts of average power is a lot of power, but it is still an achievable amount. New York has developed 250 megawatts

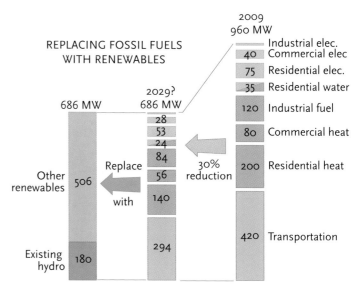

REPLACING FOSSIL FUELS
WITH RENEWABLES

2009
960 MW

	Industrial elec.
40	Commercial elec
75	Residential elec.
35	Residential water
120	Industrial fuel
80	Commercial heat
200	Residential heat
420	Transportation

686 MW

2029?
686 MW

28
53
24
84
56
140
294

Replace with

30% reduction

Other renewables 506

Existing hydro 180

of renewable power in the last 5 years.* Certainly the Adirondacks can develop 500 megawatts in 20 years. The question is no longer "Can we do it?" but rather "How shall we do it?"

The first step to answering this question is to compare the costs and the amounts of land required. Using the numbers from the graphs on p. 128, the graph below gives rough estimates of what it would cost, *at today's prices*, to install the equipment to generate 500 megawatts of average power from each of the different renewable sources.

*Again, this is the average power, not the installed capacity. Northern New York installed 830 megawatts of wind power in the last 4 years. With a capacity factor of 0.3 this produces about 250 megawatts of average power.

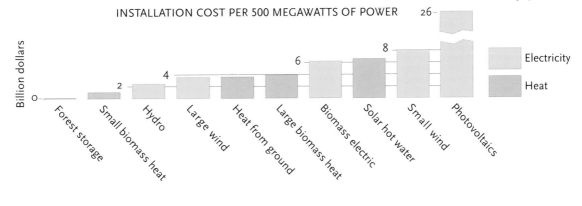

INSTALLATION COST PER 500 MEGAWATTS OF POWER

Billion dollars

Forest storage, Small biomass heat, Hydro, Large wind, Heat from ground, Large biomass heat, Biomass electric, Solar hot water, Small wind, Photovoltaics

Electricity
Heat

There are several things to note about this graph. First of all, it is just the installation costs: it does not include financing or operating costs. The costs of borrowing money, maintaining wind turbines, and fueling biomass boilers are not included. Second, nuclear is not included, because no one really knows how much it would cost. The Department of Energy estimates $2 billion for 500 megawatts, but no one has started a new nuclear plant in this country for 30 years, and nuclear plants are famous for costing two or three times what the investors expected. And third, the costs of most renewables are dropping, often fairly quickly, as the markets grow. All the major renewables will likely cost less 10 years from now than they do today.

One new category, forest storage, is included. This is the cost of buying land and taking it out of commercial production, thus creating new forest storage that can be used to offset emissions (say, from diesel trucks) for which no good source of alternative power exists. Forest storage is cheap, because no equipment is required. All that is needed is to buy heavily cut land and stop cutting it, and so it is a very cost-effective way of offsetting emissions.

The areas needed to generate 500 megawatts of average power can be calculated from the power densities given in Chapter 10. The results are shown at right. Each square is the area that would be required, by itself, to generate 500 megawatts of power. Nuclear

AREAS NEEDED TO GENERATE 500 MEGAWATTS

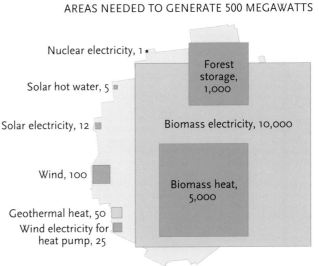

Nuclear electricity, 1
Solar hot water, 5
Solar electricity, 12
Wind, 100
Geothermal heat, 50
Wind electricity for heat pump, 25

Forest storage, 1,000
Biomass electricity, 10,000
Biomass heat, 5,000

Areas in square miles

is included here: even though we have no idea what it might cost, we do know that the footprint will be small. The square for wind assumes the turbines are grouped in a wind farm. The area would be smaller if the turbines were sited individually or in small groups. The small square for wind below the square for geothermal heat is the area required to produce the electricity to run the heat pumps.

A Renewable Energy Strategy

The cost and area diagrams, along with the analysis in Chapter 11, suggest some general principles. Wind, hydro, and geothermal heat have relatively low costs and small footprints. They are clearly winning strategies, and we are likely to use a lot of them. Biomass heat is attractive for its low cost, but requires significant amounts of forests to supply the fuel. We have the forest areas, and so will likely use a lot of it.

Biomass electricity, on the other hand, is costly and has a large footprint. We are likely to use only a little of it. Likewise, solar hot water, small wind, and solar electricity are compact technologies, but relatively costly. We will probably use them in small quantities where we need compactness, and hope their prices come down.

Many different combinations of renewables could supply the 506 megawatts of new power that we need. The diagram below shows one. It has four major features.

1 It replaces fossil fuel heat with biomass and geothermal heat. Both are proven technologies with comparable costs. Biomass will dominate in industrial situations where steam or process heat is required, and in commercial or residential situations where there is someone to tend the furnace. Geothermal will dominate in situations where automated heating and cooling are required.

2 It uses a few small biomass plants to supply both heat and electricity for municipal power.

3 It generates a total of 30 megawatts of electricity through photovoltaics and small hydro plants at existing dams. Both are excellent sources of power and could be developed further if photovoltaic prices fall or there turn out to be more sites for hydro plants.

4 It replaces the fossil fuels currently used in transportation with electricity from wind and existing hydro. Some of this electricity will be used directly in electric cars. Some will be sold to pay for biofuels, including biodiesel for trucks. And some, in time, may be used to power local biofuel plants.

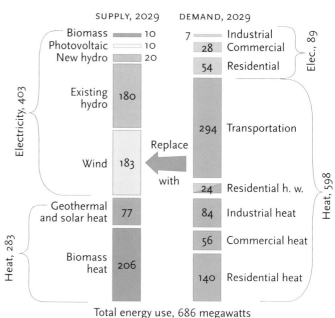

REPLACING FOSSIL FUELS WITH RENEWABLES

Total energy use, 686 megawatts

The first three of these are straight-forward extensions of existing technology, and are already happening in our area. All that is required is to make them happen faster. If we can replace fossil fuel heat at a rate of 5% a year, we will be there in 20 years.

The fourth is more radical: it assumes that three developing industries–electric vehicles, cellulosic biofuels, and biodiesel–can mature and replace their fossil predecessors in 20 years. This certainly might happen: all of the technologies show great promise. But it also might not. This is a country where it took 50 years for the tractor to replace the mule.

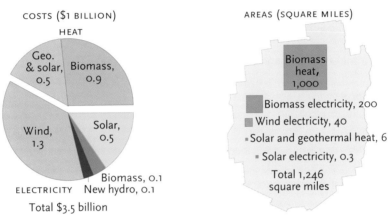

COSTS AND AREAS FOR 506 MW OF NEW RENEWABLE POWER

Land and Money

How much would an additional 500 megawatts of renewables cost, and how much land would they require? My rough estimate is that they would cost $3.5 billion to install, not counting financing, and would require 1,246 square miles of land. These are large numbers, but thinkable ones. Spread out over 20 years, the cost would be $175 million per year. This is about half what the Adirondack towns collect in property taxes, and about a quarter of what it costs to run the public schools.

The land required would be about 800,000 acres. Most of this would be used to supply biomass for heat and electricity. Supplying the biomass would use about a third of the private timberlands in the park and require harvesting something like 10,000 acres a year.

With the exception of wind, the other landscape impacts would be small, and likely cause no troubles if done carefully. The heat-generating units would mostly be small and located inside or adjacent to buildings. The biomass electricity would come from relatively small heat-and-power plants located in towns. The solar electric power would be mostly on rooftops or adjacent to buildings.

The greatest landscape impact would be from the wind turbines. To generate 180 megawatts of continuous wind power would require about 400 full-size turbines. This is not that big a number–450 turbines have been installed on the wind farms in the St. Lawrence and Tug Hill valleys since 2004. But the Adirondacks are a special place, and siting 400 turbines in the largest park in the lower forty-eight is a very different problem from siting them in farm country. And turbines evoke strong feelings. Some people, including myself, find them powerful and beautiful. Others dislike them. A few hate them. All three views will have to be respected and accommodated.

There are several ways that substantial wind development in the Adirondacks could be managed. One way would be to create a large wind farm of about 40 square miles (6 to 7 miles on a side) somewhere in the western Adirondacks where the winds are good. This would keep wind turbines out of the rest of the park, but might require clearing new utility corridors to distribute the power. This is difficult to do in the Adirondacks because of the interspersion of state and private lands, and could have much more landscape impact than the turbines themselves. One goal of any Adirondack energy plan should be to disperse power generation and avoid constructing any more power lines than are necessary.

A second way to site wind turbines in the Adirondacks would be to do what is widely done in Europe, and encourage local ownership of individual turbines placed near villages and settlements. With the guaranteed wholesale rates that prevail in Europe (p. 156), a full-sized turbine pays for itself in 8 or 10 years and after that generates $1 to $1.5 million a year for the owners. This kind of revenue stream has made a lot of friends for local wind power. The idealistic Germans regard citizen-owned wind turbines as symbols of independence and ecological responsibility, and have a word, *bürgerbeteiligungun,* for the local cooperatives that own 40% of the wind power in the country. The practical Dutch say simply, "Your own pigs don't stink."

Imagine something like this happening in the Adirondacks. New York, following the examples of Vermont and Ontario (p. 157), institutes guaranteed wholesale rates for wind-produced power. Each of the 90 settlements in the Adirondacks buys its own turbine, uses the power it needs from it, and sells the rest. Another 310 turbines are distributed in an arc along the windy west border of the Adirondacks, something like the famous *Middelegrunden* wind farm in the ocean off Copenhagen. Like the *Middelegrunden* they are owned by local electrical cooperatives, who sell shares to individuals, organizations, and governments. The 400 turbines, after operating costs, feed $340 million dollars into the regional economy.

Summary

Energy independence is possible in the Adirondacks in 20 years. The technology exists, the land base is there, and the rate of replacement of existing technology required–5% a year–is large but not impossible.

To make it happen we will need to do two new things: first, devote serious attention to improving the efficiency of vehicles and buildings. And second, begin producing serious amounts of renewable energy from wind, biomass, and geothermal.

If we succeed in making it happen, our energy supply will change in three ways. We will use less heat and more electricity and be on our way to eliminating combustion engines and becoming an electrical society. We will have left petroleum behind and be independent of both fossil fuels and foreign energy. And we will own much of the renewable energy we generate and have gained a significant measure of economic independence as well.

All three are fundamental changes. The third is the most so, because it can make the others happen. This is the subject of the next chapter.

Meachem Lake, August, 2009

13 HOW CAN WE FINANCE ENERGY INDEPENDENCE?

To achieve energy independence, the Adirondacks will need roughly $3.5 billion in capital investment over 20 years. This is a large but hardly impossible number. It is equal to what Adirondack school systems spend in 10 years, or what it would cost to build 100 miles of the Northway at today's prices.

To determine whether we can afford this, we must look at two things: how much benefit the investment will generate, and whether there are ways of borrowing against these benefits to get the capital needed.

Benefits

The capital costs of energy independence will be financeable only if there are corresponding benefits. Fortunately, there are.

The most direct benefit will be the money saved on fuel. Every watt of fossil fuel power we use costs about $0.70 per year. If we replace 500 megawatts of fossil fuels with renewables, that is a savings of $350 million a year, enough to repay the $3.5 billion cost in 10 years. Further, since the prices of fossil fuels are growing at an average rate of around 10% per year, the increase in savings over time could be more than enough to cover a 7% per year finance charge.

A second benefit will be savings in carbon. Every watt of fossil fuel power we use emits about 6 lbs of carbon dioxide. If we replace 500 megawatts of fossil fuels with renewables, that is a savings of about 1.5 million tons of carbon dioxide a year.

Currently, there is no direct way to get paid for saving carbon. If the United States adopts a carbon tax or a cap-and-trade system, this may change. If, for example, reducing carbon dioxide was worth $2 per ton (the current price on the Chicago Carbon Exchange), our savings would be worth $3 million per year. If the price was $20 per ton (the current price in the European Carbon Exchange), our savings would be worth $30 million a year. Either way, this would be only a small part of our direct savings from not buying fossil fuel.

This is an important result. On the national level, cap-and-trade programs and carbon taxes can have large effects. On the local level, it is the price of fuel and not the price of carbon that will determine the benefits of renewable energy.

A third benefit to energy independence is that much of the money we invest in it will stay in the Adirondacks. When we buy fossil fuels, most of our money leaves the Adirondacks and much of it leaves the United States. When we invest in efficiency and renewables, the money stays much closer to home; we stimulate domestic industry and generate U.S. and Adirondack jobs.

Besides economic benefits there are political and ecological ones. Acquiring and paying for fossil fuels involves a world-wide military presence and subsidizes regimes that many Americans would prefer not to support. Burning fossil fuels releases acids and mercury as well as carbon dioxide. The acids and mercury have damaged many ecosystems, including our own.

The balance of costs and benefits seems clear. The longer we use fossil fuels, the more it costs us in cash, changes the climate, and damages ecosystems. The sooner we become independent of them, the sooner we benefit. But to benefit requires a significant investment. How do we get the money to invest?

Financing Renewable Electricity with Subsidies

Financing renewable energy, like financing other businesses, gets start-up cash from banks and investors and pays it back from the profits on what it sells. The main difference is that because fossil fuels are both well established and heavily subsidized, renewables need subsidies to compete with them.

The extent to which fossil fuels are subsidized is sometimes not appreciated. Fossil fuels are cheap not only because they are concentrated and easy to produce, but because their users never have to pay their true costs. Fossil fuel producers receive tax breaks, low-cost mining leases, and free military protection. Fossil fuel users are not charged for the carbon they emit or the damage it causes. If fossil fuel prices reflected the real costs—if, say, oil companies had to pay for middle-eastern wars and Australian droughts, or if coal users had to capture the carbon, sulfur, and nitrogen they emit and put it back in the ground—then fossil fuel energy would be costly indeed.

Because of the subsidies, fossil fuels are inexpensive sources of energy in the short term. But they may be much more expensive in the long term, when scarcity drives their prices up and the environmental costs have to be paid.

Renewable energy, on the other hand, is more dilute and more expensive to collect, and so its short-term costs are high. But compared to fossil fuels, its long-term costs are much lower. Renewables do not become depleted, generate dangerous wastes, cause environmental damage, or require military protection. Their prices are less volatile and hence their long-term costs more stable. And, as the windy northern European countries have found, renewables are good national investments because they keep capital at home and generate jobs.

Thus while fossil fuels are a good short-term investment, renewable energy is a better long-term one. If the market, which in this case means the investors and lenders, is asked to choose, it will choose short-term benefits. As a result everyone, including the lenders and investors who made the choice, suffers in the long term. The function of subsidies—compulsory public investment if you like—is to adjust the short-term costs to secure long-term benefits.

FINANCING COMMERCIAL WIND

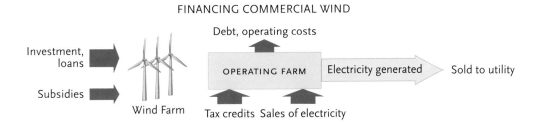

Subsidies and Their Limitations

Commercial wind energy illustrates how this works. Large wind projects typically need to sell their electricity at somewhere between $0.10 and $0.13 per kilowatt-hour to make a profit. Current wholesale electric rates are only about half this. In the United States, the difference is made up through a mixture of subsidies, including direct grants to cover construction expenses, tax credits based on the amount of electricity produced, and direct payments for "environmental attributes"—things like the amount of fossil fuel replaced or a reduction in the peaking power that the grid needs.

Together, the subsidies reduce the up-front costs by 30% or more and pay the producers an additional 2 to 4 cents per kilowatt-hour of electricity produced. With them, a large wind farm in a good site can pay for itself in less than 10 years and make handsome profits for its investors in the next 10.

This financing model is clearly working: the U.S. wind industry added 8.5 billion watts of capacity in 2008, its biggest year thus far. But nonetheless it has several important limitations that need to be thought about.

The first is that it does not encourage energy conservation. Subsidies keep prices artificially low and encourage consumption. The net result of subsidizing wind is that we now have two kinds of subsidized electricity instead of one. This is good for coal companies and consumers but not for the environment.

The second limitation is that current subsidies are designed to promote large-scale wind development, typically corporate owned, with big, efficient turbines on sites with high wind speeds. Smaller projects by nonprofit owners like cooperatives and municipalities are excluded. They can't use the tax credits, are too small to compete for the large government grants, and may not have exceptionally windy sites. And yet in the Adirondacks, where large projects will be unpopular and the highest terrain is out of bounds, small and medium-sized projects may be more promising than large ones.

The bias in U.S. wind subsidies towards large commercial projects has good and bad effects. The good effect is that it encourages big, productive developments on optimal sites. This puts wind development in the places where the pay-back is the fastest, and has built U.S. wind capacity quickly. The bad effect is that most of these wind farms are owned by national or international corporations. As a result, most of the money that they make is exported from the region where the farm is located. Big

CASH FLOW FOR A CORPORATE WIND FARM

Sales, tax credits

Loan payments, dividends, profits

Exported from region

Remain in region

Rents and payments to towns

Local staff

farms are good for the environment and contribute significantly to local economies. But their principal economic effect is on the greenness of the national economy and not the greenness of the local one.

An alternative to large corporate-owned wind farms is smaller, community-owned ones. These have been very successful in northern Europe. They are rare in the United States, not because they would not work here but because there is no way to finance them. If it turns out, as suggested on p. 152, that small, locally owned wind farms are the most appropriate way of developing wind power in the Adirondacks, we will need a to find a way. Fortunately, there are excellent models close by.

OWNERSHIP OF WIND TURBINES

Billion watts of capacity

Local

Corporate

Germany   United States   Denmark

Funding Renewable Electricity with Guaranteed Rates

Our current subsidies decrease the costs of installing renewable electricity and increase the producer's revenues by a few cents per kilowatt-hour. But they do not guarantee the price will be high enough to repay the investment and return a profit.

Guaranteed rates, in contrast, do just that. They require that the utilities purchase renewable power at a fixed rate for 20 years or more. The rates are set by the government, and paid by the utilities' customers; the more power a customer uses, the more he pays. (This is quite different from subsidies, in which the taxes of those of us who don't use much power are used to make electricity cheaper for the people who do.) In return, the customers get a guaranteed supply of renewable electricity at a fixed rate. Thus guaranteed rates are a hedge in which customers pay more for power now but are protected against future rises in their rates.

Guaranteed rates, technically known as *feed-in tariffs,* are widely used by countries with successful renewable programs. They have several key features. They are available to everyone, large or small, and so are inherently democratic. They guarantee a continuing revenue stream and so make it easier to get loans and attract investors. They can be adjusted to allow for the costs of different systems. (In Germany, for example, owners of solar electric systems are paid 45 cents per kilowatt-hour for systems on the ground, and 47 to 61 cents per kilowatt-hour, depending on the system size, for systems on roofs.) And, because they make electric power more expensive overall, they encourage conservation.

Currently Vermont has the most comprehensive program of guaranteed rates in the United States. Large wind turbines get 14 cents per kilowatt-hour; small residential turbines, which are less profitable, get 20 cents per kilowatt-hour, and photovoltaic systems get 30 cents per kilowatt-hour. Ontario, which has the best system of guaranteed rates in Canada, has lower rates for wind and higher ones for photovoltaics.

FINANCING WIND WITH GUARANTEED RATES

The guaranteed rates change the game for small and medium-sized producers. If a community in Vermont buys a 0.5 megawatt turbine for $1 million and generates about 1.3 million kilowatt-hours a year with it, the community will be guaranteed an income of about $160,000 after operating expenses. They can then borrow against this income, repay the loan in 10 years, and make over a million dollars in profit in the following 10 years.

The most attractive feature of guaranteed rates is that, if high enough, they really work. Almost every place that has serious rates for renewables has a success story. Germany, where a group of *stromrebellen* (electricity rebels) passed some of the first guaranteed-rate laws in Europe, now has 50% locally owned wind power and 5.4 billion watts of photovoltaic capacity, four times as much as the United States. Ontario instituted its system of feed-in payments in 2006 and was hoping to add a billion watts of renewable power capacity by 2016. It reached this goal in the next 2 years and since then has taken proposals for an additional 15 billion watts of renewables.

Given these numbers, our proposal to add 220 megawatts of renewable electric power to the Adirondacks in 20 years suddenly seems modest. Two hundred twenty megawatts of power will require somewhere around 800 megawatts of capacity. Ontario, right across the border, was able to contract for this amount in 2 years.

GUARANTEED PAYMENTS FOR RENEWABLES		
(cents per kWh)		
	PV	Wind
France	47–85	4–12
Germany	45–61	13
Great Britain	43–51	7–50
Ontario	38	10
Vermont	30	14–20
Washington State	30	12

The U.S. Way: Penalizing Renewables with Net-Metering

Except in Washington State and Vermont, there are no real guaranteed rates for renewables in the United States. Large projects, as described above, are funded by up-front subsidies and production credits. Small projects are funded by a combination of subsidies and a practice called net-metering that allows owners to deduct the amount of power they use from the amount they make. The subsidies are often surprisingly generous but, when combined with some perverse incentives that are built into net-metering, often surprisingly ineffective.

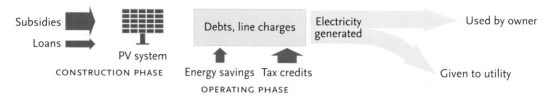

FINANCING RESIDENTIAL SOLAR AND WIND IN NEW YORK

The diagram shows how this works. A New Yorker purchases a 4.5 kilowatt photovoltaic system for $36,000. The state pays $13,000 of this directly. State and federal tax credits over the next 5 years provide an additional $12,000. The owner ends up paying $11,000 or about 30% of the total.

This is an attractive deal. But what happens after that is less attractive. The system gets turned on and produces electricity. The owner uses some of the electricity. The rest goes into the grid, which acts as an electricity bank. The meter records the net amount (the production minus the owner's use) that has gone into the grid, credits it to the owner's account, and charges him a service fee. The owner can use as much power as he wants, up to the amount banked. At the end of the year the utility confiscates the surplus power in the account and (wicked plutocrats!) sells it to other customers.

The numbers work something like this. Say a Vermont owner and a New York owner, Sarah and Sam, have identical PV systems that generate 5,000 kilowatt-hours a year. Each uses 3,000 kilowatt-hours, leaving 2,000 kilowatt-hours in the bank.

Sarah, who gets a guaranteed rate of 30 cents per kilowatt-hour, is paid $1,500 for the electricity she has generated. She is charged $450 for the power she uses, and ends up $1,050 to the good. If her system costs $11,000 after incentives, she can pay for it in 10 years and have free power plus $1,000 a year in income after that. She has an incentive to put in extra capacity because she makes money by selling her power. She has an incentive to be thrifty because she still pays for the power she uses.

Sam, under a net-metering system, gets paid nothing. He saves $500 in electricity that he would otherwise have purchased but has to pay $200 in service charges and give the utility his 2,000 surplus kilowatt-hours for free. The utility can turn around and sell this for $340. Thus Sam ends up making $300 from his investment, while the utility gets $540 without any investment at all. He has no incentive to put in a larger system and generate power for his neighbors or use less himself. It will take him 33 years to pay for his system from his electricity savings; up to that point it is costing him more than it is saving.

Net-metering is, to say the least, a miserable way of encouraging renewable power. A bank that took your money, charged you a fee for taking it, and then at the end of the year wiped your balance our would not get many customers. Likewise New York, despite 5 years of extremely generous subsidies, has only about 1,000 grid-tied solar electric systems and a few-dozen small wind systems in the state. Clearly we can do better.

Financing Renewable Heat

Thus far we have been talking about financing electrical projects. But about 60% of the new renewable energy required for energy independence is heat and not electricity. How is heat financed, and will the financing be sufficient to get the heat we need?

My quick answer, after insufficient study, is that heat is financed mostly through up-front subsidies, and the existing subsidies, though valuable, are not big enough to get us the amount of renewable heat that we will need.

Heat differs from electricity in two important ways. Most of it is used by the producers rather than being sold, and so there are no revenues to borrow against. And many of the important users of heat are nonprofits like towns and schools that don't pay taxes and so have no use for tax credits.

FINANCING BIOMASS HEAT

State and federal governments have tried, gamely, to fund renewable heat with a mixture of grants, loan funds, and tradeable tax credits. The result has been something of a hodgepodge. A lot of money has been thrown at the problem and a lot of programs created, but the eligibility rules are inconsistent and the programs come and go. The bottom line is that many important renewable heat projects are hard to fund. If you want to put in solar panels, a costly way of generating renewable energy, you have a good chance of getting 70% funding. But if you want to put in a heat pump or biomass boiler, both of which will generate much more energy per dollar of investment than solar panels, the funding levels are much lower and, especially in the case of biomass, you may not get funded at all.

Despite the uncertainties, worthy renewable heat projects are getting funded. But they do not seem to be getting funded at the level that will get us 280 megawatts of new renewable heat in the next 20 years.

Summary

Energy independence will generate substantial direct and indirect monetary benefits, and so should be fundable. To achieve it we have to have the right financing mechanisms in place. Right now we don't.

Renewable electricity is a commercial product. The easiest way to fund it is to require that the utilities buy it at a guaranteed price that will make it profitable. Developers will then know what their profits will be and can get loans and attract investors. Other mechanisms—up-front subsidies, tax credits—may also be useful. But world-wide, guaranteed rates have proven both the most successful funding mechanism, and the only one capable of encouraging the kind of community energy development we may need in the Adirondacks.

Renewable heat is mostly used where it is made and does not generate a revenue stream. It will need to be funded by up-front subsidies. Such funding currently exists but is spotty and unpredictable. What is needed is a simpler and more uniform system, analogous to the guaranteed electric rates, that reimburses owners by a fixed amount for every kilowatt of renewable heat they install.

Ampersand Lake, October, 2009

14 THE PATH FORWARD

The tone of the last few chapters has been optimistic. Yes, we have a problem, but yes, too, we have a way of dealing with it. The tools exist, our resources are excellent, the economics are favorable. A path through the mountains exists, and we can take it if we want.

This chapter is more sober. I see no sign, yet, of the will or the leadership that will take us along that path; and I see many signs to suggest that we are on, and may remain on, our old, dangerous, high-carbon path.

I hope that someday we will leave this path. When we do—when we finally see carbon emissions stabilize or drop—there will be reason for optimism. Till then, the best I can offer you in closing is a summary and a look ahead. Where are we, what are our assets, what are our obstacles, and what do we need to move forward? What can you, the reader, do to help?

Where are we?

Currently the Adirondacks use about a billion watts of direct power. Twenty percent of this is electricity; the rest, 800 megawatts, comes from petroleum. About half of the petroleum is used to run vehicles and the other half to heat buildings and supply process heat for industry.

The Adirondacks generate about 180 megawatts of renewable electricity at hydroelectric stations within the park. This offsets the electricity used in the park, and so it is only the petroleum use that results in emissions. If the Adirondacks want to become energy independent and end their carbon emissions, they have to eliminate the 800 megawatts of petroleum products they currently use.

Where do we want to go?

To lower our greenhouse emissions, we want to go to a more efficient society, where houses and cars use less energy. Also to a more renewable one, where petroleum is less common and renewable heat and electricity more common. And also, if the economic arguments in Chapter 13 are correct, to a more locally owned and powered society, where much of the Adirondacks' energy is generated inside the park by the towns and their residents.

In such a society, leaky houses, large cars, oil furnaces, and combustion engines will get rarer. Passive solar houses, small cars, wood furnaces, heat pumps, and electric motors of all kinds will be commoner. Most houses will have a continuous insulating shell and efficient windows. Many will have solar hot water heaters and photovoltaic panels. Wind-generated electricity and wood chips will be the principle energy carriers and will be relatively cheap. Liquid fuels will be less common, and petroleum-based fuels relatively rare and expensive.

What are our assets?

Our largest tangible assets are our hydroelectric stations, which currently supply about 20% of our power; the wind energy available at the edges of the park, and, even more, to its north and west; and the extent and growth rate of our forests. Together they can supply enough energy for our direct energy needs, plus surplus energy and carbon credits that we can trade for biofuels and use to offset the carbon we still emit.

Our intangible assets, which will be equally important, include our competence with structures and machines; our tradition of using forest and water resources; our willingness to experiment and innovate; and, perhaps most of all, the young people who see climate change as the challenge of their generation and are prepared to tackle it head on.

What are the key steps toward eliminating petroleum?

They are the steps discussed in Chapters 7 through 10. First we, as individuals, towns, or organizations, assess our energy use and carbon emissions. Next we set goals for reducing our energy use by thrift and efficiency. This begins with eliminating unnecessary use, and then goes on to replacing furnaces and cars and reinsulating buildings. It is a large job, will require capital, and, because progress in efficiency is incremental, will be slow. But if we reduce our energy use by a few percent a year and invest the money we save in additional reductions, we can achieve a lot in 20 years.

In addition to reducing our energy use, we will also need to replace petroleum with renewables. This is also a large job but, because renewable energy comes in large packages, not necessarily a slow one. A megawatt biomass or geothermal heating system can be installed in a few weeks. A medium-sized wind farm, capable of doubling the amount of renewable energy produced in the park, could be built in a year or two.

As with energy efficiency, the key to the growth of renewables will be the return on investment. If renewable energy can pay for itself and make a profit in 5 or 10 years, and if those profits accrue to Adirondack owners and are reinvested in more Adirondack renewables, we will progress rapidly. If renewable energy is not profitable, or if the profits accrue to owners elsewhere and are reinvested someplace else, we will progress slowly if at all.

What are the obstacles to eliminating petroleum?

The obstacles are technical, economic, and behavioral. The first two can be overcome by research and re-investment. The third is daunting.

The main technical obstacles facing us are that electric cars suitable for four-season Adirondack driving do not yet exist, and there are no electrical substitutes for heavy diesel vehicles at all. Both of these may change as better batteries and fuel cells develop. In the meantime, some combination of electric vehicles, extended-range hybrids, and biodiesel will allow us to lower our emissions.

The main economic obstacle is capital. This is solvable: efficiency creates savings and renewable electricity generates revenues. What we need is an effective way of borrowing against these to cover the up-front costs. This has been done elsewhere through a combination of subsidies, loan funds, and guaranteed rates (Chapter 13). We should be able to do the same thing here. The key will be to have a uniform program of incentives and rates, available to everyone and for every sort of renewables, that will subsidize efficiency, and make renewable electricity profitable.

The main behavioral obstacles are our local opposition to wind power, and our national love of big houses and big machines.

The opposition to wind energy may be reduced in several ways. One, which I favor, is by local ownership. Avoid big wind farms and keep turbines off the high ridges. Put up medium-sized, community-owned turbines on medium-sized hills, and use them to lower electric rates and pay for community services. Another way would be to put large turbines on commercial forest lands where they would not be visible to the public. Neither alternative has been investigated; a park-wind survey of wind resources would be extremely useful.

Changing American habits of energy consumption will be the most difficult of all. Americans regard big cars, meat-and-dairy diets, 75-degree houses, cheap air travel, and cheap access to a quarter of the world's petroleum as birthrights. The environmental movement has been trying for half a century to tell them that these are not good things to want. Thus far it has had little effect.

Fuel prices, on the other hand, have had a large effect, and many think they may be our most effective way of encouraging efficiency and reducing petroleum use. "Get the carbon costs right," they say, "and we will be on our way." If this is true, it is important, and needs a careful look.

Can high fuel prices affect petroleum consumption?

Definitely, and in fact they are probably the best known way of affecting fuel consumption. In the 1973–1974 oil embargo, the price of crude oil quadrupled, from $3 per barrel to $12 per barrel, and never fell below $10 per barrel again. Demand for petroleum fell, and Congress passed a national speed limit and other conservation laws. Between 2006 and 2008 the price of crude oil tripled. Demand fell world-wide, airlines posted huge losses, and the market for sport-utility vehicles and light trucks, up to that point the most profitable vehicles in the world, collapsed overnight.

This principle is obvious but needs stressing. *If we want to move from petroleum to renewables, we need for petroleum to become more expensive and renewables to become cheaper.*

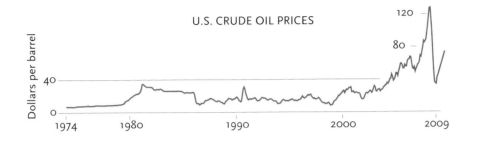

Unfortunately, because petroleum prices are very sensitive to demand, they tend not to remain high unless governments keep them high. In 2007 and 2008 U.S. crude oil prices climbed from $70 a barrel to a peak of $140 in 12 months. In July, 2008, with U.S. crude oil prices at $130 a barrel and gasoline prices over $4 per gallon, everyone was talking about energy and energy conservation. Prices then fell to $40 a barrel in six months, and then, as demand rebounded, climbed to $70 a barrel in nine months. In January 2010, with gasoline under $3 a gallon, no one is talking about conservation.

Where oil prices will go from here, no one knows. We will probably not see $25-a-barrel oil again, but we also may not see a sustained period of $120-a-barrel oil either. If this is true, it means that the market is not likely to maintain the kind of prices we need for real conservation. If we want prices high, we will need to make them high ourselves. Unfortunately, like health care, this is something that the United States is not good at.

Could we increase petroleum taxes to keep prices high?

Yes, we could, and in fact much of the developed world does. Britain and the European Union keep gas and oil prices at levels two to three times those in the United States. This stabilizes prices, reduces demand, and generates billions of dollars in revenues that support energy conservation and renewable energy.

We could certainly do the same here. But given the clout of the oil companies and the demand of consumers and industry for cheap energy, the chance of us doing it seems very low. When congressional leaders are asked about, say, a $1 tax on oil and gas they say, simply, that it is "Off the table."

This is unfortunate. In the last 10 years, the general trend in oil prices has been upward. If we don't curb demand, sooner or later high oil prices are likely to come back and stay. When they do, the profits will go overseas and our economy will suffer. If we raise prices in advance and use the revenues to build a renewable economy, we will be in a much better position when the next price spike comes.

Will carbon prices and emission caps increase the price of petroleum?

Yes, they will, but probably not by very much. Carbon prices and emission caps do make it more costly to emit carbon. But they are targeted at emitters of thousands of tons of carbon a year, and, by design, have little effect on individual consumers who emit only a few tons of carbon a year. If we are trying to change the economics of power generation, they are a good tool. If we are trying to encourage ourselves to buy smaller cars, they are a bad one.

CARBON PRICES AND PETROLEUM PRICES

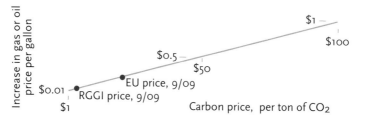

This feature of carbon prices is often misunderstood. Imagine, for example, that we have some sort of national cap-and-trade program, like that proposed in the Waxman-Markey Bill currently in Congress, or like the existing Regional Greenhouse Gas Initiative (RGGI). Under this program, carbon emitters are required to have emission allowances, which they buy from the state and then can trade on a carbon exchange. The number of allowances available is fixed, creating an *emission cap*. Over the years the cap will be reduced, reducing the total carbon emissions.

Under a cap-and-trade system, energy producers add the cost of emission allowances to the retail price of fuels. Since a gallon of gasoline emits 0.01 ton of carbon dioxide, a price of a dollar per ton of CO_2 would add 1 cent to the cost of a gallon of gasoline.

Currently carbon prices are fairly low. The current European Union price of about $20 per ton adds 20 cents to the cost of a gallon of gas. The current RGGI price of $3, if it applied to gas, would add 3 cents. To get gas prices up to $4 per gallon, the emission price would have to be over $120 a ton.

The cost of emission permits is expected to increase as emission caps are reduced. But (politics!) there are no plans to reduce the existing caps quickly. No one expects to see $100-per-ton or $200-per-ton carbon prices any time soon, and certainly the U.S. Congress is unlikely to pass any bill that would have the remotest chance of generating those kind of prices.

Thus, paralleling our conclusion about the effect of carbon prices on renewables on pp. 153–154, we conclude that: *carbon prices and emission caps, however important as instruments of national energy policy, are likely to have little effect on petroleum prices and petroleum use in the near future.*

How then can we encourage energy conservation and renewable energy?

The conclusion of the preceding section is discouraging. It says that in the near future, U.S. petroleum prices will fluctuate with the world market and may not, if the past

THE REGIONAL GREENHOUSE GAS INITIATIVE (RGGI), A REGIONAL CAP-AND-TRADE PROGRAM

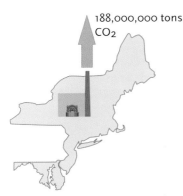

In 2008, electric generation stations in the ten-state RGGI area released about 188 million metric tons of CO_2. Any station could release as much as it wanted, for free.

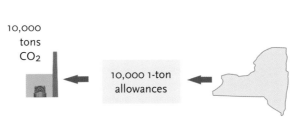

Starting in 2009, every station must hold allowances for the CO_2 it will emit in the next three years. The states sell the allowances to the stations. The total number of allowances is *capped* at 188 million per year.

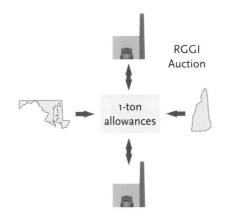

Every three months, RGGI runs an auction at which allowances may be bought and sold. The allowances are currently running about $3 per ton, for a total value of over $500,000,000 per year.

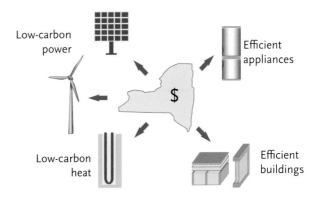

The states invest the money from selling allowances in energy-efficiency and alternative-energy programs, thus reducing the demand for electric power.

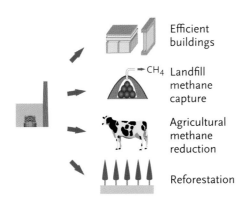

Utilities may also invest in offsets (carbon reductions elsewhere) to reduce the number of allowances they must hold.

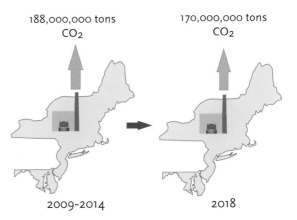

Starting in 2015, the cap (number of new allowances sold per year) will be reduced by 2.5% per year. In 2018 total emissions will have declined 10%, to 170,000 tons.

is any guide, get high enough or stay high long enough to encourage conservation and drive a rapid switch to renewables.*

Fortunately, there are other ways of encouraging them. Incentives for conservation and renewables also work. They leave petroleum artificially cheap (p. 154), and this is not good, but at least they allow renewables to compete.

If the analysis in Chapter 13 is correct, the current system of incentives is not working as well as it might. The reasons for this are the patchwork of subsidies offered for conservation and renewable heat, and the lack of guaranteed rates for producing renewable electricity. Both could be fixed.

A fix for conservation and heat would be to merge the current welter of subsidies into a single subsidy based on the amount of energy saved or the amount of heat generated. The subsidy needs to be high enough, somewhere around $5 per watt, to allow projects to pay for themselves in under 10 years.

The fix for renewable electricity is to require the utilities to buy it at guaranteed rates. The rates should be high enough to attract investors and allow the project to make a profit in under 10 years and available to all projects, large or small, private, commercial, or nonprofit. Based on the experiences of Europe and Ontario, where guaranteed rates have been quite successful, they will probably need to be around $0.12 per kilowatt-hour for commercial wind, $0.20 for small wind, and $0.30 for photovoltaic power.

Both of these strategies are practical. The first is simply an improved and less restrictive version of what we are already doing. The second is already being done in Ontario and Vermont. Both would require legislative action, and that is never fast. But New York already has a substantial legislative commitment to conservation and renewables, and with enough lobbying and support, both could be accomplished within 5 years.

What should we do in the meantime?

If my assessment is right, we are not yet at the point where economic incentives and low-energy technology line up and let us make rapid progress. Wind, biomass and geothermal heat, and high-efficiency renovations of buildings are ready to work for us; all we need are the right rates and incentives to make them take off. Photovoltaics are still too expensive for what they produce. Electric cars are promising and the incentives are good; the main problem is that we can't buy them yet.

With good political leadership and continuing technical development, all this could change. Commercial wind has already passed a tipping point, and is growing rapidly. In the next 5 or 10 years, the same could happen with community wind, heat pumps, biomass heat, and electric cars. But it also might not happen. In any event, carbon emissions are growing, and waiting to see what other people do gets us nowhere. So what should you and I—concerned, unpowerful individuals in small towns in an energy-wasting country—do in the meantime?

I have thought about this the whole time I have been writing this book, and only in the last few days have felt that I have an answer. It is this: *We should try to prove that efficiency and renewables do in fact save money. If they do, we should tell people. If they don't, we should tell even more people, and lobby for the changes that will make them pay.* I call this a demonstrate-and-communicate strategy.

* It is, of course, not in the oil producers' interests to allow oil prices to rise so high that people don't buy oil.

Demonstrate and Communicate

The logic goes like this. If efficiency and renewables are to spread, they need to be profitable. If owning, say, a hybrid car is a life-style choice or an act of philanthropy, then not many people are going to own them. But if owning a hybrid saves you money—and saves it today, not just down the road—then a lot more people might want to own one.

If they do, it will not be because the hybrid saves 26 tons of CO_2 compared to a conventional car of similar size. That is nice—most people don't mind wearing a white hat—but it will not be enough to make a lot of people buy one. What will make people buy one is that the hybrid uses half as much gas for the same distance as the conventional car.

This suggests a strategy: if we want to sell energy efficiency and renewables, we should talk about economics rather than climate. There are plenty of people around who are prepared to tell you that climate change is nonsense and carbon doesn't matter. There are far fewer who will tell you that paying \$12,000 to drive 100,000 miles is better than paying \$6,000.

The moment, however, we start to talk about economics, we encounter a problem. We know a lot about how much energy we *might* be able to save, but very little about how much we actually *can* save, or how much it will cost to do it. There are many books, including this one, that will tell you that investments in efficiency and renewables can save lots of energy and pay for themselves in a reasonable period of time. There are far fewer ones that tell you which investments have actually done it, and how much energy they have saved and how fast they paid their owners back.

The problem, simply, is a lack of good data. There is a lot of information about what things like cars and furnaces and windows and solar panels cost retail and how they work in tests. There is very little information about what they really cost to finance and install and service and operate, or how much money and energy they actually save. The information is not particularly hard to collect—all that is required is a notebook and diligence. But thus far it has rarely been done.

As a result, our discussions of energy and renewables tend to the theoretical. If someone says, "How much energy will I save?" we say, "You should be able to save a lot." But we can't say, "You will save this much by doing A, but it will be hard to finance and your return will be only 5%, while if you do B you save almost as much and your return will be 10%."

My proposal is that over the next 5 years we remedy this. Let's get the data, put it up on the web, cross-check it, and put it in a book. We could call it: *Which Renewables Work: Proven Strategies for Energy Investment.*

Our Assignment

Suppose five, or fifty, of us wanted to test and report on energy investment strategies. How would we proceed? The answer would likely be different for each of us. But there would be several common elements. We would each:

> Do an energy and carbon audit, using a form like that on p. 170. If we can break down our energy use by months, all the better.

Commit to reducing our carbon emissions by 3% or 5% per year, over the next 5 years.

Look at carbon-reducing options, and try to estimate their costs, savings, and payback periods. Throw out the ones that take longer than 10 years to pay back. That would be philanthropy and we can't sell philanthropy.

Pick the options that make sense to us and develop an energy investment strategy based on them. The strategy would be like building any other investment portfolio: we would devote a certain percentage of our income to building the portfolio, balancing safe low-return investments against riskier high-return ones.

Monitor the performance of these investments by keeping track of costs, energy purchases, and energy savings.

Create a website to share our findings and tell people what worked and what didn't. Four years from now, publish a book about what we learn.

To a scientist, and one trying to stay hopeful about climate and energy in the face of much discouraging news, this sounds like good fun. Are you interested?

This then, the notion that we have capability and resources and that it is time to start using them, is where I will leave you and the Adirondack story. We are Yankees and know about work and climate and getting things done. And as for discouragement, we know about that too, and how to face it down. Thoreau said that the mind has clouds, and we should pay them no heed. Dickinson said that hope perches in the soul and sings without words. And at Shiloh, with the Union Army routed and in disarray, when Sherman said, "Well, Grant, we've had the devil's own day, haven't we?" Grant replied, "Yes. Lick 'em tomorrow, though."

Cedar River Flow, August, 2009

APPENDIX: CALCULATING ENERGY AND EMISSIONS

The calculations in this book are, for the most part, quite simple and can be easily duplicated or adapted by anyone who is interested. Here are some basic units and quantities that were used frequently. Other data are available from the sources given in the notes (pp. 171–177), and www.convertunits.com is a convenient site for converting units. The tilde (~) is used for approximate equality.

Size kilo (k) = 10^3 mega (M) = 10^6 giga (G) = 10^9 tera (T) = 10^{12} peta (P) = 10^{15} exa (E) = 10^{18}

Length 1 foot = 0.305 meter 1 mile = 5,280 feet = 1,609 meters = 1.61 kilometers

Area 1 square foot = 0.0929 square meter 1 acre = 43,560 square feet = 4,047 square meters = 0.405 hectare 1 square mile = 640 acres = 2.59 square kilometers

Volume 1 cubic foot = 0.0283 cubic meter 1 gallon = 3.79 liters 1 barrel of petroleum = 42 gallons = 159 liters 1 cord of logs ~ 80 cubic feet of wood

Weight 1 pound = 0.454 kilogram 1 short (American) ton = 0.907 metric tonnes

Time 1 hour = 3,600 seconds 1 day = 86,400 seconds 1 year = 8,766 hours = 31.6 million seconds

Energy 1 kilowatt-hour (kWh) = 1,000 Watt-hours = 0.114 Watt-year = 3,600,000 joules = 3,412 BTUs = 860,421 calories

Power 1 Watt (W) = 1 joule/second = 8.76 kilowatt-hours/year = 3.41 BTUs per hour = 29,910 BTUs per year = 860 calories per hour 1 horsepower = 746 watts

Temperature 1 degree Fahrenheit = 0.556 degree Celsius

Energy Content and Carbon Emissions

	Energy (kWh)	CO_2 Emitted (lbs)	CO_2 per Energy (pounds per kWh)
1 tonne oil equivalent	12,000		
1 barrel crude oil	1,700		
1 gallon gasoline	37	20	0.5
1 gallon kerosene	40	21	0.5
1 gallon 85% ethanol	29	12	0.4
1 gallon diesel	40	22	0.5
1 gallon heating oil	39	22	0.5
1 gallon #6 oil	42	26	0.6
1 gallon propane	27	13	0.5
1 cubic foot natural gas	0.30	0.12	0.4
1 ton hard coal	7,400	5,700	0.8
1 lb hardwood, 20% moisture	1.7	1.5	0.8
1 lb hardwood, 40% moisture	1.2	1.1	0.9
1 cord hardwood, 20% moisture	6,300	5,600	0.9
1 kilowatt-hour NYS electricity	1	0.85	0.85
1 kilowatt-hour electricity from coal	1	2.3	2.3

Because fuels vary in composition, the energy and carbon values in the table are approximate, and the carbon-to-energy ratios even more so. The values for wood are "low heat values" which assume that the stove or boiler will not recover the energy in the steam.

Calculating Energy and Carbon Budgets

The table on p. 169 can be used to create energy and carbon budgets. For example:

If a family uses 100 gallons of gas this equals 100 gal * 37 kWh/gal * 1 W/8.7 kWh = 420 watts of power, and 100 gal * 20 lbs CO2/gal = 2,000 lbs CO2 = 1 ton.

If the family drives 10,000 miles in a car that gets 25 miles per gallon, this requires 10,000 miles/25 mpg = 40 gallons of gas. By a calculation similar to the one above, this is 168 watts of power and 0.4 ton of carbon.

Here is a worked-out example, based on the imaginary Adirondack family introduced on p. 21. The calculations have been simplified by using a power factor and a carbon factor. You can use these factors to do your own calculations.

SAMPLE WATTAGE AND CARBON BUDGETS

FUEL		POWER FACTOR	WATTS	CO2 FACTOR	TONS CO2	
50	Gasoline, gallons	4.2	210	0.001	0.5	
500	Fuel oil, kerosene, gallons	4.6	2,330	0.011	5.5	
30	Propane, gallons	3.0	90	0.0064	0.2	
2	Wood, full cords	720	[1,440]	[2.8]	[5.6]	
	Coal, tons	820		2.8		
	Total fossil fuel		2,630		6.2	

ELECTRICITY

4,000	Kilowatt-hours from grid	0.11	440	0.00043	1.7	
	Kilowatt-hours from renewables	0.11		0		

TRANSPORT

15,000	Miles, car 1	4.2/mpg	2,400	0.01/mpg	5.8	
5,000	Miles, car 2	4.2/mpg	1,050	0.01/mpg	2.5	
	Miles, train	0.03		0.00004		
1,000	Miles, bus	0.04	40	0.0001	0.1	
	Miles, intercontinental air	0.05		0.00011		
12,000	Miles, domestic air	0.08	960	0.00017	2	
1,000	Miles, bicycle	0.003	[3]	0.00001	[0.01]	
	Fossil fuel transport		4,450		10.4	
TOTAL FOSSIL FUEL			7,520		18.3	

The values for the wood and the bicycle are bracketed because they don't go into the fossil fuel totals.

SOURCES AND NOTES

Frequently Used Sources

AA Jenkins, J., 2004. *The Adirondack Atlas: A Geographic Portrait of the Adirondack Park.* Syracuse University Press. Syracuse, NY.

BP British Petroleum Company, 2007. *BP Statistical Review of World Energy, June, 2007.* British Petroleum Company, www.bp.com/statisticalreview.

CCNE Frumhoff, P.C., McCarthy, J.J., Mellilo, J.M., Moser, S.C., and Wuebbles, D.J., 2007. *Confronting Climate Change in the U.S. Northeast: Science, Impacts, Solutions.* Union of Concerned Scientists. Cambridge, MA. http://www.ucsusa.org/publications/.

CW Climate Wizard, www.climatewizard.org.

DCC Schellnhuber, H.J., Cramer, W., Nakicenovic, N., Wigley, T., and Yohe, G., ed., 2006. *Avoiding Dangerous Climate Change.* Cambridge University Press. Cambridge, England.

DM MacKay, D.J.C., 2009. *Sustainable Energy—Without the Hot Air.* UIT. Cambridge, England.

EE Ecology and Environment, 2009. *Draft Adirondack Park Greenhouse Gas Inventory.* Ecology and Environment. Lancaster, NY.

EIA Energy Information Agency of the United States Department of Energy, www.eia.doe.gov.

GF McMartin, B., 1994. *The Great Forest of the Adirondacks.* North Country Books. Utica, NY.

HCN United States Historical Climatology Network, http://cdiac.ornl.gov/epubs/ndp/ushcn/ushcn.html.

HLM Hendrickson, C.T., Lave, L.B., and Matthews, H.S., 2006. *Environmental Life Cycle Assessment of Goods and Services: An Input-Output Approach.* Resources For the Future Press. Washington, DC.

IEA International Energy Agency, 2007. *Key World Energy Statistics.* International Energy Agency. Paris, France. www.iea.org.

IPCC Intergovernmental Panel on Climate Change, 2007. *Climate Change 2007. Volume I, The Physical Science Basis. Volume II, Impacts, Adaptation, and Vulnerability. Volume III, Mitigation of Climate Change.* Cambridge University Press. Cambridge, England.

LB Jenkins, J., 2004, 2007. *The State of the Adirondack Lowland Boreal, Part I: Composition and Geography: Part II: Changes and Threats.* Wildlife Conservation Society and Adirondack Nature Conservancy. Saranac Lake, NY.

MK McKinsey and Company, 2007. *Reducing U.S. Greenhouse Gas Emissions: How Much at What Cost?* McKinsey and Company. New York, NY.

ML Lynas, M., 2008. *Six Degrees: Our Future on a Hotter Planet.* National Geographic. Washington, DC.

NECIA Northeastern Climate Impacts Assessment, 2006. *Climate Change in the U.S. Northeast.* Northeastern Climate Impacts Assessment. Cambridge, MA. www.northeastclimateimpacts.org, www.northeastclimatedata.org.

NSIDC National Snow and Ice Data Center, http://nsidc.org.

VS Smil, V., 2008. *Energy in Nature and Society: General Energetics of Complex Systems.* MIT Press. Cambridge, MA.

WEB Gipe, P., 2009. *Wind Energy Basics: A Guide to Home- and Community-Scale Wind Systems.* Second Edition. Chelsea Green. White River Junction, VT.

WM Weber, C.L., and Matthews, H.S., 2008. "Food-miles and the relative climate impacts of food choices in the United States." *Environmental Science and Technology* 42: 3508-3513.

Other Useful Sources

Bioenergy Conversion Factors, http://bioenergy.ornl.gov/papers/misc/energy_conv.html.

Convert Units, www.convertunits.com.

Database of State Incentives for Renewables, www.dsireusa.org.

Dot Earth, http://dotearth.blogs.nytimes.com.

Input-output life-cycle analysis software, www.eiolca.net.

New York State Energy Research and Development Authority, www.nyserda.org.

New York State Power Naturally, www.powernaturally.com.

Real Climate, www.realclimate.org.

Wind Works, www.wind-works.org.

Sources of Graphs and Illustrations

Except as noted below, all graphs, illustrations, and photographs are by the author.

Preface

p. viii Data for graph from EIA.

p. ix-x Maps from AA, updated by author. *For more detail:* See Terrie, P.C., 1997. *Contested Terrain: A New History of Nature and People in the Adirondacks.* Adirondack Museum and Syracuse University Press. Blue Mountain Lake and Syracuse, NY; GF; Porter, W.F., Erickson, J.D., and Whaley, R.S., 2009. *The Great Experiment in Conservation: Voices from the Adirondack Park.* Syracuse University Press. Syracuse, NY; and AA.

p. xi Map based on images from the NASA MODIS program, http://earthobservatory.nasa.gov/Newsroom/view.php?id=22585.

p. xiii *hypothetical Adirondack family:* Described on p. 21.

PART I: THE CLIMATE PROBLEM

1 Introduction: We Have a Climate Problem

p. 1 *average temperatures:* Data from HCN. The red line used here and in other climate graphs is a type of sliding average (p. xiii) called a locally weighted scatterplot regression (LOESS regression) that weights the datapoints so the ones farther away from the year whose value is being estimated count less.

p. 2 *Yearly Flows of Carbon*: Data from IPCC I, p. 515. *World Carbon Emissions, Atmospheric Carbon Dioxide*: Data from IPCC I.

p. 3 *Average Northern New York Temperatures*: The observed temperatures are computed from HCN. The high- and low-emission predictions are from NECIA, p. 10. They are computed by taking high-emission and low-emission scenarios, similar to those illustrated on p. 27, running them through three widely used climate models and averaging the results. *With 5 to 10 degrees of rise*: See p. 28. *An Adirondack rise of 10 degrees requires a world temperature rise of 6 degrees*: Obtained by comparing the predictions of NECIA and IPCC II for similar scenarios. *This conclusion is now widely accepted by climate scientists*: ML, DCC, IPCC II, and Lenton, T.M. et al., 2008. "Tipping elements in the earth's climate system." *Proceedings of the National Academy of Sciences* 105(6): 1786-1793; and Krieglera, E., et al., 2009. "Imprecise probability assessment of tipping points in the climate system." *Proceedings of the National Academy of Sciences*, in press. For calculations suggesting that we have already reached the point of dangerous and accelerating change, see Hansen, J., et al., 2008. "Target atmospheric CO$_2$: Where should humanity aim?" *Open Atmospheric Science Journal* 2: 217-231.

2 The Weather Is Changing

Except as noted, the graphs in this chapter use data from HCN and NSIDC. The trend lines are LOWESS regressions; see note to p. 3.

p. 4 *spring, summer, and winter averages*: The meteorological seasons are DJF, MAM, JJA, and SON. *statistically significant*: With the probabilty of 0.05 or less that a trend this great could be obtained by chance. *2.7 degrees per 100 years.* This and other trends are obtained by linear regression.

p.5 *annual, summer, and winter trends are statistically significant*: Stager, J.C., et al. "Historical patterns and effects of changes in Adirondack climates since the early 20th century." *Adirondack Journal of Environmental Studies* 15(2): 14-24, found that the trends in individual months for a similar group of Adirondack HCN stations were not statistically significant but did not examine seasonal or annual trends.

p. 6 *Change in Average Winter Temperature*: Burakowski, E., and Wake, C., 2009. *The Changing Character of Winter Climate in the Northeast United States.* Clean Air Cool Planet. New Canaan, CT, redrawn with permission. See also Burakowski, E., et al., 2008. "Trends in wintertime climate in the northeastern United States: 1965-2005." *Journal of Geophysical Research Atmospheres*: 113 D20114.

p. 8 *Heavy Precipitation Events*: Graph by Art DeGaetano, redrawn with permission. *Climate models suggest.* See NECIA or www.climatewizard.org.

p. 9 *Days with Snow on the Ground*: Graph from Burakowski, E., and Wake, C., op.cit., redrawn with permission. *Center-of-Volume Dates*: Graph from Hodgkins, G.A., Dudley, R.W., and Huntington, T.G., 2003. "Changes in the timing of high river flows in New England over the 20th century." *Journal*

of Hydrology 278: 244-252, redrawn with permission. All the curves show an inflection point around 1965, suggesting that the change to warmer winters began abruptly and synchronously across northern New England. *more transport of the nitrogen acids that accumulate in forests impacted by acid rain*: See Jenkins, 2007. op. cit., Chapter 5.

3 The Climate Problem Is an Energy Problem

The national and world data used in the graphs in this chapter are from EIA. Useful general treatments are BP, VS, and Cleveland, C.J., et al., 1984. "Energy and the U.S. economy: A biophysical perspective." *Science* 225: 890-897.

p. 11 *In 1800 the human energy supply was 90% biomass*: VP, p. 375.

p. 12 *New hydroelectric reservoirs emit greenhouse gases*: VS, pp. 249-256.

p. 13 *a few pieces of toast*: Ten watts of power is about a quarter of a kilowatt-hour per day. This would run a toaster or a hot plate for about fifteen minutes.

p. 14 *do not have enough to live comfortably*: VS, pp. 346-349, shows that a number of basic measures of human welfare rise quickly with rises in per capita energy up to two kilowatts, more slowly from two kilowatts to five kilowatts, and then flatten off and hardly change between five and ten kilowatts.

p. 15 *Horsepower and Person Power*: The input power is the rate at which an animal or an engine is consuming fuel; the output power is the rate at which mechanical work is being done. The numbers are from VP, pp. 138, 155-156. I assume that horse and man are working steadily at a rate they can keep up for much of the day and convert about 20% of the energy in their food into mechanical work.

p. 16 *Water Power and Wood Heat*: For sizes of waterwheels see VS, p. 183. Forges came in all sizes. I have pictured a forge near the small end of those reported in McMartin, B., 1994. *The Great Forest of the Adirondacks.* North Country Books. Utica, NY, p. 35, and assumed a consumption of 300 bushels of charcoal per ton of iron. The heat input is the heat from the charcoal; the energy in the wood used to make the charcoal would be three to six times more. *Half of a kilowatt-hour of mechanical work in a day*: VP says that human beings at peak output can do 2.8 kWh of work in a day. Most farm activities are less intense and might total 0.5 kWh of work per day. A pint of gasoline in a combustion engine yields 1.2 kWh of mechanical energy.

p. 17 *Adirondack Heat Engines, ca. 1900*: These numbers are mostly guesses. The output power of 19th-century engines was rarely measured directly, and even more rarely reported. *The largest ones.* The largest engines used in commercial planes have a thrust of 500,000 Newtons and are about 30% efficient. If this thrust was applied at cruising speed, it would represent an output power of over 100,000 watts. The largest ship diesels have output powers of about 80,000 watts and, at 50% efficiency, are the most efficient internal combustion engines ever made.

p. 18 *Adirondack Heat Engines, 2000*: The powers are estimated from published rates of fuel consumption. All of these are average powers under cruising or light working conditions. *Thomas Edison's first U.S. powerhouse*: VP, pp. 235-236.

p. 19 *Energy Inputs to an Acre of U.S. Corn*: Data from Pimentel, D. and Pimentel, M.H., 2008. *Food, Energy and Society*. Third edition. CRC Press. Boca Raton, FL, p. 142. *Energy Embedded in Foods and Materials*. Compiled from energy densities cited in DM and VS. *The computer…has about 1,500 kilowatt-hours of embedded energy*. For the embedded energy in computers and cars, see HLM, DM, p. 94, and VS, p. 289. I assume here that a year of hard manual work might produce 300 kilowatt-hours of energy.

p. 20 *Direct Energy Use of an Adirondack Fossil Fuel Household*: The household is imaginary, but based on real ones we sampled. The conversion factors used to get the wattage are given on p. 169. *an average American diet represents an energy flow of about 750 watts per person*: Back-calculated from the carbon emissions given in WM. An alternate calculation assuming a diet of 2,400 kilocalories per day, split equally between meat, fats, and carbohydrates and using the values for embedded energy from the graph on p. 19, gives 550 watts. If you add an additional 1.3 kWh per pound for processing and retailing, you are up to 700 watts. DM, p. 79, estimates the average British diet at 600 watts. None of these estimates include energy in the food that is wasted: by some estimates this is 25% or more of all the food produced in the United States.

p. 23 *Resources Required to Replace 2.8 Trillion Watts of Fossil Fuels*: Assumptions: 1.5 MW wind turbines with a capacity factor of 0.3, capable of extracting 2 W of power per square meter of land; solar panels with a power density of 20 W/ sq. m; 1 GW nuclear plants with a capacity factor of 95%, each using a square mile of land; forests producing biomass energy at at the rate of 0.1 W/sq. m; croplands producing, 0.2 W/sq. m. The conversion factors for power densities are 1 W/sq. m = 4,040 W/acre = 2,600,000 W/sq. mile. *area the size of Vermont*: Vermont is 9,600 square miles, Oregon 98,000 square miles, the lower forty-eight 2,900,000 square miles, and the whole United States 3,500,000 square miles.

p. 24 *coal mines and oil fields produce energy at densities of 2,000 watts per square meter*: VS, p. 376.

4 How Much Could the Adirondacks Change?

General references: CCNE, CW, DCC, IPCC II, ML. Two useful syntheses are Hayhoe, K., et al., 2008. "Regional climate change projections for the Northeast U.S." *Mitigation and Adaptation Strategies for Global Change*, in press; and Hayhoe, K., et al., 2007. "Past and future changes in climate and hydrological indicators in the U.S. Northeast." *Climate Dynamics* 28(4): 381-407.

p. 25 *Estimated Reserves of Fossil Fuels*: Data from IPCC III, p. 264. See Smil, V., 2003. *Energy at the Crossroads: Global Perspectives and Uncertainties*. MIT Press. Cambridge, MA, for a discussion of the uncertainties involved.

p. 26 *Chemical Removal of Carbon Dioxide From the Atmosphere*: Based on Sarmiento, J.L., and Gruber, N., 2006. *Ocean Biogeochemical Dynamics*. Princeton University Press. Princeton, NJ, p. 403. Archer, D., et al.., 2009. "Atmospheric lifetime of fossil fuel carbon dioxide." *Annual Review of Earth*

and Planetary Sciences 37: 117-34, is a recent review and Chapter 6 of Archer, D., 2009. *The Long Thaw: How Humans Are Changing the Next 100,000 Years of Earth's Climate*. Princeton University Press. Princeton, NJ, an accessible summary.

Results of Using Up Fossil Fuels: Assumptions: that 50% of the carbon emitted from the burning of fossil fuels will be removed by forests and the ocean, and that atmospheric CO_2 will rise 1 ppm for every 7.6 billion tonnes of CO_2 that stay in the atmosphere. Since the percentage of CO_2 removed will decline as forests saturate and the seas become more acid, this underestimates the rise in CO_2 that may occur.

p. 27 *Three Scenarios for Stabilizing CO$_2$*: Based scenarios III, IV, and VI from IPCC III, p. 16. Actual emissions from EIA.

p. 28 *Adirondack Temperature Versus CO$_2$*: Original figure based on a similar figure for world temperatures in IPCC III, p. 16. Assumes, as per NECIA, that our temperature rise will be 1.7 times the world temperature rise.

p. 30 *Number of Adirondack Forest Species*: Mammals are not included because they have wide ecological latitude and can't be separated into forest and nonforest species. Overall, about 60% of our mammals are found in the southern Appalachians.

p. 31 *Predicted Changes in Winter Snow Cover*: Based on maps from NECIA. *Changes in Suitability*. Data from Iverson, L., Prasad, A., and Matthews, S., 2008. "Potential changes in suitable habitat for 134 tree species in the northeastern United States." *Mitigation and Adaptation Strategies for Global Change*, in press. The suitability of the habitat is modeled as a combination of soil and climate factors that predict a species' current abundance. The models don't take competition into account and don't predict how fast the species will respond.

p. 32 *Most of the others migrate slowly*: In the last major warming, in the postglacial, trees moved northwards at 20 miles per century or less. Recent studies of the dispersal of forest interior plants show that many of them may move less than a kilometer in a century.

5 What We Might Lose

General sources: AA; LB; Scott, D., Dawson, J., and Jones, B., 2008. "Climate change vulnerability of the U.S. northeast winter recreation-tourism sector." *Mitigation and Adaptation Strategies for Global Change*, in press; Rodenhouse, N.L., et al., 2008. "Potential effects of climate change on birds of the Northeast." *Mitigation and Adaptation Strategies for Global Change*, in press.

p. 35 *Alpine Vegetation in the High Peaks*: From data supplied by Tim Howard of the New York Natural Heritage Program.

p. 36 *forest and krummholtz plants are moving uphill*: See Lenoir, J., et al., 2008. "A significant upward shift of plant species optimum elevation during the 20th century." *Science* 320: 1768-1771; Lesicaac, P., and McCune, B., 2004. "Decline of arctic-alpine plants at the southern margin of their range following a decade of climatic warming." *Journal of Vegetation Science* 15(5): 679-690.

p. 37 Maps from AA, based on National Wetlands Inventory maps prepared by the Adirondack Park Agency. *I have written about it*: LB.

p. 40 *Rare and Uncommon Plants*: From data gathered by the author, 1982 to 2007. *Temperature Limits*: Prepared by plotting published distribution records against isotherms of temperature.

p. 41 *Rare Plants in the Hudson River Ice Meadows*: From research by the author, 1988-1996. *Recent studies have found this is happening in many places in the north*: LB.

p. 42 *WCS Boreal Bird Survey Records*: From research done by Michale Glennon of the Wildlife Conservation Society and her colleagues. *Temperature Limits*: Prepared by plotting published distribution records against isotherms of temperature.

p. 45 *Winter Sports I*: Photos courtesy of the New York State archives, the Adirondack Collection at the Saranac Lake Free Library, and the 1932 & 1980 Lake Placid Winter Olympic Museum, used with permission.

p. 46 *Adirondack Winter Sports*: From material gathered by Elizabeth McKenna.

p. 47 *Winter Sports II*: Photos © Nancie Battaglia, used with permission.

p. 48 *Old Forge area*: Data gathered by Elizabeth McKenna.

p. 49 Maps adapted from AA.

p. 50 *New York Ski Areas*: Snow cover from the NECIA. Ski areas and clubs from www.nensa.net/clubs/club_list1.php and other ski associations. Small ski areas open and close frequently, and the existing maps tend to be out of date and do not always agree with each other.

p. 50 Photo from the 1932 & 1980 Lake Placid Winter Olympic Museum, used with permission.

6 Biology and Recreation Are Changing

General references: Parmesan, C., 2006. "Ecological and evolutionary responses to recent climate change." *Annual Review of Ecology and Systematics* 37: 637-69; Barnosky, A.D., 2009. *Heatstroke: Nature in an Age of Global Warming.* Island Press. Washington, DC, and other references cited in these publications.

p. 53 *Changes in Average Dates When Frogs Begin Calling*: Data from Gibbs, J.P., and Breisch, A.R., 2001. "Climate warming and calling phenology of frogs near Ithaca, New York, 1900-1999." *Conservation Biology* 15(4): 1175-1178. *Dates of Spring Wildflowers*: Data from Miller-Rushing, A.J., and Primack, R.B., 2008. "Global warming and flowering times in Thoreau's Concord: A community perspective." *Ecology* 89(2): 232-241.

p. 54 *Bird migration dates are also changing*: Miller-Rushing, A.J., et al., 2008. "Bird migration times, climate change, and changing population size." *Global Change Biology* 14: 1959-1972. *Several Adirondack data sets*: Stager, J.C., et al. "Historical patterns and effects of changes in Adirondack climates since the early 20th century." *Adirondack Journal*

of Environmental Studies 15(2): 14-24. *Days of Snow During Deer Season*: Data from HCN.

p. 55 *An analysis of the Concord Flowering dates*: Willis, C.G., et al., C.C., 2008. "Phylogenetic patterns of species loss in Thoreau's woods are driven by climate change." *Procedings of the National Academy of Sciences* 105(44): 17029-17033. *Pied flycatcher*: Both, C., et al., 2006. "Climate change and population declines in a long-distance migratory bird." *Nature* 44: 81-83. *Expansion of Southern Species*: References for this section are the general references for the chapter, plus Gibbons, J.W., et al., 2000. "The global decline of reptiles, déjà vu amphibians." *BioScience* 50(8): 653-666; Hickling, R., et al., 2006. "The distributions of a wide range of taxonomic groups are expanding polewards." *Global Change Biology* 12: 450-455; Myers, p., et al., 2009. "Climate-induced changes in the small mammal communities of the Northern Great Lakes Region." *Climate Change Biology,* in press; Pauli, H., et al., 2007. "Signals of range expansions and contractions of vascular plants in the high Alps.'" *Global Change Biology,* 13: 147-156; and Woodall, C.W., et al., 2009. "An indicator of tree migration in forests of the eastern United States." *Forest Ecology and Management* 257: 1434-1444.

p. 56 *Expansion of Southern Birds*: Based on an analysis of checklists and breeding bird atlases by the author.

p. 57 *Mountain Pine Beetle*: Kurz, W.A., et al., 2008. "Mountain pine beetle and forest carbon feedback to climate change." *Nature* 452: 987-990. *Hemlock wooly adelgid*: Paradis, A., et al., 2008. "Effect of winter temperatures on the survival of hemlock woolly adelgid, *Adelges tsugae*, and the potential impact of global warming on its future range in eastern North America." *Mitigation and Adaptation Strategies for Global Change*, in press.

p. 58 *Lyme Disease Risk*: Data from American Lyme Disease Foundation, www.aldf.com/usmap.shtml. Rick Ostfeld is preparing a book on the ecology of Lyme disease, to appear in 2010.

p. 59 *Distances of Southern Animals*: Data from published range maps.

p. 60 *Decline of the Cut-Leaved Anemone*: Data gathered by the author and Debbie Benjamin. *Are cold-climate species dying off*: For the examples mentioned here, see Parmesan, 2006. op. cit. and Barnosky, 2009. op. cit.

p. 61 *Adirondack Spruce Grouse*: Data from Ross, A. M., and Johnson, G., 2008. *Spruce Grouse in the Lowland Boreal Forests of New York State: Distribution, Movements, and Habitat.* N.Y.S. Department of Environmental Conservation, Report AMO5122.

p. 62 *Number of Blocks Occupied by Boreal Species*: Data from the NY.S. Breeding Bird Atlas, www.dec.ny.gov/animals/51030.html.

p. 65 *Retreat of Boreal Trees*: Data from Beckage, B., et al., 2008. "A rapid upward shift of a forest ecotone during 40 years of warming in the Green Mountains of Vermont." www.pnas.org/cgi/doi/10.1073/pmas.0708921105. *Changes in Boreal Communities*: For a review, see LB.

p. 65 *Snowmobile Trail Passes*: Data supplied by the town of Webb.

p. 66 *Downhill Ski Areas in Western New England*: Data from the New England Lost Ski Areas Project, www.nelsap.org, and personal communications from ski areas. For a similar decline in New Hampshire, see Hamilton, L.C., et al., 2003. "Warming winters and New Hampshire's lost ski areas: An integrated case study." *International Journal of Sociology and Social Policy* 23:52-73; and Hamilton, L.C., Brown, C., and Keim, B.D., 2007. "Ski areas, weather, and climate: Time series models for New England case studies." *International Journal of Climatology* 27: 2113-**2124.**

PART II: AN ADIRONDACK STRATEGY

7 Assessment: Adirondack Carbon Emissions

pp. 69-72 General emissions data from EIA. For a summary of emission factors, see pp. 169-170.

p. 72 *Carbon Emissions From Transport*: Data from DM and the author's estimates.

p. 73 *trains are skinny compared to their length*: For vehicles at constant speed, much of the energy goes to overcoming air resistance, which depends on the frontal area. Long vehicles have about the energy requirements as short ones but spread it over more passengers. *Food Availability*: Data from USDA Economic Research Service, http://ers.usda.gov/data/foodconsumption. *Greenhouse Emissions From This Food*: Data from WM.

p. 74 *Greenhouse Gas Emissions From the U.S. Food Supply*: Data from WM.

p. 75 *Carbon Emissions from Producing Goods and Services*: Data from eiolca.net. *input-output analysis*: An input-output analysis divides the U.S. economy sectors and tabulates how much energy each sector uses, how much pollution each emits, and what materials and services each sector buys from every other. Using this information, it is possible to estimate the average greenhouse emissions of each sector, per $1,000 of product. See HLM for details.

p. 76 *Carbon Costs of Life*: Data from www.eiolca.net.

p. 77 *Estimating a Household Carbon Budget*: Estimate uses the emissions factors on p. 169.

pp. 77-79 *Real Adirondack Households*: Data gathered by the Wildlife Conservation Society Adirondack Program.

p. 80 *Hamlet of Wanakena*: Data gathered by author.

p. 81 *Estimated Carbon Emissions for the Town of Fine*: Data from Paul Alioto, Mark Hall, EIA, and U.S. Census.

p. 82 *The Whole Park*: Data from EE, with additional information from Levi Durham.

8 Reduction: Low-Carbon Transport

General references: DM; Davis, S., Diegel, S.W., and Boundy, R.G, 2008. *Transportation Energy Data Book*. Edition 27. Oak Ridge National Laboratory. Oak Ridge, TE, www.cta.ornl.gov/data.

p. 84 *When used in vehicles it will produce about 4,000 kilowatt-hours of mechanical energy*: Based on an average efficiency of about 25% for combustion engines.

p. 85 *Energy Cost of Transport*: From DM, p. 128, and fuel-consumption data gathered by the author. The vehicles are assumed to be at cruising speed; those in the right-hand column are assumed to be carrying a single passenger. Since energy per mile depends sensitively on speed, the numbers are only approximate.

p. 86 *Public Transportation*: Data from www.amtrack.com, www.trailways.com, and www.tupperlakeinfo.com/community/publictransport.htm.

p. 87 *Three Strategies to Emit Less Carbon*: Assumptions: gas is $2.96 per gallon, the Prius costs $23,000 and gets 48 miles per gallon. Financing costs are not included. *Where the Energy in the Gas Goes*. The analysis is based on DM, chapter A, and is approximate; it assumes that the rolling resistance is 0.01, the effective drag area is 0.95 square meters the mileage at 60 mph is 25 mpg, and the engine efficiency is 25%.

p. 90 *Toyota Prius*. Assumptions: rolling resistance = 0.01, effective drag area = 0.66 sq. m, mileage at 60 mph = 52 mpg, and the engine efficiency is 28%.

pp. 90-93 *Electric Cars*: Data from en.wikipedia.org/wiki/Chevrolet_Volt; www.phoenixmotorcars.com; www.think.no; www.miniusa.com/minie-usa; www.teslamotors.com; www.goingreen.co.uk/store; www.aptera.com; www.mitsubishi-motors.com/special/ev.

pp. 94-95 *The Bottom Line*: Data from manufacturer's web sites; carbon and economic assumptions shown in notes to graphs.

9 Reduction: Low-Carbon Buildings

General references: DM, chapter E; Harley, B., and Gifford, A., 2005. *Field Guide: Residential New Construction*. Conservation Services Group. Westover, MA, www.dos.state.ny.us/code/energycode/Forms_code/NYguide.pdf; and Low Energy House, www.lowenergyhouse.com.

p. 97 *Energy Used in Buildings*: Back-calculated from carbon data in EE. *80,000 private houses*: Data from AA.

p. 98 *Energy Use by an Average Household*: Data from EIA residential survey.

p. 99 *The Heating Demand in Lake Placid*: Data from HCN.

p. 100 *Energy Consumption for Different Indoor Temperatures*: Calculated from the demand curve for Lake Placid on p. 99. *Average Size of New Single-Family Houses*: Data from EIA.

p. 101 *having a more efficient machine has no effect if you turn around and use it more*: This is what economists call a rebound effect or Jevon's Paradox, for William Stanley Jevons, a 19th-century British economist who discovered that as steam engines grew more efficient, British industry used more coal.

p. 102 *Heat Losses From Two New Houses*: Data from Harris, J., and Blasnik, M., 2007. *Reference Design Guide for Highly Energy Efficient Residential Construction*. Vermont Energy Investment Corporation. Burlington, VT.

p. 103 *Solar Gain and Solar Design*: Based on Kachadorian, J., 2006. *The Passive Solar House*. Chelsea Green. White River Junction, VT; and Mazria, E., 1979. *The Passive Solar Energy*

Book: A Complete Guide to Passive solar Home, Greenhouse, and Building Design. Rodale Press. Emmaus, PA.

p. 104 *Heat Pump*: General references: Banks, D., 2008. *An Introduction to Thermogeology: Ground Source Heating and Cooling.* Blackwell Publishing. Oxford, U.K.; and Ochsner, K., 2008. *Geothermal Heat Pumps: A Guide for Planning and Installing.* Earthscan. Sterling, VA. For efficiency measurements on a heat pump system just north of the Adirondacks, see www.fs.fed.us/sustainableoperations/susops-summit-2008/Tyree_Net-Zero_Energy_Houses-OurFuture.ppt.

p. 107 *Energy Needed to Heat Houses*: based on Harris and Blasnik, 2007. op. cit.; Aulisi, S., and McGilvray, D., n.d. *House Warming.* Adirondack Alternate Energy. Edinburg, NY; and data collected by the author.

p. 109 *Hot Water*: Data for average households from EIA residential survey.

p. 111 *Hot Water Systems Compared*: Assumed efficiencies are given in the text. The total power requirements of solar hot-water systems are poorly documented and uncertain; my estimate is based on data from www.energystar.gov/index.cfm?c=solar_wheat.pr_solar_wheat and www.solar-rating.org.

p. 112 *Energy Consumption of Refrigerators*: Data from www.energystar.gov/index.cfm?c=refrig.pr_refrigerators.

10 Replacement: Low-Carbon Energy

General references: DM; WEB; American Wind Energy Association, www.awea.org; Biomass Energy Resource Center, www.biomasscenter.org; Goodall, C., 2008. *Ten Technologies to Save the Planet.* Profile Books. London; National Renewable Energy Laboratory, http://www.nrel.gov/; New York State Power Naturally, www.powernaturally.com; Nuttall, W.J., 2005. *Nuclear Renaissance: Technologies and Policies for the Future of Nuclear Power.* Taylor & Francis. New York NY.; Pahl, G., 2007. *The Citizen-Powered Energy Handbook: Community Solutions to a Global Crisis.* Chelsea Green. White River Junction, VT; Ramlow, B., 2006. *Solar Water Heating: A Comprehensive Guide to Solar Water and Space-Heating Systems.* New Society Publishers. Gabriola Island, BC, Canada; Renewable Energy Laboratory, n.d. *Community Wind Power Fact Sheets 1–7.* University of Massachusetts. Amherst, MA, www.ceere.org/rerl; Smil, V., 2005. *Energy at the Crossroads: Global Perspectives and Uncertainties.* MIT Press. Cambridge, MA; Union of Concerned Scientists, 2007. *Biofuels: An Important Part of a Low-Carbon Diet.* Union of Concerned Scientists. Cambridge, MA, www.ucsusa.org; and Wind Works, www.wind-works.org.

p. 115 *Average Solar Energy in the Adirondacks*: Data on solar beam from www.nrel.gov; penetration of solar heat into the ground approximated with a solution to the 1-dimensional diffusion equation given in DM, p. 306. *A 15-mile-per hour wind has a power of about 300 watts per square meter*: WEB.

p. 116 *average power produced by a PV system*: Data gathered by the author.

p. 117 *a liberal program of incentives*: Based on information from www.nyserda.org and recent quotes from solar install-

ers. *Solar Hot Water*: Section based on Ramlow, op. cit. and data from www.solar-rating.org.

p. 118 *Hydropower*: Data on the Adirondack stations from the EIA generator database; capacity factor for New York calculated from EIA data on renewables.

p. 119 *Big Wind*: Data from EIA, www.windpoweringamerica.gov/wind_installed_capacity.asp and www.awea.org.

p. 120 *Northern New York got its first commercial wind farm in 2004*: Data from www.horizonwind.com/projects/whatwevedone/mapleridge and www.noblepower.com/our-windparks/index.html.

p. 121 *Bergey 10-Kilowatt Turbine*: Drawing based on http://bergey.com/Products/Excel.Description.html. *With state and federal incentives*: As given by www.powernaturally.com and www.dsireusa.org.

p. 122 *Woody Biomass*: Prices and general information supplied by Kamalesh Dushi of the Biomass Research Institute, Montpelier, VT.

p. 123 *To get a sense of the amount of land involved*: See p. 135 for an estimate of the growth rate of Adirondack forests.

p. 124 *Biomass electric plants burning green wood are about 30% efficient*: Based on data from the McNeil Generating Station in Burlington, VT, www.burlingtonelectric.com. *Biodiesel*: See Pahl, G., 2008. *Biodiesel: Growing a New Energy Economy.* Second edition. Chelsea Green. White River Junction, VT. *Cellulosic ethanol*: See Goodall, op. cit.

p. 125 *Shallow Geothermal Energy*: Data on costs gathered by the author. For the power density, see the note to p. 115; the capacity factor is uncertain.

p. 126 *Nuclear Energy*: Data from www.world-nuclear.org/info/inf41.html. For general discussions of safety issues and nuclear prospect, see Goodall, op. cit.; Nuttall, op. cit.; and Gronlund, L., Lochbaum, D., and Lyman, E., 2007. *Nuclear Power in a Warming World: Assessing the Risks, Addressing the Challenges.* Union of Concerned Scientists. Cambridge, MA, pubs@ucsusa.org. *Major civilian reactor accidents*: Information from www.atomicarchive.com.

pp. 128–129 *Renewables Compared*: The graphs use the costs and power densities given in previous sections of the chapter.

11 Offsets: Carbon in Adirondack Forests

p. 130 *Computer-generated map from forest inventory data*: From Ruefenacht, B., et al., 2008. "Conterminous U.S. and Alaska forest type mapping using forest inventory and analysis data." *Photogrammetric Engineering & Remote Sensing* 74(11): 1379–1388. *World forests absorb 3 billion tons of carbon a year*: From IPCC I. Note that, following ecological practice, carbon flows in this chapter are given in tons of carbon, not tons of CO_2.

p. 133 *Carbon Flows in a Hemlock Stand*: Data from http://harvardforest.fas.harvard.edu:8080/exist/xquery/data.xq?id=hf103. *Carbon Storage in a Northeastern Maple-Birch-Beech Forest*: Data from Smith, J.E., et al., 2006. *Methods for Calculating Forest Ecosystem and Harvested Carbon With*

Standard Estimates for the Forest Types of the United States. United States Department of Agriculture, Forest Service, General Technical Report NE-343.

p. 134 *Annual Flow of Carbon in Two-Hundred-Year-Old Temperate and Boreal Forests*: Data from Luyssaert, S., et al., 2008. "Old-growth forests as global carbon sinks." *Nature* 455: 213–215. *The Adirondacks have about 2.6 million acres of forested private land*: Data from AA. *Great fires that burned a sixth of the Adirondacks*: AA, p. 103.

p. 135 *Modeled Carbon Storage in Five Research Forests*: Data from Ollinger, S.V., et al., 2008. "Potential effects of climate change and rising CO_2 on ecosystem processes in northeastern U.S. forests." *Mitigation and Adaptation Strategies for Global Change*, in press. *An analysis…by Charley Canham*: Personal communication. *A growth model developed by Scott Ollinger*: Op. cit. In contrast, Colin Beier, in EE, gives an estimate of 600,000 tonnes of $CO_2(e)$ stored in Adirondack forests per year. This is 0.04 ton per acre per year, ten times lower than our estimate.

pp. 135–136 *Estimated carbon emissions from fossil fuels*: From EE. *Predicted Carbon Storage in Five Research Forests*: Data from Ollinger et al., op. cit.

p. 136 *Many ecologists think*: See, for example Angert, A., et al., 2005. "Drier summers cancel out the CO_2 uptake enhancement induced by warmer springs." *Proceedings of the National Academy of Sciences* 102(31): 10823–10827.

p. 137 *Carbon Flows From a Clear-Cut Harvest*: Forest carbon flows from Smith et al., op. cit.; fossil fuel carbon releases estimated using www.eiolca.net.

p. 138 *Carbon Pools After a Clear-Cut*: Data from Smith et al., op. cit.

p. 139 *Materials and Energy in a Medium-Sized House*: Data from Meil, J., et al., 2004. *Environmental Impacts of a Single-Family Building Shell—From Harvest to Construction.* Consortium for Research on Renewable Industrial Materials. Seattle, WA, www.corrim.org.

p. 140 et seq. *Managing Forest Carbon*: The models used here are based on the carbon-accumulation curve from Smith et al., op. cit., shown on p. 133.

12 *Can the Adirondacks become Energy Independent?*

The calculations in this chapter use the costs and power densities for renewables estimated in Chapter 10; these costs do not include any subsidies or financing costs. The graphic presentation, using energy stacks, is adapted, gratefully, from DM.

p. 146 *Reducing the Stack*: I do not give any cost estimates for the energy-efficiency measures I describe here because I have no local data on which to base an estimate. For a national estimate see MK.

p. 148 *Northern New York as a whole probably produces 940 megawatts of hydropower and 250 megawatts of wind power*: Total installed capacity from EIA generator database and www.horizonwinDCom/projects/whatwevedone/mapleridge and www.noblepower.com/our-windparks/index.html; capacity factor assumed to be 0.5 for hydro and 0.3 for wind.

p. 152 *The idealistic Germans regard citizen-owned wind turbines as symbols of independence*: WEB, p. 107 et seq.

13 *How Can We Finance Energy Independence?*

p. 153 *The most direct benefit will be the money saved on fuel*: I assume here that fossil fuels cost about $3 per gallon or $0.70 per watt.

p. 155 *Subsidies and Their Limitations.* For databases of subsidies for renewable energy, see www.dsireusa.org. and www.wind-works-org. For New York State subsidies, see www.nyserda.org and www.powernaturally.com. For program reports, see New York State Energy Research and Development Authority, 2009. *New York Energy Smart Program Evaluation and Status Report: Year Ending December 31, 2008.* www.nyserda.org; and New York State Energy Research and Development Authority, 2009. *New York State Renewable Portfolio Standard: Performance Report, Program Period Ending March 2009.* www.nyserda.org.

p. 156 *An alternative to large corporate-owned wind farms*: See WEB, Chapter 7.

pp. 156–157 *Funding Renewable Electricity With Guaranteed Rates.* For an extensive on-line collection of articles, see www.wind-works.org. Gipe, P., 2009. *Evolution of Feed-in Tariffs,* wind-works.org/FeedLaws/EvolutionofFeed-inTariffs.html is a useful introduction. For Ontario's guaranteed rates see, comments submitted by the New York Solar Energy Industries Association to the New York Public Service Board, www.wind-works.org/FeedLaws/USA/NYSEIA Comments_03E0188SA-18-19.pdf. For Vermont's new law, see Gipe, P., 2009. *Vermonts FITs Become Law: The Mouse That Roared,* www.wind-works.org/FeedLaws/USA/VermontFITsBecomeLawTheMouseThatRoared.html.

p. 158 *New York…has only about 1,000 grid-tied solar electric systems*: New York State Energy Research and Development Authority, 2009. op. cit.

14 *The Path Forward*

p. 162 *"Get the carbon costs right"*: See MK and Cleetus, R., 2007. *We Need a Well-Designed Cap-and-Trade Program to Fight Global Warming.* Union of Concerned Scientists. Cambridge, MA., www.usc.usa.org. *1973-1974 oil embargo*: See Smil, 2005. op. cit., p. 149 et seq.

p. 163 *U.S. Crude Oil Prices*: Data from EIA.

p. 164 *national cap-and-trade program*: See, for example, Cleetus, R., 2007. op. cit. *Regional Greenhouse Gas Initiative*: see Regional Greenhouse Gas Initiative, 2007. *Overview of RGGI CO$_2$ Budget Trading Program*, www.rggi.org.

p. 168 *Thoreau*: The quote is from the journals; I don't remember where. *Dickinson*: Poem 254, "Hope is the thing with feathers." *And at Shiloh*: From Keegan, J., 1987. *The Mask of Command.* Penguin Books. London.

Old growth near the Cedar River Flow, October, 2009

Jerry Jenkins lives in White Creek, New York, and works as a researcher with the Wildlife Conservation Society Adirondack Program. He is also the founder and director of the White Creek Field School. He was trained in physics and philosophy and has worked as a botanist and geographer for 40 years. His specialties are botanical survey and forest ecology. He has done botanical work in all 254 towns in Vermont, inventoried some 500,000 acres of Adirondack land that are now under conservation easements or in the Forest Preserve, and written extensively about plant identification and natural resource geography. His most recent books are the *Adirondack Atlas,* the *Harvard Forest Flora,* and *Acid Rain in the Adirondacks.* His next two will be graphic guides to winter trees and northeastern mosses.

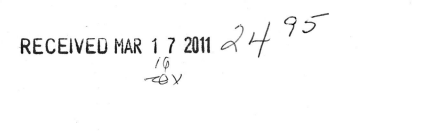